Imagining Africa

There has been a long history of idealism concerning the potential of economic and political developments in Africa, the latest iteration of which emerged around the time of the 2007–8 global financial crisis. Here, Clive Gabay takes a historical approach to questions concerning change and international order as these apply to Africa in Western imaginaries. Challenging traditional post-colonial accounts that see the West imagine itself as superior to Africa, he argues that the centrality of racial anxieties concerning white supremacy make Africa appear, at moments of Western crisis, as the saviour of western ideals, specifically democracy, bureaucracy and neo-classical economic order. Uncommonly, this book turns its lens as much inwards as outwards, interrogating how changing attitudes to Africa over the course of the twentieth and early-twenty-first centuries correspond to shifting anxieties concerning whiteness, and the growing hope that Africa will be the place where the historical genius of Whiteness might be saved and perpetuated.

CLIVE GABAY is Senior Lecturer at Queen Mary University of London, where he has taught since 2010. He has been the recipient of a number of prestigious grants and awards, including British Academy Conference Award and a two-year UK Arts and Humanities Research Council Early Career Leaders Fellowship. Among other outlets, he has published in *Globalizations*, *Review of African Political Economy*, and *Interventions: The International Journal of Postcolonial Studies*. His previous books include *Exploring an African Civil Society: Development and Democracy in Malawi, 1994–2014* (2015) and *Civil Society and Global Poverty: Hegemony, Inclusivity, Legitimacy* (2012).

Imagining Africa

Whiteness and the Western Gaze

CLIVE GABAY
Queen Mary University of London

CAMBRIDGE
UNIVERSITY PRESS

CAMBRIDGE
UNIVERSITY PRESS

University Printing House, Cambridge CB2 8BS, United Kingdom

One Liberty Plaza, 20th Floor, New York, NY 10006, USA

477 Williamstown Road, Port Melbourne, VIC 3207, Australia

314-321, 3rd Floor, Plot 3, Splendor Forum, Jasola District Centre, New Delhi - 110025, India

79 Anson Road, #06-04/06, Singapore 079906

Cambridge University Press is part of the University of Cambridge.

It furthers the University's mission by disseminating knowledge in the pursuit of education, learning and research at the highest international levels of excellence.

www.cambridge.org
Information on this title: www.cambridge.org/9781108461924
DOI: 10.1017/9781108652582

© Clive Gabay 2018

First published 2018
First paperback edition 2020

A catalogue record for this publication is available from the British Library

ISBN 978-1-108-47360-6 Hardback
ISBN 978-1-108-46192-4 Paperback

Cambridge University Press has no responsibility for the persistence or accuracy of URLs for external or third-party internet websites referred to in this publication, and does not guarantee that any content on such websites is, or will remain, accurate or appropriate.

Contents

Figures

Table

Acknowledgements

This book has taken a long time to write, emerging partially formed through a series of conversations and observations during the latter part of 2012. There followed a series of draft papers presented at a variety of conferences; discussants and co-panellists too numerous to mention, but whose questions, criticisms and collegiality contributed in important ways to the final manuscript.

There are, though, some specific individuals who I would like to mention without whom the book would not have emerged. Carl Death, Saul Dubow, Reuben Loffman, Toussaint Nothias, Lisa Tilley, Engin Isin, Sophie Harman, David Williams and Robbie Shilliam all read various iterations of particular chapters and related papers. I am deeply indebted to all of my colleagues and mentors in the School of Politics and International Relations at Queen Mary University of London. In particular, I must thank all the members of my departmental reading group on race and racism. Spaces such as these are so rare to find, so vital to nurture and, in this case, has been fundamental to the trajectory of this book. Having said all of this, none of these individuals shoulder any responsibility for any flaws that exist over the following pages.

Andrew Loveland, Alex Challis and Lisa Pilgram have aided me in applying for, monitoring and reporting back to the various funds and pots of money that have enabled me to carry out the research for this book. Worth particular mention in this regard is the Faculty of Humanities and Social Sciences at Queen Mary University of London, who have provided me with sabbaticals and other forms of financial support, and the United Kingdom Arts and Humanities Research Council, who generously funded one year of full-time buy-out and another year of partial buy-out from my teaching and administrative responsibilities in order to carry out the archival research central to many of the chapters presented in the book.

This book would certainly not be here was it not for the efforts of my commissioning editor at Cambridge University Press, Maria Marsh, who took a very early interest in the project over a coffee, before anything had been committed to paper, stayed on board when the focus completely shifted, and shepherded the manuscript through the various stages of review, most of which was all done from a completely different time zone to me in Singapore. As a result, I have spent many a breakfast catching up on the latest developments of the manuscript's progress through CUP's internal processes. A big thank you is also owed to Maria's colleagues at CUP, especially Abigail Walkington and Cassi Roberts, who were endlessly helpful in assisting me in tying up a variety of loose ends.

A very special mention indeed is owed to Emma Dabiri, who spent two years of her life following up arcane and uncomfortable sources, helping me shape the project and providing a model of what a real public intellectual looks like. Finally, Daniella and Mika, who bear with me, support me, make me laugh and for whom it is all for.

1 Whiteness, the Western Gaze and Africa

Without specifically addressing white ethnicity, there can be no critical evaluation of the construction of the other[1]

... whiteness needs to be made strange[2]

What is the relationship between Whiteness and Africa? How do changing ideas about Africa reflect changing ideas about White racial and civilisational vitality in the West? This is a book that challenges conventional critical and post-colonial accounts of what we might call the Western gaze, and subsequent imaginaries and constructions of Africa. Many critical scholars argue that such imaginaries and constructions, whereby the continent is conceived of as being out-of-time, empty, savage and/or childlike, have been driven either by the material demands of Western capital and crises of over-accumulation in Western capitalist economies,[3] or by civilisational paternalism conjoined with a highly racialised understanding of world order.[4] Both of these impulses can, and have gone, hand-in-hand. However, in both of these accounts Africa is held to be in a directly negative hierarchical relationship with the West. Africa is, in these accounts, and to greater and lesser extents, emptier, more savage, more childlike, less modern, and less civilised than the West. How then can these kinds of approaches account for those times when Africa is not portrayed in such terms, when it seems that Africa is held in important segments

---

[1] Coco Fusco, 'Fantasies of Opportunity', *Afterimage Magazine*, December 1988, p. 9.

[2] Richard Dyer, *White: Essays on Race and Culture* (London, New York, NY: Routledge, 1997), p. 10.

[3] See for instance: Bram Büscher, 'The Political Economy of Africa's Natural Resources and the "Great Financial Crisis"', *Tijdschrift voor Economische en Sociale Geografie*, 103:2, 2012, pp. 136–49.

[4] See for instance: James Heartfield, *The Aborigines' Protection Society: Humanitarian Imperialism in Australia, New Zealand, Fiji, Canada, South Africa, and the Congo, 1837–1909* (London: Hurst Publishers, 2011).

of elite Western opinion (i.e., government, media, non-governmental organisations [NGOs], etc.) to be more socially, politically, culturally and/or economically dynamic than the West? What do these accounts miss about the historical engagement and representation of the continent among mainstream Western scholarship and policy-making if we begin to problematise the degree to which Africa has always been held as a denigrated and 'less-than' place with respect to the West? And why is it, given the overwhelming opinion otherwise, that Africa has at times been held, by mainstream commentators, scholars, politicians and others, in superior relation to the West? This book addresses these questions by taking a different approach to exploring constructions of Africa in popular and elite Western imaginaries. In doing so, the book engages in terrain normally under-appreciated by scholarship on the place of Africa and the West in imaginaries of international order. Although there is much to recommend about materialist and paternalist accounts of these imaginaries, this book seeks to supplement such accounts by arguing that over the past century major transitions have occurred which have reset these imaginaries and begun, in specific conjunctures, to place Africa in superior relation to the West, embedded in growing anxieties concerning the ability of phenotypical whites[5] to perpetuate their mythologised historical genius in gifting to the world liberal economy and democracy. It is this mythologised genius, and the way that it has structured social political and economic realities for white and non-white people alike, that I will call 'Whiteness'.

To be clear then, over the following pages I will seek to make a distinction between structures of Whiteness on the one hand, and phenotypical presentation on the other (whereby some people with lighter skin pigmentation may or may not identify themselves as being white, a decision-making process that itself is a privilege of possessing a lighter skin tone). The argument thereafter will suggest that it is racial anxiety, in greater and lesser amounts, rather than simply material or paternal inclinations, that drives shifting imaginaries of Africa. Whiteness, understood as a historical and structural force, has always needed a place called Africa, and the latter has become an increasingly

---

[5] I use iterations of the term 'phenotypical whiteness' throughout the book, fully aware that having a lighter skin pigmentation has not always, and continues not always, to be a marker of racial supremacy in Western societies. Jews, Irish and Poles are just three groups to have been historically deprived the social benefits that other groups of phenotypical whites have accrued due to their skin colour. I engage with these debates in more detail later in this chapter.

important component in the ways by which Western elites of many different political affiliations have constructed Whiteness over the past century and invested their hopes for the perpetuated vitality of its related and mythologised social, political and economic historical genius. There has been a rhizomatic quality to the degree to which these anxieties have been foregrounded and backgrounded, mirrored across a range of debates concerning the make-up of international order, many of them unconcerned with Africa.[6] Nonetheless, as far as Africa is concerned, a major high point in considerations of the place of the continent in the international order emerged following the 2007–8 financial crash, with assertions among policy-makers, scholars, management consultancies, NGOs, international organisations and cultural and literary sectors that Africa was 'rising'.[7] An important point to be made about all of this celebratory fascination is that

---

[6] For insight into this rhizomatic quality in the context of debates concerning US decline, see Michael Cox, 'Is the United States in decline – again?' *International Affairs*, 83:4, 2007, pp. 643–53. In this book, I do not engage with the debate over United States' decline, primarily because it does not concern itself with Africa. However, as Cox argues, these debates also have historical provenance, dating at least as far back as NSC 68, the 1950 US National Security Council memo that helped to usher in the Cold War. In its more contemporary iteration, much of this literature is far more bullish than the literature concerned with Africa (see note 7 for examples of this). Examples of the more bullish attitude concerning US decline include John Ikenberry, 'Is American Multilateralism in Decline?' *Perspectives on Politics*, 1:3, 2003, pp. 533–49; Robert Kagan, 'Not Fade Away: The Myth of American Decline' *The New Republic*, 11 January 2012, available at: https://newrepublic.com/article/99521/america-world-power-declinism, accessed on 21 August 2017). There are however exceptions – i.e., Charles Kupchan, *No One's World: The West, the Rising Rest, and the Coming Global Turn* (Oxford: Oxford University Press, 2012).

[7] A brief sample: Jean-Paul Severino and Olivier Ray, *Africa's Moment* (Cambridge: Polity Press, 2011); Steven Radelet, *Emerging Africa: How 17 Countries Are Leading the Way* (Washington, DC: Center for Global Development, 2010); Charles Robertson, *The Fastest Billion: The Story behind Africa's Economic Revolution* (London: Renaissance Capital, 2012); McKinsey & Company, 'The Rise of the African Consumer: A Report from McKinsey's Africa Consumer Insights Center', available at www.mckinsey.com/~/media/McKinsey%20Offices/South%20Africa/PDFs/Rise_of_the_African_consumer-McKinsey_Africa_Consumer_Insights_Center_report.ashx, accessed on 14 January 2015; Deloitte, 'The Rise and Rise of the African Middle Class', available at www2.deloitte.com/content/dam/Deloitte/au/Documents/international-specialist/deloitte-au-aas-rise-african-middle-class-12.pdf, accessed on 15 January 2015; Goldman Sachs, 'Africa's Turn', Equity Research Fortnightly Thoughts (Goldman Sachs newsletter), Issue 27, 1 March 2012, available at http://allafrica.com/download/resource/main/main/idatcs/00031978:a218704b4806a5136c18f03d75a4529c.pdf, accessed on 15 January 2015.

while the titles of the reports, books and blogs all deploy 'Africa' as their locus of analysis, as we will see in Chapter 7 where this literature is explored, Africa north of the Sahara is barely mentioned. Implied by this is a resonance with older ideas about the continent that divided it between a 'dark', 'Black' Africa south of the Sahara, and a more complex form of civilisation North of the Sahara, although, as we will see, arguably in the post-crash conjuncture these roles have been flipped somewhat.

The racial anxieties underpinning this plethora of upbeat analysis will be explored in further detail in Chapters 6 and 7. More broadly however, the book sets out to make four core contributions. First, it foregrounds Whiteness as a constitutive element in the construction of imaginations about international order. Secondly, the book overturns the conventional post-colonial critique of Western imaginaries of Africa by problematising the sense in which the former consistently holds the latter in inferior relation to it. Third, through a series of contextual and historical case study chapters, the book provides a historicisation of contemporary debates about Africa's economic, political and cultural 'rise', embedding them in a rhizomatic genealogy of anxiety-driven idealisations of the continent that have patterned imaginations of Whiteness for at least the past century. Lastly, in doing this, the book provides a sociology of significant shifts in how Whiteness has been (re)constructed over the past century, shifts that began to take place after World War II, and that began to manifest more openly following the 2007–8 financial crash in the context of major anxieties about White civilisational vitality. Importantly then, I do not propose to write a full history of changes in Whiteness, instead taking several illustrative or provocative moments over the past century to illustrate the centrality of racial anxiety to White supremacist understandings of international order and the West's and Africa's relative place therein.

The following section expands on the question of how I seek to deploy Whiteness in this book. Before that, a brief reflection on where this book began will help in understanding how the above contributions have, over time, been formulated. During the summer of 2012 I was grappling with a project exploring the contemporary nature of sovereignty in Africa (which never went anywhere) when I stumbled across something quite different. It began to strike me that there were two very different perspectives that were emerging on the state of African states. One was a more pessimistic, or at least constructively sceptical account, found in the arguments of, for instance, Pierre Engelbert, when he asserts that African states at a fundamental level simply do not work.[8] In a similar vein, others have argued that African state sovereignty in the sense of manifesting as coherent territorial states is ultimately mythical.[9] On the other hand, a literature was emerging that trumpeted African state agency in shaping international order, ranging across climate change treaties, responses to HIV and Aids, poverty reduction and trade.[10] These two positions were not mutually incompatible; the latter foregrounding the place of African governing elites in international affairs, the former on the lack of writ these elites exert domestically.[11]

It was not, however, this debate on African statehood that really stood out. Rather, it was the breathlessness of some of the arguments being put by some advocates of 'African agency'. Arguments asserting Africa's 'agency', or its 'rise', did seem unusual. Indeed, if we were to take the conventional critique of Western representations of Africa, which suggests that Africa has historically served as the image of the degenerating old man in the youthful Dorian Gray's mirror,[12] then proclamations such as '[a]n Africa of 1.8 billion inhabitants will rapidly impose itself in the globalization game',[13] or assertions that Africa is 'Leading the Way'[14] and undergoing an 'Economic Revolution'[15] would seem to suggest that Africa's place in Western narrations of the continent were perhaps undergoing something of a transition. Moreover, it

[8] See especially, Pierre Engelbert, *Africa: Unity, Sovereignty, and Sorrow* (Boulder, CO: Lynne Reinner, 2009), p. 1.
[9] Oliver Jutersonke and Moncef Kartas, 'The State as Urban Myth: Governance without Government in the Global South' in Robert Schuett and Peter M. R. Stirk (eds.) *The Concept of the State in International Relations: Philosophy, Sovereignty, Cosmopolitanism* (Edinburgh: Edinburgh University Press, 2015) pp. 108–35.
[10] Sophie Harman and William Brown (eds.), *African Agency in International Politics* (Abingdon: Routledge, 2013); Sophie Harman and William Brown, 'In from the Margins? The Changing Place of Africa in International Relations', *International Affairs*, 89:1, 2013, pp. 69–87.
[11] In many senses, therefore, these debates reproduce an older argument about Africa's 'quasi states'. See Robert Jackson, *Quasi-States: Sovereignty, International Relations and the Third World* (Cambridge: Cambridge University Press, 1991).
[12] Chinua Achebe, *An Image of Africa* (London: Penguin, 1977/2010), p. 19.
[13] Severino and Ray, *Africa's Moment*, p. 3.
[14] Radelet, *Emerging Africa*.
[15] Robertson, *The Fastest Billion*.

was not just one or two books that were making these claims. A quick glance at the bookshelves in the O. R. Tambo International Airport in Johannesburg, always a purveyor of popular 'state of the continent' literature; a perusal of the investment guides produced by some of the big management consultancies and accountancy firms;[16] a note of the prominent 'Africa Rising' conferences being held by international organisations;[17] the rise of African film, food and fashion festivals in the capitals of former imperial powers; or even seeing the fictional character Clare Underwood, one of the main protagonists in the popular drama *House of Cards*, reading a copy of Jean-Michel Severino and Oliver Ray's *Africa's Moment*,[18] tells us that something was going on here that, while faddish, guilty perhaps of 'a triumph of hope over experience',[19] and in many respects quite short-lived, undone by the bursting of Africa's commodity boom since 2014–15, nonetheless represented a burgeoning field of knowledge and construction site of ideas about a place called 'Africa', as well as an insight into the state of racial anxiety in the post-financial crash era – the conjuncture in which all of these manifestations of Africa's rise began to appear.

Notwithstanding that much of this 'Africa Rising' literature had a whiff of what Peter Vale has called 'airport literature' to it, which, devoid of any serious conceptual or theoretical reflection, describes a homogeneous relationship between Africa and 'globalisation',[20] the turnaround from pessimism to optimism in popular coverage of the continent had been stark, something I reflect on in more detail in Chapter 7. For now, it is important to note that only eleven years separated an infamous front cover of the Economist magazine from a very different one. In 2000, under the headline 'The Hopeless Continent', a black front page featured, adorned simply by the figure of a young

---

[16] For instance: McKinsey & Company, 'The Rise of the African Consumer'; Deloitte, 'The Rise and Rise of the African Middle Class'; Goldman Sachs, 'Africa's Turn'.
[17] See for instance, the International Monetary Fund's www.africarising.org.
[18] Series One, Episode Nine.
[19] Keith Somerville, 'Africa Emerges, but from What into What?', available at: http://africanarguments.org/2013/09/04/africa-emerges-but-from-what-and-into-what-a-triumph-of-hope-over-experience-in-robert-rotbergs-new-assessment-of-contemporary-africa-by-keith-somerville/, accessed on 18 November 2014.
[20] Peter Vale, 'The Movement, Modernity and New International Relations Writing in South Africa', *International Affairs*, 78:3, July 2002, pp. 585–93.

African man carrying a rocket or grenade launcher, transposed over the shape of the African continent. In 2011, the Economist returned to the continent with a very different message (although similarly problematic front cover – see Chapter 7). Under the headline 'Africa Rising' we saw an empty savannah at sunrise, with a young boy in the foreground running with an Africa-shaped, rainbow-coloured kite.[21] Such a turnaround was emblematic more broadly of the shift I have already described, and its starkness demanded an analysis. That the emergence and prevalence of this narrative seemed to match with growing tensions and unrest in Europe and the United States – not least the 2007–8 financial crash and its aftermath – seemed to reinforce the need for further investigation and contextualisation.

One way of interrogating all of this is to focus our attention on what kind of Africa is being constructed, and to an extent, this book does do this. However, of more interest perhaps, is what these ideas and proclamations say about the social context from which they emerge. Toni Morrison has suggested that what she calls 'Africanism'[22] serves a particular and, indeed, primary function for those who deploy it, namely 'a way of contemplating chaos and civilization, desire and fear, and a mechanism for testing the problems and blessings of freedom'.[23] As such, we should expect imaginaries and projections of 'Others' to be in a state of almost constant flux, from positive to negative and back again – or to be positive in some quarters and negative in others. Indeed, and despite claims from some who suggest that there is a reasonably constant historical and hierarchical relationship in Western imaginaries of Africa,[24] flux is a persistent feature of these historical imaginaries of the continent, whereby 'there were drastic changes in

---

[21] Images and references are provided in Chapter 7.
[22] '[A] term for the denotative and connotative blackness that African peoples have come to signify, as well as the entire range of views, assumptions, readings, and misreadings that accompany Eurocentric learning about those people', Toni Morrison, *Playing in the Dark: Whiteness and the Literary Imagination* (Cambridge, MA: Harvard University Press, 1992), p. 6.
[23] Ibid., at p. 11.
[24] See for instance, Valentin Yves Mudimbe, *The Idea of Africa* (Bloomington, IN: Indiana University Press, 1994), p. xi; Stuart Hall, 'The West and the Rest: Discourses and Power' in Stuart Hall, David Held, Don Hubert, Kenneth Thompson (eds.) *Modernity: An Introduction to Modern Societies* (Cambridge, MA: Blackwell, 1992), p. 308.

the imagery [of Africa] even in periods when Europeans had no contact whatsoever with black Africa'.[25]

None of this is to suggest that there is not a discursive unity to such
fluctuating imaginaries. However, this unity is not always to be found in
the geo-politics of the West/Africa relationship that asserts the West and
its largely phenotypically white elites as better than the 'Rest' (including
sub-classes of whites in the West,[26] but with Africa at the bottom of the
pile[27]). Rather, and because imaginaries of Africa are best seen as being
determined by a form of ethnocentric self-referentialism,[28] this unity is
to be found in the degree to which such imaginaries and projections
redraw the boundaries of Whiteness. As such, this book is not particularly concerned with the veracity of analyses suggesting that Africa
has 'arisen'.[29] Nor is it particularly concerned with acclamations of
African political and economic power that have emerged from the
continent itself.[30] Rather the book is concerned with the claims that

---

[25] Jan Nederveen Pieterse, *White on Black: Images of Africa and Blacks in
Western Popular Culture* (New Haven, CT: Yale University Press, 1992), p. 29;
See also Phillip Curtin, *The Image of Africa: British Ideas and Action 1780–
1850* (Madison, WI: University of Wisconsin Press, 1964).

[26] Dyer, *White*, p. 8.

[27] Hall, 'The West and the Rest'.

[28] Pieterse, *White on Black*, p. 29; See also Harrison's argument concerning
British attitudes when he argues that 'representations of Africa are best
understood as narratives about Britishness first and about Africa second',
Graham Harrison, *The African Presence: Representation of Africa in the
Construction of Britishness* (Manchester: Manchester University Press, 2013),
p. 71.

[29] For counter arguments to this assertion based on African public opinion
see Boniface Dulani, Robert Mattes, and Carolyn Logan, 'After a Decade of
Growth in Africa, Little Change in Poverty at the Grassroots', Afrobarometer,
October 2013, available at: www.afrobarometer.org/files/documents/policy_
brief/ab_r5_policybriefno1.pdf, accessed 1 November 2013; For an analysis
based on the bursting of Africa's commodity boom see Ian Taylor, *Africa
Rising? BRICS – Diversifying Dependency* (Oxford: James Currey, 2014).

[30] The past two decades have been replete with iterations of these, often for
instrumental reasons. In 1998 former President of South Africa Thabo Mbeki
declared an 'African Renaissance' (Thabo Mbeki, 'The African Renaissance
Statement of Deputy President, Thabo Mbeki, SABC, Gallagher Estate, 13
August 1998', available at: www.dfa.gov.za/docs/speeches/1998/mbek0813
.htm, accessed on 1 October 2015) although this was widely thought to
mask South African hegemonic aspirations (Rok Ajulu, 'Thabo Mbeki's
African Renaissance in a Globalising World Economy: The Struggle for the
Soul of the Continent', *Review of African Political Economy*, 28:87 (2001),
pp. 27–42). Interestingly though the term 'renaissance' implies a re-entry
onto the stage of world history, rather than a first appearance, as implied by

have emerged specifically among policy and political elites beyond Africa (or settled in Africa), during the post-crash period, historicising some of these claims, examining what they can reveal about the evolving social construction of Whiteness, and foregrounding Whiteness as a constitutive principle in imaginaries of Africa and relatedly international order.

'whiteness' and 'Whiteness'

Returning to some of the questions that opened this book, I want to dwell on what Whiteness represents in this current work, and how it relates to other key terms that will also appear, such as 'Western' and 'Eurocentric'. Most centrally, the book rests on the distinction between whiteness as a form of phenotypical presentation (itself historically fluid), and Whiteness as a system of privilege that has historically made some people of a phenotypical white presentation more likely to experience social and economic upliftment than their non-white,[31] or non-white-enough counterparts, although it is important to note that this is a process that continues to unfold unevenly and inter-sectionally. Importantly, as perceptions of the failure of this system to work even for those who consider themselves to be phenotypically white grows[32] (despite most indicators pointing in the other direction in terms of the overrepresentation of non-white groups in incarceration figures, gaps in educational attainment, low incomes, etc.), this system of privilege becomes more and more untethered from phenotype and projected

---

much of the post-financial crash 'Africa Rising' narrative. Rwanda's President Paul Kagame has also often talked of Africa's rising power, although again, some have seen in this an attempt to mask Rwandan regional hegemony and Kagame's domestic authoritarianism (Danielle Beswick, 'Managing Dissent in a Post Genocide Environment: The Challenge of Political Space in Rwanda' *Development and Change*, 41:2 (2010), pp. 225–51). This is discussed further in Chapter 7.

[31] Charles Mills, *The Racial Contract* (Ithaca, NY: Cornell University Press, 1997), p. 106.

[32] See for instance, research in an United States context which suggests that over half of white working class people 'believe discrimination against whites has become as big a problem as discrimination against blacks and other minorities', Daniel Cox, Rachel Lienesch, and Robert P. Jones, 'Beyond Economics: Fears of Cultural Displacement Pushed the White Working Class to Trump', *Public Religion Research Institute*, 9 May 2017, available at: www.prri.org/research/white-working-class-attitudes-economy-trade-immigration-election-donald-trump/, accessed on 22 August 2017.

onto peoples and territories where it might be seen to function effectively again, thus at least safeguarding the mythologised historical genius of Whiteness, previously assigned solely to Western political, economic and cultural practices, as a form of bequeathment.

The importance of the conceptual distinction between phenotypical whiteness and socio-political and economic Whiteness is relevant here to a discussion concerning international order, and the discipline that claims to study and explain it – International Relations – because of the discipline's failure to address this latter form of Whiteness head-on. The past two decades have seen a proliferation of work on race and international order, and global studies more broadly.[33] Such scholarship has worked to uncover both the racialised and normative assumptions that underpin much mainstream theoretical modelling about international order, and the variety of silences and erasures that these assumptions have manifested under the pretence of universality. For instance, Robert Vitalis argues that mainstream International Relations (IR) historiographies that locate the birth of the discipline in interwar debates concerning security and cooperation have erased the radical anti-imperial analyses of IR that were being generated by African-American scholars in the early part of the twentieth century,[34] thus rendering race absent (in both authorial and subject terms) in canonical debates, what Vitalis earlier called 'a norm against noticing'.[35] However, the study of race and international order has largely held up a homogeneous and pre-social conception of Whiteness as the backdrop for racial hierarchy in international order. This has been a necessary step in the valuable work of interrogating and isolating the

---

[33] A brief but indicative list includes: Alex Anievas, Nivi Manchanda, and Robbie Shilliam, *Race and Racism in International Relations: Confronting the Global Colour Line* (London: Routledge, 2014); Branwen Gruffydd Jones, 'Race in the Ontology of International Order' *Political Studies*, 56(4), 2008, pp. 907–27; John H. Hobson, *The Eurocentric Conception of World Politics: Western International Theory 1760–2010* (Cambridge: Cambridge University Press, 2012); Robbie Shilliam (ed.), *International Relations and Non-Western Thought: Imperialism, Colonialism and Investigations of Global Modernity* (London: Routledge, 2010); Robert Vitalis, 'The Graceful and Generous Liberal Gesture: Making Racism Invisible in American International Relations', *Millennium – Journal of International Studies*, 29:2, 2000, pp. 331–56; Robert Vitalis, *White World Order, Black Power Politics: The Birth of American International Relations* (Ithaca, NY: Cornell University Press, 2015).
[34] Vitalis, *White World Order*, pp. 7–11.
[35] Vitalis, 'The Graceful and Generous', p. 353.

ways in which conceptually, ideationally and materially international order has been constructed along what W.E.B. Du Bois famously noted was 'the color line'.[36] And yet as valuable as all this work has been, it has not paid enough attention to the ways in which Whiteness itself is a social construct, mutating and resetting its own boundaries in ways that do not necessarily conform to skin phenotype alone. To put it another way, scholarship of the relationship between race and international order has understandably been focussed on trying to unpick the racism and double standards inherent in a hierarchy that asserts that some ('Black', 'Brown', 'Yellow', 'Eastern', 'Third World') peoples and states lack 'development',[37] 'modernity'[38] or 'sovereignty'[39] while other ('Western') states do possess these characteristics, and thus the right and historical mission to intervene and uplift everyone else. However, in justifiably maintaining this focus, such studies overlook the mutability of 'Whiteness' and, therefore, various and changing projections of racial hierarchy. Indeed, this was not something that escaped the attention of Du Bois himself, when, having visited the site of the Warsaw Ghetto in Poland he wrote that 'the problem of slavery, emancipation and caste ... was not ... solely a matter of color and physical and racial characteristics'.[40]

Much of the critical scholarship in IR has tended to locate the absence of race in understanding the history of the discipline and the way its categories have been formulated with reference to eurocentrism. However, for all the explicit texts written about eurocentrism since 2000,[41] very few of these have explicitly tied eurocentrism into

[36] W. E. B. Du Bois, *The Souls of Black Folk* (New York, NY: New American Library, Inc, 1903), p. 19.
[37] Arturo Escobar, *Encountering Development: The Making and Unmaking of the Third World* (Princeton, NJ: Princeton University Press).
[38] Gurminder K. Bhambra, 'Historical Sociology, Modernity, and Postcolonial Critique', *The American Historical Review*, 116:3, 2011, pp. 653–62.
[39] Siba Grovogui, 'Regimes of Sovereignty: Rethinking International Morality and the African Condition,' *The European Journal of International Relations*, 8:3, 2002, pp. 315–38.
[40] W. E. B. Du Bois, 'The Negro and the Warsaw Ghetto', in Phil Zuckerman (ed.) *The Social Theory of W. E. B. Du Bois* (Thousand Oaks, CA: Pine Forge Press, 2004), pp. 45–6.
[41] An inexhaustive but instructive list: Dipesh Chakrabarty, *Provincializing Europe: Postcolonial Thought and Historical Difference* (Princeton, NJ: Princeton University Press, 2000); Hobson, *The Eurocentric Conception of World Politics*; Meera Sabaratnam, 'Avatars of Eurocentrism in the Critique of the Liberal Peace', *Security Dialogue*, 44:3, 2013, pp. 259–78.

logics of race and Whiteness. Race is of course present in these texts,[42] and yet it is often backgrounded, or partially erased by a focus on eurocentrism as an autonomous form of power and/or social, political and economic comprehension. John H. Hobson's widely regarded 2012 book on eurocentrism for instance offers a discussion of two variants of what he calls 'Eurocentric institutionalism', but remains embedded in a partial erasure of race. Hobson labels his two variants of Eurocentric institutionalism as paternalist and anti-imperialist. Paternalist Eurocentric institutionalism rests on a racial imaginary of world order, whereby Western societies are awarded 'a pioneering agency such that they can auto-generate or auto-develop into modernity while conversely, Eastern societies are granted conditional agency and are unable to auto-generate or self-develop'.[43] Anti-imperialist Eurocentric institutionalism on the other hand rejects the intervention by Western societies in the affairs of non-Western territories, and suggests that 'non-European peoples will evolve naturally and spontaneously – or auto-develop – into civilization', but only by following the 'naturalized Western path' that had been pioneered by the Europeans through their 'exceptional institutional genius'. That is, the West remains the original pioneer of development'.[44] As such, the anti-imperialist modus operandi of this variant of eurocentrism should not blind us to its deeply racialised nature. Indeed, this is something Hobson himself notes, although only in what the non-Western Other is thought to lack (i.e., a set of cultural, political and economic standards and practices of its own that renders the 'Western path' irrelevant). However, this is also a perspective that racialises the West, in terms of what it is thought to possess, namely a system that is deemed superior based on its ability to produce various degrees of wealth and status for people who are largely phenotypically white. This wealth and development is not just considered as happenstance, but is intrinsically tied to the racial characteristics of people in the West. It is this characterisation of Western historical development as being endogenous, that makes what Hobson calls Europe's 'exceptional institutional genius'[45] fundamentally raced.

---

[42] See for instance Chakrabarty's discussion of Franz Fanon in *Provincializing Europe*, p. 5.
[43] Hobson, *The Eurocentric Conception of World Politics*, pp. 5–6.
[44] Ibid.
[45] Ibid., at p. 6.

This sense of endogenous genius erases the historical reliance of these phenotypically white-majority societies and their wealth on systems of slavery and imperialism.[46] As such it has been possible to generate a belief in the universal utility of this system for the whole world. It is this universalism (rather than the existence of that system itself and its supposed markers, i.e., individualism, secular rationality, etc.) that in this book I call 'Whiteness'. What distinguishes Whiteness from, for instance, eurocentrism, is precisely the superiority located in 'Eurocentric institutionalism' vis-à-vis the institutions possessed by the rest of the world. This is what racialises eurocentrism; what makes it White. As a self-referential set of attitudes, eurocentrism on its own does not necessitate a superior self-analysis vis-à-vis the rest of the world. Narcissism does not necessarily imply a sense of superiority. It is the desire to reproduce that system universally, to think of it as superior to any other system of social and economic reproduction (a process incidentally beset by fundamental contradictions[47]), which makes this process White.

In practice, this means making a distinction between a sense of Western decay that has been prevalent among policy and media elites in the years since the 2007–8 financial crash (a sense of decay that, as we will see in the following chapters, has often been present in elite conceptions of international order) and the continuation of efforts to export those same decaying institutional practices to the rest of the world via modalities of democracy promotion, good governance, technical assistance, among others. This is not simply Eurocentric self-regard (which might explain the elite sense of Western decay), but the valorisation of a system that serves to flag the historical racial genius of the West. As such, this represents an effort to shore up this historical genius from domestic Western decay, by maintaining those self-same standards of racialised historical genius in the rest of the world.

---

[46] For attempts to redress this auto-blindness see Bhambra, 'Historical Sociology'; Partha Sarathi Gupta, *Imperialism and the British Labour Movement, 1914–1964* (New York, NY: Holmes & Meier Publishers, 1975).

[47] For instance, until every state in the world develops its own empire (a logical fallacy), it will be impossible for them to accrue wealth and power in the same way as Imperial Western states have done – Ray Kiely, 'Development and Modernisation', in J. Scott (ed.) *Key Sociological Concepts* (Abingdon: Routledge, 2006), pp. 107–10.

For all this, it remains the case that in much of the literature on race and international order the nuances of Whiteness remain unexplored. As such, Whiteness risks becoming either under-analysed, or itself reified as only being ascribable to people of a certain skin colour (or sub-sets thereof), rather than a series of logics that operate to structure attitudes, spaces, modes of behaviour and so on. It is in this sense that phenotypical whiteness, even given the history of exclusion from white supremacy experienced by various phenotypically white groups (i.e., Jews, Irish, Roma, Polish, etc.) and a socially coded form of Whiteness begin to diverge. In part this reticence to make Whiteness explicit may be to do with the difficulty of fixing Whiteness down among a plethora of other identifications that have historically been deployed to cordon off and defend the privilege of some phenotypically white people. In a purely British context (the context from which I am writing) these identifications have included 'The Crown, the Empire, Greater Britain, Anglo Saxendom, "kith and kin", pan-Europeanism',[48] among others. Nonetheless, and as I will argue, it is possible to see through these various forms of identification to a deeper set of logics that construct Whiteness as something that goes beyond phenotype. In this sense Whiteness becomes something that goes beyond the colour of a person's skin to structure ways of acting and being in the world that are normalised, all the while that such norms are held to have derived from people with a particular racial phenotype, and that act to abnormalise people who do not act according to these (White) norms of social behaviour. In this sense, Whiteness is both narrower and broader than phenotype, excluding some phenotypically white people according to class, geographical, ethnic or religious criteria, while embracing some non-white people according to similar standards. This is how some groups of people can 'become' white (by acting White).[49]

Importantly, the perpetuation of a system that has historically privileged some groups of largely phenotypically white people does not mean that all phenotypically white people are white supremacists,

---

[48] Josiah Brownell, 'Out of Time: Global Settlerism, Nostalgia, and the Selling of the Rhodesian Rebellion Overseas' *Journal of Southern African Studies*, 43:4, 2017, p. 810, EarlyView, p. 5.

[49] See for instance: Noel Ignatiev, *How the Irish Became White* (London, New York, NY: Routledge, 1995/2009); David Roediger, *Working toward Whiteness: How America's Immigrants Became White: The Strange Journey from Ellis Island to the Suburbs* (New York, NY: Basic Books, 2006).

nor that people who are not phenotypically white do not perpetuate structures of Whiteness. At the same time, limiting the usage of the term 'white supremacy' to white Fascists and assorted white ethno-nationalists means that we risk missing how Whiteness operates as a structuring system that accrues privilege in white-majority and/or white governed societies, primarily to people who are phenotypically white (even if firstly, this is uneven among different groups of white people based on class, ethnicity, gender, etc., and secondly, not all white people see it that way). Indeed, if the focus remained purely on those who explicitly pursue white supremacism, then one might conclude that white supremacism had been lurking in the shadows prior to the ascension of white supremacists to the Government of the United States, rather than existing front and centre in the form of a set of institutional practices that discriminate against non-white peoples in many different white-majority societies across educational attainment, employment, incarceration rates and so on.[50]

This all rests on the distinction between structural White supremacy and the more individualising term white suprema*cist*. It is the former this book is largely concerned with, although the terminology is not without its problems. For instance, a set of institutions designed around principles that have historically privileged phenotypically white people does not preclude someone who is not phenotypically white from absorbing those principles and acting accordingly, even if they will still find it harder than someone who is phenotypically white to access the highest echelons of those institutions. We see this most clearly in how many institutions in white-majority or white-governed societies are designed around the idea and practice of meritocracy, a system that in effect largely precludes affirmative action (or at least becomes a site of political contestation over the meaning of meritocracy when it is

---

[50] For differences in educational attainment, employment and health outcomes in the United Kingdom based on ethnic categorisation see 'How Fair is Britain?' *Equality and Human Rights Commission*, 2010, available at: www.equalityhumanrights.com/en/publication-download/how-fair-britain-report, accessed on 22 August 2017. Although harder to ascertain, estimates suggest that the proportion of Muslims in French prisons (most of whom have a sub-Saharan or North African heritage) sits anywhere between 40 and 70 per cent – see Jonathan Laurence and Justin Vaïsse, *Integrating Islam: Political and Religious Challenges in Contemporary France* (Washington, DC: Brookings Institution Press, 2006), p. 41.

not precluded[51]) and other modes of recognition of the largely socially constructed manner in which privilege operates.[52] That all said, it is clear that institutions established on principles that have historically privileged some groups of phenotypically white people do not entirely exclude people who are not phenotypically white from ascending to their highest echelons, former President of the United States Barack Obama being one of the most evident contemporary examples. As a self-proclaimed political Liberal,[53] a political creed Charles Mills has argued rests on the perpetuation of white supremacy,[54] is Obama a white supremacist? The answer should clearly be, 'no'. And yet as a participant in and a perpetuator of a system that, however unwittingly, continues to privilege in many respects (if not always, as evidenced by Obama's ascension to the presidency) phenotypically white people, we can still think of Obama as perpetuating a mode of political and social ordering that is White. Of course, in this sense this is what most of us do, to different extents in different spaces, regardless of our ethnic background. Again, this rests on the distinction between systemic White supremacy and individual white suprema*cists*.

Although Du Bois was writing about the peculiarities of Whiteness in *Black Reconstruction* in 1935,[55] the distinction between being phenotypically white, and being 'White', is one made by Mills in 1997 in *The Racial Contract*, and refers to the manner by which one can distinguish 'whiteness' as a phenotypical classification from '"Whiteness" as a politico-economic system committed to white supremacy … one could then distinguish "being white" from "being White"'.[56] In subsequent years we have seen this distinction stretched even further whereby Whiteness has also become a means by which to safeguard the

---

[51] See for instance: Christopher Sebastian Parker, 'Trump's Affirmative-Action Rollback: A Promise Kept', available at www.chronicle.com/article/Trump-s-Affirmative-Action/240842, accessed on 21 August 2017.
[52] Jo Little, *Against Meritocracy: Culture, Power and Myths of Mobility* (Abingdon, New York, NY: Routledge, 2017).
[53] 'Obama's final UN speech: 'I believe in a liberal political order', available at: www.theguardian.com/us-news/video/2016/sep/20/obamas-final-un-speech-i-believe-in-a-liberal-political-order-video, accessed on 21 August 2017.
[54] Mills, *The Racial Contract*.
[55] W. E. B. Du Bois, *Black Reconstruction in America: An Essay toward a History of the Part Which Black Folk Played in the Attempt to Reconstruct Democracy in America, 1860–1880* (San Diego, CA: Harcourt Brace, 1935), especially chapter 12.
[56] Mills, *The Racial Contract*, p. 106.

historical genius of the West in places beyond the West, namely Africa. In order to understand how this has happened, it is useful to develop Mills' provocation concerning Whiteness as signifying structural racial supremacy. Ruth Frankenberg for instance argued that Whiteness is, first 'a location of structural advantage, of race privilege. Second, it is a "standpoint," a place from which white people look at ourselves, at others, and at society. Third, "Whiteness" refers to a set of cultural practices that are usually unmarked and unnamed'.[57] Although presented as a triptych, Frankenberg's depiction of Whiteness can also cohere around a duality, one invoked, one not. As an invocation, Whiteness is the process by which people who are phenotypically white may *self-consciously* identify with *some* phenotypically white people while simultaneously excluding others who are phenotypically white, as well as those who are not, cutting across national and class boundaries. Such a form of identification might take on the label of 'British', or 'European', but in each of these instances, and others, these labels generally only refer to people who are phenotypically white, even if they also exclude other phenotypical whites, depending on individual or collective standpoint (i.e., communists, feminists, Jews, working classes, etc.). As a non-invoked phenomenon, Whiteness speaks to the features identified in Frankenberg's second and third categorisations, as a position of structural privilege, and a related set of norms that serve to reinforce that privilege, because it is people who are phenotypically white who are most able, through their structural privilege, to perform those norms. In this sense Whiteness has to be understood as a dynamic social process, linked to processes of domination, rather than a purely ontological category linked to skin colour. 'Whiteness is dynamic, relational, and operating at all times and on myriad levels',[58] and thus can be thought of as operating at many levels and scales of political and social being, whether through belief systems, organisational practices, or international rules and regulations. As we will see throughout the chapters of this book, Whiteness moves across this duality of invocation and non-invocation very fluidly, and is very often present simultaneously.

[57] Ruth Frankenberg, *White Women, Race Matters: The Social Construction of Whiteness* (Minneapolis: University of Minnesota Press, 1993), p. 1.
[58] Robin DiAngelo, 'White Fragility' *International Journal of Critical Pedagogy*, 3:3, 2011, p. 56.

In the sense of being a set of norms that do not explicitly invoke race, Whiteness is everywhere, and yet is rarely named as such. It is also what produces fixity and rigidity, it is the universal that ignores particularity; it is 'a category of experience that disappears as a category through experience ... this disappearance makes whiteness "worldly"'.[59] Yet, at the same time Whiteness *is* fluid. It constantly seeks to expand itself through an incorporation of non-White bodies (and in this sense bears a resemblance and relationship to capitalism and its inherent drive to incorporate non-capitalist zones into itself in the name of its own survival). This fluidity is perfectly encapsulated in Dyer's association of Whiteness with the Christian cosmology of incarnation, which, in relation, produced White people whose being 'is in the body yet not of it', and non-White people (who might still be phenotypically white, for instance Roma, or European Jews) whose being is entirely corporeal. White people thus develop a special and transcendental relationship to race, whereas non-White people do not.[60]

In this sense, then, Whiteness (as a set of social codes and practices in addition to, and sometimes beyond phenotype) becomes Godly, with sacred qualities. And yet incarnating as White presupposes the possibility of conversion, and it is here that Whiteness becomes fluid, even though converts to Whiteness – those who seek to embody the characteristics of Whiteness – are simultaneously condemned to live under the suspicion of the convert, no matter how zealous their conversion. Indeed, it is interesting to reflect that when Du Bois chose *The Souls of Black Folk* as the title of his 1903 book,[61] he might arguably have not simply been signposting to the content of the work, but also to the shared humanity, and Godliness, of 'Black Folk', and to his rejection of the need of such people to 'convert' into a supposedly more Godly way of being.

Of course, while Whiteness may be a fluid construct, open to conversion in theory, in practice, those not considered White, for phenotypical or other reasons, continue to face racist discrimination based on the colour of their skin, and/or their assumed racial habitus. Nonetheless, from the perspective of Whiteness, racism is merely pathological, a disease that can, and indeed largely has been eradicated

---

[59] Sara Ahmed, 'A Phenomenology of Whiteness', *Feminist Theory*, 8: 149, 2007, p. 150.

[60] Dyer, *White*, p. 14.

[61] W. E. B. Du Bois, *The Souls of Black Folk* (New York, NY: Bantam Classic, 1903).

in contemporary meritocratic societies. As such, the more people that sign up to the universalistic pretensions of Whiteness, the 'styles, capacities, aspirations, techniques, habits' that Whiteness puts 'within reach' of certain (familiarised, racialised as-White) bodies, the merrier[62] (and it is precisely this tendency that informs much contemporary analysis of Africa's place in the international order, which will be explored in greater detail in Chapter 7).

This works in the opposite direction too, 'whereby those phenotypically/genealogically/culturally categorized as white fail to live up to the civic and political responsibilities of Whiteness, they are in dereliction of their duties as citizens'.[63] This indeed has been the story for all kinds of phenotypically white people, not considered 'White' by those who own and perpetuate 'this overarching hegemonic Whiteness'.[64] These have included Greeks, Italians, Poles, Jews, Roma, Irish, etc. If we stand these groups next to the multi-racial cosmopolitan elites sitting in the offices of the World Bank, United Nations, or large international management consultancies, then we can see that distinctions based *purely* on phenotype start to break down, although, because of the discrimination faced by non-white bodies no matter their social status, these distinctions cannot be ascribed simply to class.

That Whiteness may be fluid, and that White hegemony may hold (and indeed, as I will argue, by necessity mandate) that Whiteness is both accessible to all, and also increasingly becoming dislocated from those phenotypically white people in Western societies held to most embody White supremacy, is in no way in contradiction with the daily racism faced by people who are not phenotypically white. The focus of this book then is not on the 'real' of racism as it is experienced by its victims. Rather, it is about the constant redrawing of the boundaries of Whiteness, as refracted through Western imaginaries of Africa, by some of those who consider themselves acting in the best interests of Western civilisational vitality, and indeed the whole of humanity (because of the inherent superiority of Western civilisation), not all of whom may necessarily be phenotypically white.

This will be a central feature of this book, as it seeks to understand how, over the course of the past hundred years, important transitions

[62] Ahmed, 'Phenomenology', p. 154.
[63] Mills, *The Racial Contract*, p. 14
[64] Dyer, *White*, p. 13.

have occurred in the ways in which the gatekeepers of 'Whiteness', political and cultural elites, including settler colonisers, government officials, liberal humanitarians, authors and film-makers, have slowly loosened the ties between skin-pigmentation and the kinds of qualities that have been historically imagined to constitute White supremacy (not that these qualities have ever extended to all those people with a lighter skin pigmentation) . These qualities (the codes and logics of Whiteness) range across entrepreneurialism, individualism, hygiene, monogamy, and a variety of social and political rules and regulations, which also embed themselves into international regimes of law,[65] collective security[66] and beyond. Again, it is not these characteristics as such that should be labelled White, but rather their valorisation as principle universal characteristics, a valorisation that ignores the racial privilege that has historically made these characteristics more attainable/desirable/dominant for certain phenotypically white groups in the West, *and* erases other ways of being, living and ordering. As a series of military, political and economic crises have rocked the idea that ties Western civilisation umbilically to phenotypical whiteness, there has been a concomitant decrease in the belief that such a phenotype is a necessary precondition for Western civilisational greatness on an individual, societal and international level, all the while that such greatness remains the standard by which individual, societal and international spheres are defined and demarcated. Importantly, as a rhizomatic tendency, this has been an uneven and not always visible process, often operating in the background. The ensuing chapters will focus on those times when such tendencies have been foregrounded.

As I have previously argued none of this is to suggest that skin pigmentation does not remain central to the manner by which race operates socially. Nonetheless, historically race *has* operated in ways that suggest that understanding race as a series of codes and logics that demarcates civilised borders between 'moderns' and 'non-moderns'[67] is a fruitful path with which to explore the changing ways in which Africa has been imagined over the past century. It is within this frame

---

[65] Grovogui, 'Regimes of Sovereignty'.

[66] Robbie Shilliam, 'Intervention and Colonial-Modernity: Decolonising the Italy/Ethiopia Conflict through Psalms 68:31', *Review of International Studies*, 39:5, 2013, pp. 1131–47.

[67] Robbie Shilliam, *The Black Pacific: Anti-Colonial Struggles and Oceanic Connections* (London: Bloomsbury Academic, 2015), p. 10.

that, for example, we can mark out the ground upon which it was possible for British eugenicists in the 1920s to generate a series of descriptors about working class people (habitual criminals, prostitutes, lunatics, drunkards, welfare dependents, feeble-minded, etc.) that were easily and quickly applied to the waves of immigrants that began to arrive in the United Kingdom after World War II. Indeed, in this way British eugenicists 'caught up' with their US counterparts, who had been more explicitly preoccupied with race ever since the mass migration of African-Americans from the South to the North in the early part of the twentieth century.[68]

This book therefore argues that it is too simplistic to suggest that post-crash proclamations of African agency, and the continent's rise, simply reflected a changing material reality – i.e., an Africa stabilising after years of internecine warfare and stagnating economic growth (however selective an interpretation of Africa's contemporary political economy this might be). Nor is it adequate to explain these assertions as a reflection of a softening of the Western gaze, which has often seen Africa as a space of exceptional 'barbarism' and pre-modernity.[69]

The core argument of the book is, therefore, that the idea that Western civilisation is the preserve and vocation of certain groups of phenotypically white people is one that has become increasingly unsteady over the past century, all the while that such civilisational standards have remained central to the structuring of international and social order, and thus continue to deny the legitimacy of difference within that order. As the chapters unfold, the book will illustrate that the relationship between civilisational practice (Whiteness) and phenotypical whiteness began to fracture after World War II, something that is now being seen more fully as a result of a range of anxieties concerning Western civilisational vitality. Even though materialist accounts of how phenotypically white elites have considered similarly pigmented labouring classes to be inferior to other 'races' suggests that who gets

---

[68] Michael G. Kenny 'Racial Science in Social Context: John R. Baker on Eugenics, Race, and the Public Role of the Scientist', *Isis: A Journal of the History of Science Society*, 95:3, 2004, p. 403.

[69] Scarlett Cornelissen, Fantu Cheru, and Timothy Shaw, 'Introduction – Africa and International Relations in the Twenty First Century: Still Changing Theory?' in Scarlett Cornelissen, Fantu Cheru, and Timothy Shaw (eds.) *Africa and International Relations in the Twenty First Century* (New York, NY: Palgrave MacMillan, 2012), p. 12.

to embody and reproduce White supremacy are unevenly applied;[70] it is also accurate to say that until the end of World War II, phenotypically white elites did not generally see anyone but themselves as capable of enacting Western civilisation. With Africa long-regarded as being 'the case of delinquency par excellence',[71] the post-crash proliferation of 'Africa Rising' narratives represents a prime site to begin exploring the issues posed concerning historical and present states of White self-regard and projections of racial hierarchy in international order. This is because, having long been placed at the very bottom of attempts to construct international territorial and cultural hierarchies,[72] the positive reception given to iterations of African politics, economy, culture, food and fashion in formerly Imperial metropoles this century represents a potentially inductive moment when placed in the legacy of a more familiarly dismissive and overtly racist set of characterisations that has seemed to populate Western imaginaries of Africa in previous periods.

We now turn to the two sets of debates that inform the arguments made in the coming chapters. First, the following section considers post-colonial scholarship's critiques of the Western gaze and Africa, the limitations of which have been rendered clearer by contemporary debates concerning Africa's rise. Second, the subsequent section makes the case for considering Whiteness as inherently anxious, and the implications that follow from this for considering subsequent imaginaries of Africa. Following these two discussions, the chapter will continue to present some reflections on methodology and selection, before providing a detailed chapter outline for the rest of the book.

The Post-Colonial Critique of the Western Gaze and Africa (and Its Limitations)

One of this book's key underlying contributions is to challenge and extend conventional post-colonial critiques of Western imaginaries

---

[70] See Theodore Allen, *The Invention of the White Race, Vol. 2: The Origin of Racial Oppression in Anglo-America* (London: Verso Books, 1997); David Cannadine, *Ornamentalism: How the British Saw Their Empire* (London, New York, NY: Penguin, 2001); Pieterse, *White on Black*, pp. 212–24; Diana Jeater, *Law, Language and Science: The Invention of the 'Native Mind' in Southern Rhodesia, 1890–1930* (Portsmouth, NH: Heinemann, 2007), pp. 192–3.

[71] Scarlett Cornelissen, Fantu Cheru, and Timothy Shaw, 'Introduction', p. 2.

[72] For an example, see: Samuel Huntington, *The Clash of Civilizations and the Remaking of World Order* (New York, NY: Simon & Schuster, 1996), pp. 40–6.

of Africa. These fall into two categories, the limitations of which are brought into sharp relief by post-crash 'Africa Rising' debates, and the other historical case studies considered in this book. The first of these categories looks at the denigration of Africa present in Western imaginaries of the continent.

Scholars have long argued that a racialised idea of Africa has dominated Western imaginaries of the continent, with the former historically understood and dismissed as the international 'case of delinquency' par excellence,[73] and the place where (non-racialised, White) Westerners have been able to say 'there go I but for the grace of God'.[74] V. Y. Mudimbe suggests that Africa has been 'imagined and rejected as the intimate and other side of the European thinking subject',[75] while Achille Mbembe highlights a Western impulse to 'discover the most appalling manifestations of human nature ... in Africa', a tendency in European political thought dating back to at least Georg Hegel of seeing Africa as the West's 'dark', ahistorical 'Other', alive and well in contemporary public discourse.[76] Similarly, in a British context, Harrison has argued that 'it would be difficult to make a case that representation has ever escaped from a general set of Britain/Africa dyads established in the late seventeenth century as a set of negative tropes',[77] while the novelist Chinua Achebe asserted that Western imaginaries have produced a 'need ... to set Africa up as a foil to Europe, as a place of negations ... in comparison with which Europe's own state of spiritual grace will be manifest'.[78] Arguing more broadly, Stuart Hall argued that the 'Rest' becomes defined by everything the 'West' is not, where the latter consistently takes on positive features denied to the Rest.[79] As such, ideas about Africa specifically become intertwined with attitudes towards race, whereby Whiteness (the exhibition of certain ordained behaviours and practices) becomes a signifier of civilisation, and Blackness (signifying the lack of these ordained behaviours

---

[73] Cornelissen, Cheru, and Shaw, 'Introduction', p. 2.
[74] Achebe, *Image of Africa*, p. 19.
[75] Mudimbe, *The Idea of Africa*, p. xi.
[76] Achille Mbembe, 'Nicolas Sarkozy's Africa' *Africultures*, 2007, Available at www.africultures.com/php/index.php?nav=paper&no=6816, accessed on 20 September 2015.
[77] Harrison, *The African Presence*, p. 53.
[78] Achebe, *Image of Africa*, p. x.
[79] Hall, 'The West and the Rest', p. 308.

and practices) becomes a signifier of profane childish immaturity and/ or barbarity.

These are arguments that persist in contemporary analyses of historical Western imaginaries of the continent. For instance, in a British context, Harrison has argued that the African presence in British national culture has been a result of processes of domestication, whereby the African presence is deployed to assert British national and cultural superiority,[80] and results in an idea of Africa as a place that requires British intervention and whereby Africans are passive and require saving.[81] Similarly, Mudimbe argues that this is a state of affairs that has 'always' been the case,[82] since at least the fifteenth century when Europeans first started encountering Africans. By the nineteenth century a colonial library had emerged, with the 'explicit purpose of faithfully translating and deciphering the African object' in order to domesticate it, with that object symbolically aligned with 'the concept of deviation'.[83] The problem with Mudimbe's analysis, as with other analyses presented in this section, is that this objectification seems no longer to be (and, as subsequent chapters will illustrate, has not 'always' been) predicated on Africa-as-deviant, or Africa-as-behind. Indeed, where Mahmood Mamdani argues that in the late-colonial period European imperial policy underwent a shift from rejuvenating society in non-African possessions to preserving society in African ones (in order to serve European interests),[84] this book suggests that this went alongside an increasingly manifest sensibility that saw in Africa the potential to save White vitality from a degraded West. This was not necessarily a departure from the racialisation of Africa, but it *was* a mission that would require idealised and valorised African subjects to carry the mantle of Western civilisation and enact Whiteness and African subjects who would be rendered in superior terms to phenotypically white people, substantial groups of whom were seen as becoming increasingly dislocated from, and indeed perhaps were never qualified for, Western civilisational prowess. And if

[80] Harrison, *The African Presence*, p. 8.
[81] Ibid., at p. 14.
[82] Mudimbe, *Idea of Africa*, p. xi.
[83] Ibid., at p. xii.
[84] Mahmood Mamdani, *Citizen and Subject: Contemporary Africa and the Legacy of Late Colonialism* (Princeton, NJ: Princeton University Press, 1996), pp. 50–1.

this is the case, then we need to reappraise our critical tools, for taking the analyses presented in this section to their logical conclusion would not leave us with any better an understanding of post-crash 'Africa Rising' debates, their historical provenance and why it is that they might be problematic.

The second category of post-colonial literature concerning the Western gaze and imaginaries of Africa I wish to briefly consider here does provide more analytical purchase, and yet does not answer important questions concerning the significant issue of *why* contemporary and historical narratives of Africa's 'rise' or 'emergence' became prominent when they did (i.e., the sociology of these narratives). This is predominantly found in more recent literature that explores the ways in which humanitarian and development organisations and campaigns tend to idealise Africa as a way to enact liberal fantasies. For instance, Williams[85] and Williams and Young[86] have noted that the project at the heart of World Bank development policy is to construct a fantasy of the homo oeconomicus liberal subject in Africa. This has happened via a process that has worked to act against familial and kin ties in public office, to deregulate property and banking markets and services, to establish micro-finance initiatives, and so on, all of which are projects that persist, despite the regularity with which they fail on their own terms to produce macro-economic growth and/or entrepreneurial individuals.[87] In the sphere of the moral economy, Julia Gallagher has argued that humanitarian campaigns peddle experiences where 'encounters with "morally superior" people, who have suffered and retained extraordinary levels of humanity' can 'provide a feeling of connection to a higher good than can be achieved at home, where materialism, greed, and the pursuit of self-interest make life more morally uneven'.[88] This is of course not a recent development,

---

[85] David Williams, 'Constructing the Economic Space: International Organisations and the Making of Homo Oeconomicus' *Millennium*, 28:1, 1999, pp. 79–99.

[86] David Williams and Tom Young, 'Civil Society and the Liberal Project in Ghana and Sierra Leone' *Journal of Intervention and Statebuilding*, 6:1, 2012, pp. 57–72.

[87] In the case of micro-finance, which has been a pet project of the World Bank for a number of years, see Centre for the Study of Financial Innovation, 'Microfinance Banana Skins: Facing Reality' (New York, NY: CSFI, 2014).

[88] Julia Gallagher, 'Healing the Scar? Idealizing Britain in Africa 1997–2007', *African Affairs*, 108:432, 2009, p. 440.

with a strain of trying to find the sunlit uplands of life in Africa to ameliorate perceived depressed domestic conditions being a consistent historical feature of Western imperial imaginaries and projects. In the late-eighteenth century for instance, the British Home Office sanctioned and financed projects to seek out suitable lands in Africa for the settlement of, to be sure, convicts,[89] but which were yet 'designed from the beginning to produce both wealth and a degree of human happiness which would be harder to achieve in the corrupt "Old World" of Europe'.[90] Such projects that were established were almost uniformly failures.[91] However, this did not prevent later colonial officials from harbouring similar ideas, driven by similar hopes of finding morally unspoilt utopias in Africa. For instance, some British colonial officials in the 1920s saw in their African postings the possibilities of erecting 'new Jerusalems', where they could resurrect the green and pleasant lands of Britain's past among the simple folk to be found in the African hinterland.[92]

Post-crash narratives about Africa's 'rise' engaged in similarly idealistic tropes. Celebrations of the 'African middle class', whose consumerism would drive them to demand transparency and stable economies from their governments,[93] or a growing number of 'mature' African democracies[94] all spoke to this sense in which Western imaginaries continued to fashion African subjectivities that reflected Whiteness and the vitality of supposedly phenotypically white achievements and standards. And yet while the above analyses of idealisation in Western imaginaries of Africa do shed important light on the breathlessness of post-crash debates about Africa's 'rise', we are still not left with a sociology of these debates (or indeed older examples); a sense of *why* these debates emerged at the precise point that they did, and not earlier, or indeed at all.

---

[89] Curtin, *The Image of Africa*, p. 92.
[90] Ibid., at p. 89.
[91] For a broader discussion on such projects see Curtin, *The Image of Africa*, pp. 88–119.
[92] Christopher Prior, *Exporting Empire: Africa, Colonial Officials and the Construction of the Imperial State c. 1900–39* (Manchester: Manchester University Press, 2013), p. 111.
[93] For instance, Robert Rotberg, *Africa Emerges* (Cambridge: Polity Press, 2013), pp. 5–6.
[94] For instance, Radelet, *Emerging Africa*, passim.

Some scholars have attempted to explore this question. Bram Büscher, for example, explains contemporary instances of Western idealisation of African resources and eco-tourism as intimately wrapped up in the political economy of the continent, which tends to be viewed either as 'left behind' (when Africa's economic potential is deemed insignificant), or at times of Western economic deterioration, as capable of producing 'win–win' scenarios for Western economies and African peoples.[95] This political economy approach is shared by scholars who have analysed attempts to 'brand' Africa as a place of ethical investment and tourism.[96] However, when we survey the entire range of ways in which Africa has penetrated the public consciousness of formerly imperial societies this century, a purely material approach does not really seem to provide enough explanatory rigour. For instance, the rise of African fashion as a feature of mainstream metropolitan nightlife[97] cannot be explained simply by recourse to Western economic vitality, or lack thereof. Similarly, the explosion in popularity for African film, food and literature festivals cannot be explained in these terms either. Even more straightforwardly political issues, such as the fervent belief one finds among some commentators in Africa's 'demographic dividend',[98] or its 'maturing democracies',[99] cannot be explained with recourse to purely material arguments.

Chapters 6 and 7 will explore these post-crash debates in greater detail, but for now it is important to note that this is precisely where one of this book's contributions lies; in pushing against the boundaries of conventional post-colonial and materialist critiques of Western

---

[95] Büscher, 'The Political Economy of Africa's Natural Resources,' p. 137.

[96] Lisa Ann Richey and Stefano Ponte, 'Brand Aid and the International Political Economy and Sociology of North-South Relations', *International Political Sociology*, 7:1, 2013, pp. 92–3.

[97] See: Time Out, 'V&A Friday Late: Afropolitan', Thursday, 11 October 2012, available at www.timeout.com/london/shopping/v-a-friday-late-afropolitan, accessed on 4 February 2016; MoMa, 'King Britt presents MOONDANCE, A Night in the AfroFuture', Sunday, 13 April 2014, available at http://momaps1 .org/calendar/view/498/, accessed on 4 February 2016.

[98] For instance: Severino and Ray, *Africa's Moment*, p. 1; Rotberg, *Africa Emerges*, p. 12; Vijay Mahajan, *Africa Rising: How 900 million African Consumers Offer More Than You Think* (New Jersey: Pearson Education, 2009), pp. 127–47; David Mataen, *Africa: the Ultimate Frontier Market* (Peterman: Harriman House, 2012), pp. 7–21; Robertson, *The Fastest Billion*, pp. 126–14.

[99] For instance: Radelet, *Emergent Africa*; Rotberg, *Africa Emerges*.

imaginaries of Africa. Some scholars within this group fail to furnish us with the critical tools to understand how Whiteness, understood as not always connected to territory and phenotype, can invert the negative relationship that has seemingly defined the way that Africa has been historically envisaged in Western intellectual and popular traditions; while other scholars get some of the way there by focussing on the ways in which the desire to universalise Whiteness can produce idealisations of Africa, but without providing a clear map or set of coordinates to understand precisely why it is that these idealisations appear at particular times. For as we will see, post-crash debates about Africa's rise did not channel ideas about the continent that were new. Both in form (books talking about Africa's 'rise' or 'emergence' were being published as far back as the 1940s)[100] and substance, these debates were neither post-stereotypical nor *sui generis*. And yet these are insights that we would not necessarily glean from conventional post-colonial critiques of Western imaginaries of Africa. In short, what we lack is a sociology of this imagination, one that this book aims to provide by presenting a series of case studies that illustrate how transitions in anxieties concerning White economic, political and social vitality during the twentieth century have produced shifting sets of idealisations about Africa in Western imaginaries of the continent and international order, as well as a rupture in the relationship between phenotypically white exclusivity and civilisational prowess.

The Inherency of Anxiety to Whiteness

If it is indeed the case that post-crash 'Africa Rising' narratives and other cultural and social phenomena represent not simply a post-stereotypical form of representing Africa, but a deeply ethnocentric Western set of imaginaries of the continent, then a question follows. How is it possible that positive idealisations of Africa, which in some instances assert Africa's primary status in aspects of international order, might be ethnocentric, given that Whiteness, commonly understood, trumpets its own supremacy and the superiority of 'European

---

[100] See for instance: William MacMillan, *Africa Emergent* (Harmondsworth: Pelican Books, 1938/49); Joseph Oldham, *New Hope in Africa* (London: Longman, 1955); William Ward, *Emergent Africa* (London: George Allen and Unwin Ltd, 1967).

institutional genius',[101] assigning the rest of the (non-white and non-White) world to the 'waiting room of history'?[102]

The answer to this question will be broken down into two components. Firstly, the book will substantiate the fact that Western imaginaries of Africa have always relied on idealisations of various definitions of African subjectivity, in some cases to reassert the principle of phenotypical white supremacy, in others, to validate the supremacy of Whiteness, even where phenotypical whites might be in civilisational decline. This explains the historical nature of some of the subsequent chapters, which set out to highlight illustrative instances of when optimism about various forms of hyper-idealised African subjects have been conjoined with the second component of the answer to the question above, namely anxieties concerning White vitality, and the uneven, but gradual, detachment of phenotypical whiteness from Western civilisational prowess over the past century (or the detachment of whiteness from Whiteness). Put another way, the book will argue that post-crash narratives concerning Africa's rise represent the latest staging post in the belief that Western civilisational characteristics are universal and irreproachable, all the while that phenotypical whiteness is no longer a guarantor of access to, and the social reproduction of, these civilisational characteristics. What follows will briefly deal with each of these components in turn.

From the earliest Imperial encounters, positive idealisations about the 'savages' of newly colonised territories went hand-in-hand with pessimism concerning their intellectual or productive capacities, with these assessments at times contradicting each other. Tzvetan Todorov for instance argued of Christopher Columbus that he had 'decided to admire everything ... These people are good, Columbus declares at the start, without any concern to ground his affirmation ... This admiration [is] determined in advance'.[103] Columbus's optimism was informed by a sense of self-superiority that those he encountered shared his cosmology, and it was only later, when the reality of native resistance punctured Columbus's idealised vision of them, that he inverted his opinions of them into the perhaps more familiarly racist

---

[101] Hobson, *The Eurocentric Conception of World Politics*, p. 6.
[102] Chakrabarty, *Provincializing Europe*, p. 8.
[103] Tzvetan Todorov, *The Conquest of America: The Question of the Other* (New York, NY: Harper and Row, 1984), p. 36.

tropes of barbarity and uncivility.[104] A similar process occurred in Africa, whereby some of the earlier missionaries 'tended to gloss over the tensions the imperial encounter created for missionary culture', and were hugely optimistic about the African capability for Christian conversion, and that Africans could thus be 'civilized'.[105] Once again, this only changed when, by the middle of the nineteenth century, the reality of African resistance to conversion disrupted the fantastical idealisations of missionary endeavour.[106]

Therefore, even though White supremacy might typically be characterised by a straightforwardly superior self-confidence vis-à-vis the rest of the world, in a historical sense a '"first Europe, then elsewhere" structure of global historical time',[107] positive idealisations of Africa have been 'quietly re-presenting [themselves]' as an avatar of Whiteness for a very long time.[108] Writing about European Imperialism more broadly, Richard Price argues that it was a project that was 'always heavily contoured by optimism and hope. Empire carries with it a prescription for change that must be conveyed with self-confidence and certainty'.[109] So even though European imperialism was fundamentally ethnocentric, envisioning the rest of the world as lagging behind the West, these paragraphs have illustrated that because the imperial project has also been concerned with reshaping the world in its image, particular Western imaginaries have had to be optimistic about the ability of Others to achieve or even surpass phenotypical whites in reproducing Whiteness in the form of Western civilisational standards, codes and logics. This is something that becomes even more pronounced when this self-referential fantasy of white phenotypical exceptionality (for some phenotypically white people) and privileged

---

[104] Ibid., at p. 44.

[105] Richard Price, *Making Empire: Colonial Encounters and the Creation of Imperial Rule in Nineteenth-Century Africa* (Cambridge: Cambridge University Press, 2008), p. 56.

[106] Ibid., at p.57; see also Jan Vansina, *Being Colonized: The Kuba Experience in Rural Congo, 1880–1960* (Madison, WI: The University of Wisconsin Press, 2010), p. 278.

[107] Chakrabarty, *Provincializing Europe*, p. 7.

[108] Sabaratnam, 'Avatars of Eurocentrism', p. 274. Sabaratnam is here talking explicitly about Eurocentrism, and not Whiteness, although as noted earlier on in this chapter, Eurocentrism often stands as a placeholder for race and Whiteness in the critical literature on Eurocentrism.

[109] Price, *Making Empire*, p. 57.

status vis-à-vis the reproduction of Western civilisational standards becomes undermined.

This brings us to the second component of the answer to the question that opened this section. What we have seen thus far is that it is entirely possible for Western imaginaries to invert the superiority of phenotypical whiteness over phenotypical blackness, and place the former in an inferior position to the latter, all the while maintaining notions of White standards at the top of a civilisational hierarchy. But why does this occur? In short, because the superiority historically inherent to Whiteness is riddled with, and constantly undermined by, anxieties concerning the ability of the phenotypically 'white race' to perpetuate itself as the boundary-keeper for Western civilisation, the apogee of Whiteness. As we will see in several of the forthcoming chapters, idealisations about various forms of valorised African subjectivity in different periods ('tribal', 'bureaucrat', 'entrepreneurial middle class') have been intimately related to metropolitan social, political, economic, cultural and fundamentally racial anxieties.

Existential anxieties have long-informed positive Western imaginaries of an idealised Africa and the colonised world more broadly. In a previous section, I mentioned the ways in which Africa has always been imagined as a place where the social and moral decay of the West could be escaped. This is a product of the pendulum-like way with which Whiteness produces ideas about both the West and Africa (assigning negative and positive traits to each, sometimes in turn, more often simultaneously), which is underpinned by a set of ethnocentric anxieties concerning White vitality, and occurs simply because of the hard work required to maintain enough evidence to sustain the optimism inherent to Imperialism and the idea of White 'European institutional genius'.[110]

Such work requires the creation of an insulating layer against the real of racial injustice necessitated by the sustenance of white privilege. But this insulation is weak, and results in what Robin DiAngelo calls 'White fragility'. This fragility operates in a number of ways and produces a range of emotions when bodies demarcated as White (bodies that might not always be phenotypically white) are confronted by the injustices that sustain them as such, including, most obviously, angry denial, but also 'withdrawal, emotional incapacitation, guilt,

---

[110] Hobson, *The Eurocentric Conception*, p. 6.

argumentation, and cognitive dissonance'.[111] In itself this is an operation designed to avoid the confrontation between Whiteness and injustice. Ultimately, 'White bodies do not have to face their Whiteness; they are not orientated towards it, and this "not" is what allows Whiteness to cohere'.[112] Arguably, it is in this 'not' that we find the idealisations of Africa considered in the coming chapters. For it is from this 'not' that the variety of cognitive dissonances that produce these idealisations emerge. Not facing the true nature of Whiteness and the injustices that constitute Whiteness involves constructing an edifice of fantasy, one that operates almost constantly in a state of psychopathic denial and cognitive dissonance, whereby '[o]ne has to learn to see the world wrongly ... [producing] a particular pattern of localized and global cognitive dysfunctions...producing the ironic outcome that whites will in general be unable to understand the world they themselves have made'.[113]

This is a historical feature of Whiteness. Colonial officials and Imperial agents went to many lengths to maintain their illusions of grandeur and unique genius, seeking to avoid appearing inferior[114] or elderly[115] in front of the colonised, and arguably masking a deep set of anxieties about that self-same genius. With specific reference to colonial settler projects in Africa, there were constant tensions between the self-assured sense that 'civilization, race and fitness to rule could not be pulled apart', the optimistic belief that Africans could be tutored into civilisation under such a triptych of privilege, and the necessity of policing the behaviour of settler communities to ensure that they did not breach the borders of 'civilised' acceptability and undermine White and white prestige,[116] presenting manifestations of phenotypical white violence as pathological, rather than constitutive of Whiteness.

---

[111] Robin DiAngelo, 'White Fragility', p. 56.
[112] Ahmed, 'Phenomenology', p. 156.
[113] Mills, *The Racial Contract*, pp. 17–18. Mills could undoubtedly be more nuanced in his language around 'whites', although even if we focus his statement on those with the power to 'make the world', his point would still stand.
[114] Sankaran Krishna, *Globalization and Postcolonialism: Hegemony and Resistance in the Twenty-First Century* (Boulder, CO: Rowman and Littlefield, 2008), p. 116.
[115] Edward Said, *Orientalism* (London: Vintage Books, 1978), p. 42.
[116] Brett Shadle, *The Souls of White Folk: White Settlers in Kenya, 1900s–1920s* (Manchester: Manchester University Press, 2015), p. 4.

For these borders were constantly being breached, and, as subsequent chapters will illustrate, resulted in increasingly desperate attempts to expand the Western civilisational frontier in an attempt to distance Western civilisation from an increasingly feckless and reckless form of phenotypical whiteness. Historically, the idealised subjects to have emerged from such anxiety have ranged from the good, docile Africans that would flock to Christianity in the missionary era,[117] to the contemporary 'African middle class', thought more likely to demand effective and transparent governance.[118] In both cases – and others considered in subsequent chapters – these translate into attempts to expand Western civilisational frontiers at first with, and then beyond, phenotypical whiteness, with implications for how international order in a racial hierarchy is imagined.

Africa has thus always served as a site where, inspired by White anxiety and fragility, people self-identifying with Whiteness (the belief in the universality of a mythologised European institutional genius) have sought to remake better versions of the West. In seeking to displace supposedly White histories onto Africa, as a means of 'saving' these histories from phenotypical white decline, Africa has become a place in which Whiteness can seek a kind of nostalgic self-affirmation; nostalgic because this is a self-affirmation of a mythologised historical genius now looking for an outlet beyond a failing Western iteration of Whiteness. This translates into a romanticised version of White/ European/Western history, achieved not simply by defining Whiteness in relation to its opposite – the conventional argument deployed by critical and post-colonial scholarship – but also by reassuring itself of the validity of its own supposedly endogenous achievements and claims in light of anxiety about the sustainability of these things in the West itself. Holding up the picture of Dorian Gray into which Whiteness has been able to empty its own flaws[119] is thus not the *only* function Africa has served within Western imaginaries of the continent. Indeed, this book will argue that post-crash debates about Africa's 'rise' represent the latest way in which Western imaginaries

[117] Price, *Making Empire*, p. 49.
[118] Rotberg, *Africa Emerges*, pp. 5–6; for an argument which suggests that this class have not thus far sought to act beyond their own self-interest, see Nic Cheeseman, 'Does the African Middle Class Defend Democracy? Evidence from Kenya' Afrobarometer, Working Paper No. 150, December 2014.
[119] Achebe, *Image of Africa*, p. 19.

of Africa, beset by constitutive anxieties concerning White vitality in the West, reverses the situation, placing the West in the picture of the old, decrepit Dorian Gray, rather than posing, full of vigour, in front of it. The following chapters will illustrate how this is a pattern that is not unique to post-crash discussions of Africa's rise, but is rather a constitutive sociological pathology of Whiteness, which can be seen to pattern Western imaginaries of Africa and international order more broadly for at least the past century. In Chapter 4 especially, we will see that this tendency for imaginaries of Africa and international order to be driven by racial anxieties takes a significant turn, itself shaped by the events of World War II. Further details concerning the significance of this transition, as well as other methodological issues, are provided in the following section.

Some Notes on Method and Selection

This is not a straightforward history book. Rather, the book seeks to illustrate shifts in the boundaries of Whiteness through a number of historical and contemporary case studies that act as provocations to think about how and why these boundaries have shifted over the past century. An important question to, therefore, address is why it is that (the idea and image of) Africa in particular helps us to understand some of these shifting contours of twentieth and twenty-first-century Whiteness. Put another way, why is this book not about India, or perhaps, given its similarly homogeneous connotation, the Middle East?[120] Indeed, en-vogue acronyms such as BRICS (Brazil, Russia, India, China, South Africa) or MINTs (Mexico, Indonesia, Nigeria, Turkey) suggests that Africa has not been alone in experiencing feverish excitement concerning its politics and economy. Nonetheless, Africa stands out precisely because for so long it has been both so denigrated, and so much a subject of fascination for humanitarian, cultural, literary and other industries, almost standing alone as 'an aggregate continental space ... [which] is more akin to a cognitive space than one marked by state boundaries or genealogy'.[121] More than any other place on the

[120] See for instance Said, *Orientalism*.

[121] Harrison, *The African Presence*, p. 2. It is not my intention here to get into debates over how 'African' people living in Africa feel. Certainly, the map of Africa, transposed onto T-shirts, carvings, canvasses and all kinds of other materials found at markets and shops across the continent (South of the

Earth then, the West 'has been "inventing" Africa for centuries',[122] and as such Africa stands as a receptacle, long held to be devoid of its own history and culture both absolutely, and in comparison, to other non-Western territories,[123] into which the genius of Western civilisation can be poured and sustained.

There is another feature of this book that requires explaining. The historical case studies that appear in this book (Chapters 3 and 5), as well as the contextual chapters which partner them (Chapters 2 and 4) are set in an Anglophone settler-colonial context, specifically, in the case of Chapter 3, in Kenya, and then in Chapter 5 British Southern Africa more broadly. Even Chapter 7, which incorporates the analysis of contemporary 'Africa Rising' narratives, takes place in what one might call, with one or two exceptions, the 'Anglosphere' of English language news, policy reports, books, investment guides, etc. Yet throughout the book I talk about White anxieties, and Whiteness in general, as overarching social constructs.

In terms of the Anglophone and Anglospheric focus, there are personal limitations that explain this approach – i.e., mainly limitations of language and translation resources. However, there are additional reasons that justify the Anglo-centrism of the book. Although the British were of course not alone in constructing ideas about Africa, they were

---

Sahara at least) is something that exists to satisfy tourist expectations of the place they have come to. But one shouldn't assume that this is all it amounts to. The risk here is of falling into an 'Africa-as-tribal' stereotype. One only has to witness the crowds at screenings of an Africa Cup of Nations football match to witness how important national pride can be, at least some of the time (see, Thandika Mkandawire, 'Rethinking Pan-Africanism, Nationalism and the New Regionalism', in Sam Moyo and Paris Yeros (eds.), *Reclaiming the Nation: The Return of the National Question in Africa, Asia and Latin America* [Chicago, IL: University of Chicago Press, 2011], pp. 31–54). That this might also apply to a pan-African sense of identification should not be easily dismissed. See for instance the contemporary pan-African thinkers considered in Guy Martin, *African Political Thought* (London, New York, NY: Palgrave MacMillan, 2012), pp. 55–70.

[122] Mudimbe, *The Idea of Africa*, p. xv.

[123] See for example, Lothrup Stoddard, *The Rising Tide of Color against White World Supremacy* (London: Chapman and Hall, 1920), chapters 4 and 5. Stoddard, an American populist writer and eugenicist, believed that while all of the Earth's other 'races' posed a threat to phenotypical white civilisation, Africans were static, without history or culture, and thus posed no such threat. For a similar approach, see also Huntington, *Clash of Civilizations*, pp. 40–7.

the predominant colonial power, both in terms of territorial span and also in terms of administrative power and colonial expertise.[124] To take just one example of what this meant and how it manifested, in terms of popular and travel literature alone (an area the book will touch on in Chapters 2 and 4), the sheer volume of titles produced far exceeded that of any other imperial power.[125] Furthermore, the contemporary Anglophone narrative concerning Africa's rise is extensive, and is parroted by International Organisations and international consultancy firms, who, although writing in English, employ an international staff and perform for an international set of stakeholders and audiences. Relatedly, as the book progresses there will be times when American voices overlap with, and intercede with, the British focus of the book. In some cases these voices will share the anxieties of their British interlocutors, and at other times not. For instance, although driven by a similar set of geo-political anxieties in the 1950s, where British commentators often saw African independence as a rejection of Western civilisational standards, many US commentators saw an affirmation of US revolutionary history, which served to constitute Whiteness in a different manner.[126] Albeit at times in tension then (and this will be further drawn out in Chapter 4), this reinforces the sense in which rather than talking about a fixed British context, it makes more sense to talk in terms of an 'Anglosphere'[127] where similarities and differences emerge because, while 'the imagined community of white men was transnational in its reach' it was also 'nationalist in its outcomes, bolstering regimes of border protection and national sovereignty'.[128]

Nonetheless, the focus of this book on Anglophone and Anglospheric Africa means that the claims that I will make concerning White anxieties, and subsequent idealisations concerning Africa, and the shifts in the socially constructed contours of Whiteness in general, are necessarily partial and qualified. This is reinforced by the settler-colonial focus

---

[124] Mamdani, *Citizen and Subject*, p. 50.

[125] Dorothy Hammond and Alta Jablow, *The Myth of Africa* (New York, NY: The Library of Social Science, 1977), p. 15.

[126] Martin Staniland, *American Intellectuals and African Nationalists, 1955–1970* (New Haven, CT, and London: Yale University Press, 1991), p. 76.

[127] Duncan Bell, 'The Project for a New Anglo Century: Race, Space and Global Order' in Peter Katzenstein (ed.), *Anglo-America and Its Discontents: Civilizational Identities Beyond West and East* (Abingdon: Routledge, 2012).

[128] Marilyn Lake and Henry Reynolds, *Drawing the Global Colour Line* (Cambridge: Cambridge University Press, 2008), p. 4.

of Chapters 3 and 5. In one sense, one might wonder whether there is something distinctive about settler-colonial imaginaries of Whiteness. Certainly, phenotypically white settlers in British Africa were driven by a particularly psychopathic set of anxieties, resulting in a much more hard-edged, self-serving and manic set of idealisations concerning African subjectivity. As such however, we can consider settler anxieties as being indicative of broader trends in period-specific White anxieties. Underlining this, many of the main protagonists we will encounter in the following chapters transcend settler politics as members of the British aristocratic class and/or humanitarian elite. As such, class, and associated class anxieties, as much as being positioned in a particular settler colonial locale, becomes an important feature of settler idealisations over the course of the two settler colonial case studies presented in Chapters 3 and 5. This reveals Whiteness to be an intersectional phenomenon, constituted by constructed characteristics and demarcations of class as well as race. As explained more fully below, each of the case study chapters will be partnered and preceded by matching chapters that explore broader socio-cultural Western imaginaries of Africa during the relevant contemporaneous period. That the kinds of anxieties identified in Chapters 3 and 5 are borne out by these broader socio-cultural analyses reinforces the sense in which settler colonial iterations of Whiteness may have been more pronounced in their anxiety, but certainly did not represent some kind of outlier in this regard.

The final case study the book presents, in Chapter 7, is very different, being contemporary, outside of an explicitly settler-colonial context, and much more transnational than the preceding case studies. The focus of Chapter 7 is more narrative-driven, taking a series of post-2007–8 financial crash upbeat proclamations concerning Africa's rise as its point of analysis. The fact of when this narrative emerged is what links it to the other case study chapters, all three of which were selected based on the presence of 'crisis' in the production of period-specific White anxieties. Settler colonies, and their place in generating prognoses for Britain's Empire, were key drivers of various crises of governance and confidence through the first two thirds of the last century (and not just for British elites), while it was the 2007–8 financial crisis that underpinned the emergence of the contemporary Africa Rising narrative that instigated this book project. As such, 'crisis' became an important component of tracing the evolution of Whiteness back through the past century. Indeed, as Simon Gikandi has argued, it has been through international crisis that Whiteness 'has articulated the modes of inclusion and exclusion that were its condition of possibility'.[129] As the chapters proceed, it will become clear precisely how important British settler colonies in Africa were in prompting this evolution, and how all of this relates to the more contemporary conjuncture.

There is one more issue that requires an explanation, and that is the temporal boundaries that apply in this book. This is a book about White anxieties and subsequent idealisations of Africa and their limitations in the twentieth and early-twenty-first centuries; it would be legitimate then to ask: what about White anxieties and subsequent idealisations of Africa from earlier periods? Indeed, it is not that such idealisations did not exist previously.[130] However, the twentieth century marks the period when 'the British Empire in Africa, so arduously acquired in the nineteenth century, was lost',[131] and where furthermore, an important transition took place that is only really manifesting more fully today. This transition followed World War II, and was related to the realisation that what was once thought unrepeatable (World War I) was distinctly so, and in many respects worse by several degrees. This realisation reinforced a process of increasing racial anxiety concerning the decline and parochialisation of Western civilisation. This had begun at the beginning of the century, but after World War II produced a belief among Anglospheric elites that 'the global line of colour could no longer be held'.[132] This book will argue that such a realisation did not create so much a crisis of confidence in 'European institutional genius',[133] and the place of White knowledge systems in defining and operationalising international order, but rather a crisis of confidence in the phenotypical white race's ability to incubate and facilitate Western civilisational genius, and in the face of increasing levels of miscegenation, to perpetuate itself. As we will see, this led to increasingly manic searches for Africans who could be entrusted with protecting and growing White vitality and Western civilisational universality.

[129] Simon Gikandi, 'The Ghost of Matthew Arnold: Englishness and the Politics of Culture', *Nineteenth-Century Contexts*, 29:2–3, 2007, p. 196.
[130] For the nineteenth century see: Price, *Making Empire*, p. 56; for the eighteenth century see: Curtin, *The Image of Africa*, pp. 88–119.
[131] Hammond and Jablow, *The Myth of Africa*, p. 114.
[132] Frank Furedi, *The Silent War: Imperialism and the Changing Perception of Race* (New Brunswick, NJ: Rutgers University Press, 1998), p. 17.
[133] Hobson, *The Eurocentric Conception*, p, 6.

Chapter Outline

The following provides a brief outline of the chapters in this book. A quick note on selection is required before the outlines proper. The chapters that follow seek to create period-specific, socio-cultural *and* politico-economically contextualised accounts of Western idealisations of Africa and their limitations, as well as provide the material for a sociology of such idealisations (predicated on shifting anxieties concerning White vitality) and a historicisation of post-crash Africa Rising narratives. In this latter respect, then, the book is also a kind of genealogy of these post-crash narratives, although it is also more than that. It is, however, genealogical in that genealogies 'are not conventional histories', 'do not aim to reconstruct a totalisable past' and 'do not claim the status of successive moments coherent in themselves'.[134] Rather than present three distinct phases, the three different periods explored in this book produce a kind of analytic that will heighten an understanding of dynamics that might otherwise go unexplored, namely, that post-crash narratives about Africa's rise are not *sui generis*, and do have a past that tells us a great deal about the shifting contours of Whiteness.

This genealogical bent, therefore, explains the choice of historical periods and case studies that appear in Chapters 2–5. I will explain these in more detail in the outlines below, but in short, these choices were made based on a number of criteria. First, and given the account of the importance of the twentieth century, I wanted to focus on one pre- and one post-World War II case study. Second, because of the crisis which looms over much of the Africa Rising debates that have appeared since 2007–8 (i.e., the global financial crash, global terrorism, democratic deficit, etc.) I also wanted to select cases that were similarly embedded in times of perceived crisis. Again, the chapter outlines will explain these in more detail. Lastly, because post-crash idealisations of Africa emerged almost unanimously from what might be described as sources of elite liberal progressivism/social democracy (i.e., progressively aligned public policy think-tanks, social democratic politicians and political advisers, NGOs, cultural commentators, etc.) I also wanted to find case studies where similarly composed coalitions

---

[134] Wendy Larner and William Walters, 'The Political Rationality of "New Regionalism": Toward a Genealogy of the Region', *Theory and Society*, 31, 2002, p. 394.

of (relative) progressives were featured (although as we will see, the boundaries between progressive and non-progressive, radical and reactionary, have not always been so distinct).

The chapters of the book proceed as follows: I have already referred to the case studies that will appear in Chapters 3 and 5, with post-crash 'Africa Rising' narratives being explored in Chapter 7. Preceding each of these chapters will be supplementary chapters (i.e., Chapters 2, 4 and 6) that will provide a more broadly rendered, period-specific, social, cultural, political and economic contextual basis for the more focussed discussions taking place in the case study chapters.

Chapter 2, for example, explores the ways in which ideas about Africa, race and empire manifested themselves socially and culturally in Britain at the end of World War I, and what these manifestations can reveal about anxieties concerning Whiteness and subsequent idealisations of Africa during this period. The chapter takes in a broad range of post-war travel and exploration literature, fiction, major anthropological works and the expanding field of eugenics, all of which constructed positive views of Africans as loyal less-than humans, simultaneously betraying anxieties about Western civilisational decline and the sustainability of phenotypical white domination in international order. Ideas about Whiteness in this period are thus far more invoked than they will be later on in the century, whereby phenotypical whiteness in the 1920s remains self-consciously understood as being a precondition for the performance of Western historical genius, namely Western civilisation. This chapter serves a framing function for Chapter 3, which focusses down into events that occurred in the British colony of Kenya in the 1920s.

Chapter 3 considers the events that built up to, and followed on from, the arrest of Harry Thuku, an early Kenyan anti-colonial nationalist, and a protest in Nairobi against his arrest on 22 March 1922 at which at least 20 people, and possibly up to 200, were killed by members of the Colonial Police Force. This event was the high water mark of two years of developing crisis in Kenya Colony. On top of the Thuku protest, settler groups had developed plans to kidnap the British Governor and declare unilateral independence if the British Government did not back them in their dispute with Indian claims for equal representative rights in the Kenya Legislative Council and equal access to land. The settler community perceived this dispute in the context of a defence of white power and White civilisational vitality against a tide of mass Indian and minority (urban, 'semi educated')

African usurpation. Thuku and his East Africa Association (EAA) emerged during this period of crisis as a nascent Kenyan nationalist and anti-colonial movement, and the chapter will trace the various interpretations of Thuku that emerged from debates among settlers, the British colonial administration in Kenya and in London (in the Colonial Office) and British humanitarian networks. Thuku and the EAA challenged both the European settler dominance of Colony affairs, as well as the officially sanctioned chiefs and headmen who constituted the various and divided tribal associations established by missionaries to interact with the colonial administration.

As Thuku and the EAA's activities spread, and became more con-frontational, so the various groups of settlers, colonial administrators and humanitarians used the figure of Thuku as a relief against which 'good' and praiseworthy African behaviour could be delineated, either in the actions of Thuku himself, or more commonly as a response to him. In separate sections the chapter, therefore, explicates how each of these groups deployed Thuku, as well as the anxieties concerning Whiteness that drove these deployments and made them ultimately both fantastical and idealised. All of this will be shown to correspond with the broader socio-cultural attitudes detailed in the previous chap-ter. Fundamentally, these anxieties corresponded with a continuing belief in, if not the sustenance of, white power in Europe, then certainly the self-same in Africa. As such, the Whiteness on display among and across government officials, settlers, missionaries and humanitarians remained embedded in a self-referential sense of phenotypical white superiority (albeit that this did not apply to all phenotypical whites) which their idealisations of Africans served to reassure.

Chapter 4 shifts the focus by skipping over World War II and into the 1950s, placing us firmly within debates over decolonisation in Africa. The chapter addresses the resultant socio-cultural and polit-ical anxieties that characterise this period in the West, and as with Chapter 2's relationship to Chapter 3, this chapter will thematically fore-shadow the case study text presented in Chapter 5. The chap-ter considers the major social and political paradigm of the 1950s, Modernisation Theory, as a starting point for exploring socio-cultural and political anxieties of the period. Briefly, Modernisation Theory describes a set of attitudes popular from the end of World War II among influential (primarily, but not solely, American) scholars and domestic and international public policy-makers. These attitudes held that science and technology, coupled with 'modern' attitudes to savings, accumulation and consumption were the historical drivers of Western capitalism-cum-civilisation, and were thus central to development in the soon-to-be decolonising world. It was explicitly anti-communist, and explicitly anti-tradition (or rather, anti any tradition that did not cohere to ideas about Western Modernity).

Importantly, the attitudes that underpinned Modernisation Theory were not simply limited to scholarly and political debate, but also permeated through socio-cultural representations of Africa as viewed through some of the Anglospheric fiction and travel literature, film and popular art of the period. As such, Chapter 4 will incorporate an analysis of key Modernisation Theory texts, as well as popular film and travel writing of the period concerned with Africa. Again, the aim will be to explore the racial anxieties that underpinned these representations of Africa, and the idealisations concerning the continent and its peoples that were produced as a result. The chapter begins to illustrate how Whiteness became far less invoked in the post-war period, as racial forms of categorisation begin to be replaced by (racialised) cultural ones. The next chapter focusses these arguments in a particular case study, that of settler-driven inter-racial societies in British possessions in Southern and Eastern Africa in the 1950s and 1960s.

Chapter 5 explores the response of (relatively) more progressive settlers in British possessions in Southern and Eastern Africa to the prospect (and crisis) of decolonisation and independence in the 1950s and early-1960s, and how these responses were geared around staving off what they saw as the potentially catastrophic outcomes of this process – i.e., 'white racialist' or 'black racialist' domination. In the early 1950s, a number of settler-driven inter-racial associations began to establish themselves in British possessions in Southern and Eastern Africa, most notable among them the Capricorn Africa Society. These associations were founded on the principle that it was culture, rather than race, which should be the demarcation between admittance and non-admittance to civilised society, and thus a sustained set of idealisations emerged from these societies about the capacity of *some* Africans to meet the standards of Western culture/civilisation. Despite attracting some African members, these associations never sustained large numbers of members of any ethnicity, and yet by situating themselves between what they saw as the equivalent 'extremist racialism' of both overtly racist European settler and African nationalist movements, Capricorn and similar associations tapped into Anglospheric geo-political Cold War anxieties, making these societies, for a brief period, central to British imperial policy, before fading under the pressure of the growing mass and significance of African nationalist movements across the continent.

Chapter 5 will deal with the anxieties that drove these settler-driven associations to embrace some Africans (i.e., those who met the sanctioned standards of 'civilised' cultural behaviour) while rejecting others. In addition to Cold War anxieties concerning Communist take-over in Africa, these associations channelled broader racial anxieties concerning the ability of Western civilisational genius to perpetuate itself after World War II, which directly correspond with the anxieties detailed in Chapter 4. These created the grounds for ahistorical idealisations of African political agency (which the 'progressive' settlers of these associations saw themselves as being ideally situated to 'awaken') and about those Africans who were deemed to be 'civilised' (for rejecting African nationalist 'racialism'). Unlike the idealised Africans of Chapter 3, these Africans were deemed superior to (some) phenotypical whites, and with race being relegated to culture, civilisational vitality in this period started to become untethered from phenotypical whiteness, all the while that a sense of White original and institutional genius remained dominant.

Chapter 6 takes a leap into the twenty-first century, although it argues that this jump in time does not represent a meaningful transition in the characteristics which came to define anxieties concerning Whiteness in the immediate post-war period considered in Chapters 4 and 5. In this chapter (and Chapter 7) quite the opposite will be suggested– that the ethnocentric basis of post-crash idealisations of Africa simply represent a more elaborated version of those anxieties on display in Chapters 4 and 5. In this chapter, this argument will be put forward via an exploration of the broader social, cultural, political and economic milieu in which post-crash narratives of Africa's rise are embedded. It will do so by arguing that the large and growing set of African cultural industries that have emerged in Western metropolitan centres this century have attracted increasing levels of popularity because they, in effect, assuage racial anxieties about Western civilisational sustenance, by showing that a familiar-but-different[135] form

---

[135] This formulation is taken from Homi Bhabha's discussion of colonial mimicry (Homi Bhabha, *The Location of Culture* [London: Routledge, 1994], p. 86).

of White genius is being practised by Africans, even if such genius is under threat among groups of phenotypical whites in the West itself. These industries have produced fashion shows, pop-up bars, film and literary festivals, food festivals, hair festivals and so on. Chapter 6 explores the ways in which such cultural representations are received by Western audiences, and how this reception idealises and appropriates an Africa that confirms White logics and reassures anxieties concerning White vitality and universality. Of course, such an argument is complicated by the fact that in many instances it is people of African heritage who organise, participate in, consume or act as propagandists for these cultural industries. The chapter does not argue that twenty-first-century African cultural industries represent a series of homogeneous expressions of anxiety and idealisation. Rather, these industries sit at an intersection of class, race and gender that is deemed appropriate for public consumption by those publics who consume these cultural happenings, where expressions of difference are best received where they assuage anxieties about Whiteness and the historical genius of Western societies. As such, the chapter argues that contemporary African cultural industries unwittingly act to assuage majoritarian anxieties and post-colonial guilt by idealising a form of Western civilisation-lived-through-Africans, the ultimate universalisation of Whiteness. This affirms White standards concerning consumerism and materialism, by showing that even if, as a result of the 2007–8 banking and financial crises, the ability of (majority phenotypically white) Western populations to meet such standards might be slipping (due to stagnating incomes, job precarity, etc.), they are only growing in Africa. Africa here, thus, acts as a *tabula rasa* upon which Whiteness can be saved from a declining West. As such, the chapter will argue that contemporary African cultural industries shadow the politico-economic and geo-political arguments made by the 'Africa Rising' commentariat considered in Chapter 7, particularly concerning White norm-affirmation.

This final substantive chapter, Chapter 7, deals with idealisations about African politics, economies and societies as witnessed within narratives about Africa's rise, which for a period grew more prevalent after the 2007–8 financial crash, and which deployed the crash as an explicit reference point for much of their idealised analyses of Africa. As with Chapters 3 and 5, this chapter provides a focussed exploration of the themes which are explored in its 'partner' chapter (Chapter 6).

Chapter 7 relates these post-crash politico-economic idealisations about Africa to anxieties about the vitality of White economic, political and social standards in the post-financial-crash world where this appears threatened by a variety of exogenous and endogenous geo-political and economic forces ranging from China and Russia to Da'esh and Donald Trump. The chapter argues that these post-crash expressions of African idealisation were deeply ethnocentric, sought self-referential norms affirming African behaviour and practices, and were based on a series of self-deceptions that, for instance, reified the growth of an African middle class produced by the expansion of global markets, all the while ignoring both the deeply precarious and potentially anti-democratic nature[136] of this class, as well as the concomitant growth in formally criminalised behaviour that this same market expansion had produced – i.e., email scamming, piracy, and so on.

Chapter 8 seeks to draw the various threads of the previous chapters together into a coherent genealogy and sociology of Afro-idealisation as representative of the shifting contours of Whiteness and racialised ideas about international order, arguing that there are a set of relationships that can be traced between contemporary and historical idealisations about Africa, and the racial anxieties that drive them and explain their prominence at certain times. The chapter argues that these relationships cohere around their shared anxieties concerning White vitality, White dominance of international order, and exclusive claims to civilisational genius, all of which result in the sanctioning of certain idealised forms of African behaviour, which generally affirm the sustenance of White standards and explain attempts to refashion Africa in a mythologised version of the West's image. However, the chapter will also draw attention to the ways in which these idealised forms of Africanicity, which get projected and/or held up as ideal, ultimately reveal themselves to be fantastical in the face of the actually existing agency of the people subjected as 'African'. The book concludes by arguing that such subjects often act in their own interests in ways that can counter the implicit hegemonic ambitions of anxious Western idealisations of Africa, a project that has always, intentionally and otherwise, sought, and largely failed, to mould Africa into an affirmation of Whiteness.

---

[136] Cheeseman, 'Does the African Middle Class Defend Democracy?'

I have been conducting research for this book since the summer of 2013. There has been a lot of trial and error, and some of the many hours I spent, for instance, at Anti-Slavery International's wonderful library in London did not end up contributing in a visible way to this book. The same goes for the School of African and Oriental Studies' (SOAS) London Missionary Society collections. I mention these here to illustrate the many miles yet to be travelled as far as this book goes. Material that did make it into this book nonetheless came from a variety of sources. The Royal Geographic Society-Institute of British Geographers in London has a wonderful (and unavailable electronically) card catalogue that runs to thousands of titles published from the eighteenth century until the late 1990s. It is organised by continent, then by country, and lastly thematically, which means that, for instance, the researcher interested in what European botanists thought about rare flowers in Borneo in the 1920s, would likely find a treasure trove of information awaiting them. It was from this catalogue that the travel and exploration literature explored in Chapters 2 and 4 were derived, supplemented by further titles held at SOAS. The case study material in Chapters 3 and 5 was retrieved from a number of different archives, and mainly consists of government records, settler records, anti-colonial newspapers and pamphlets, private correspondences and humanitarian and settler campaign material held at the National Archive (UK), the Institute of Commonwealth Studies special collections (University of London), the University of Oxford Africa collections at the Weston Library, the Kenya National Archive (Nairobi), the Center for Research Libraries (Chicago) and the Margaret Herrick Library, Academy of Motion Picture Arts and Sciences. In addition, oral history interview recordings with settlers, 'progressive' inter-racialists and anti-colonial Kenyan nationalists were consulted at the Imperial War Museum and the Kenya National Archive. Many of the sources presented in this book have never been written about or cited in the published record before.

Rather than describe every archive and every step of the research process, I instead want to briefly flag some important staging points that shaped the general direction and development of the project that unfolds in the following chapters. Two in particular are worth noting. It was my hope that the time spent in the Kenya National Archive would yield primary material on the various insurgent and anti-colonial movements that began to grow in that territory in the

1920s. However, it became clear very quickly that the Kenya National Archive was, concerning this period in Kenyan history at least, a repository of British colonial administration records, or at least those that the retreating British colonial administration saw fit enough to leave in situ, rather than set fire to or remove back to secret repositories in the United Kingdom.[137] Material suggestive of African attitudes towards British colonial and settler governance was available (some of which is presented in Chapter 8), but not in great detail, and so it was at this point that I decided the book had to be squarely centred on Whiteness, and the construction of ideas about Africa as refracted through White self-regard.

The second significant moment in the unfolding of the research process concerns the material presented in Chapters 2 and 4, and by extension Chapter 6. I spent a great deal of time thinking about how I could contextualise the case study chapters, and help these chapters speak to broader themes. I was fortunate enough, in 2014, to participate in a workshop at the Royal Geographic Society, where I came across the card catalogue described on the previous page. Taking stock of all of the titles contained therein helped me in mapping out the kind of contextual material I would need for each of the case study chapters. This is what also led me to SOAS to explore the collections of twentieth-century travel literature and colonial administrator autobiographies contained in their collections. Working backwards from the contemporary period (presented in Chapter 6), where social and cultural attitudes can be mined in a much broader array of media, led me to consider Africa-related films and exhibitions in the West in the 1920s and 1950s. In these ways, there are some common threads running through the contextual chapters, even if such threads weave slightly different patterns in the different periods they are derived from.

The characteristics that define Whiteness, and boundaries delineating Whiteness and Western imaginaries of Africa and international order, are not the same as they were. Although White genius is still rendered paramount (thus perpetuating a fundamental racial exclusivity concerning the ways in which international hierarchies are imagined and practised), phenotypical whiteness is no longer a prerequisite for the social reproduction of this genius, although this all nonetheless

---

[137] Ian Cobain, *The History Thieves: Secrets, Lies and the Shaping of a Modern Nation* (London: Portobello Books, 2016).

remains predicated on a fundamental denial of difference. This book argues that the ways in which Africa, its territories and its peoples have been rendered in Western imaginaries provide an ideal way of exploring this transition, which has taken place over the past century. This transition has been driven by anxieties concerning White vitality and universality, and resulted in idealisations of Africa and Africans, which have become ever more frantic in the face of the agency of those subjected as 'African' in this imagination.

2 | *Finding Anti-Civilisation in Africa*

In England … there is news of Africa everywhere[1]

> Africa is a treasure house, both to Europe and
> to an unknowing Africa itself[2]

The British Empire Exhibition and the Aesthetic
Anxieties of the Interwar Period

On 23 April 1924, St George's Day, the 216 acres-site in North London
dedicated to the British Empire Exhibition threw open its doors for
public view. Costing in excess of £4.5 million, and attracting 7.5
million visitors, plus another 10 million when it reopened in 1925,[3]
the Exhibition was designed to be the largest of Britain's imperial
pleasure parks, and celebrate and point towards a future of 'imperial
cooperation'.[4] The African presence was significant, with the 'lavish
displays'[5] of the West African pavilion setting it apart from those of
other dependent colonial territories. Indeed, taken together, the South
African, West African and East African groups occupied a total area of
around nine acres of the site.[6]

---

[1] Eslanda Robeson (African American anthropologist, actor and activist reflecting
in 1946 on time spent in London in the 1920s) in Stephen Bourne, *Black in the
British Frame: The Black Experience in British Film and Television* (London:
Continuum Press, 2001), p. 15.

[2] Harry Johnston, 'The Africa of the Immediate Future', *Journal of the African
Society*, 18:71, 1919.

[3] Jonathan Woodham, 'Images of Africa and Design at the British Empire
Exhibitions between the Wars', *Journal of Design History*, 2:1, 1989, Endnote
4.

[4] Daniel Mark Stephen, '"The White Man's Grave": British West Africa and
the British Empire Exhibition of 1924–1925', *Journal of British Studies*, 48:1,
2009, p. 102.

[5] Ibid., at p. 103.

[6] Woodham, 'Images of Africa', Endnote 4.

    With American political and humanitarian elites largely eschewing
Africa during this period,[7] we need to turn to the British Empire to get
a sense of White Anglospheric attitudes towards the continent. Within
this context, and due to its size, public profile and commercial, industrial and government backing, the British Empire Exhibition provides
an unparalleled insight into both elite and broader public attitudes
towards national identity, race and empire in the 1920s. As such, the
Exhibition serves as an instructive case of how period-specific racial
anxieties concerning Whiteness and Western civilisation translated
into idealisations of the empire broadly speaking, and in particular
certain aspects of 'African culture', with these particularities emerging
in order to address material and civilisational concerns around White
vitality. The upshot of this relationship was that Africa came to be seen
as a place where Whiteness could be redeemed, through the settlement
of phenotypically white people on the continent. The settlement of
British colonies in Africa was not, therefore, simply a product of imperial prestige or commercial gain, but also, and fundamentally, about
civilisational survival. This is a theme that this chapter will return to
as it explores not just the British Empire Exhibition, but post-World
War I, Afro-centric travel and exploration literature more generally.
As such, this chapter sets the scene for the case study of Kenya Colony
discussed in Chapter 3.
    At the British Empire Exhibition, the material anxieties the various
African exhibition spaces spoke to were prominent and were framed
by the various material factors driving the Exhibition. Figure 2.1 is
emblematic of these more general drivers and is derived from a pamphlet of many similar images produced by the Colonial Office for the
Exhibition.
    In an African context, we see similar factors at play. The exhibit
guide to the South African pavilion for instance contains eighty-three
sections, all but one focussing on industrial or other economic opportunities, developments and progress.[8] Nevertheless, the volume of economic and financial opportunities being advertised and displayed at

---

[7] It was only in the post-World War II period that American journalists and
   intellectuals began to visit the continent, often bringing a large amount of
   extraneous baggage with them based on fears embedded in widespread
   ignorance of the continent. See Staniland, *American Intellectuals*, p. 19.
[8] Union of South Africa British Empire Exhibition 1924 Catalogue, Brent
   Archives, British Empire Exhibition, WHS/0/1/0/6/9.

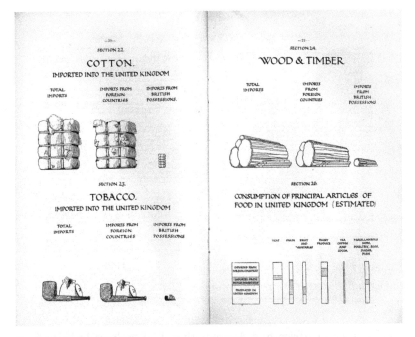

Figure 2.1 Material drivers of the British Empire Exhibition
The British Empire Exhibition Oversea Settlement Gallery, issued by the
Oversea Settlement Department of the Colonial Office, Brent Archives,
British Empire Exhibition, WHS/0/1/5/22.
(image supplied with permission from the Brent Museum and Archives)

the Exhibition should not detract from other important factors driving it, and which speak to broader metropolitan anxieties concerning
White civilisational vitality at that time. An insight into this is provided by a different image in the pamphlet referenced in Figure 2.1,
entitled 'Is this a Wise Distribution of Population within Our Empire'[9]:
    Concerns about urban overcrowding, squalor and moral feckless-
ness were not new, and had driven utopian projects for African settlement since the eighteenth century.[10] Nonetheless, such concerns were
now being brought into play with more recently produced post-War
material and civilisational anxieties to inform a broader range of

---

[9] Ibid.
[10] Curtin, *Image of Africa*, pp. 88–119.

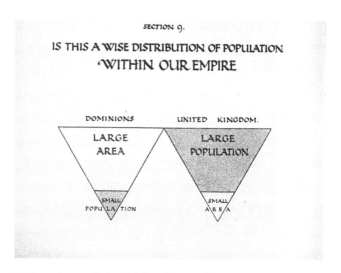

Figure 2.2 Broader anxieties driving the British Empire Exhibition
(image supplied with permission from the Brent Museum and Archives)

idealisations of Africa and Africans than had perhaps hitherto been prominent (Figure 2.2).

World War I was an obvious backdrop to the drivers behind the Exhibition; an exhibition that would serve as notice that Europe, and specifically Britain, had not succumbed to violent savagery or more intense exploitation of colonised people and territory, but rather had led to 'an improvement in imperial cooperation'.[11] And so, while the Exhibition organisers were in large part concerned with showing off Britain's economic potential, via its imperial 'commonwealth', this was done 'in the context of widespread unemployment and fears of radical degeneration and national decline'.[12] As a result, the Exhibition was part of a governing elite project that saw imperial consolidation 'as a solution to supposed problems of cultural degeneration and the declining international fortunes of the "British race"'.[13]

---

[11] Daniel Mark Stephen, *The Empire of Progress: West Africans, Indians and Britons at the British Empire Exhibition, 1924–25* (London, New York, NY: Palgrave MacMillan, 2013), p. 2.
[12] Ibid., at p. 9.
[13] Ibid., at p. 39.

Such anxieties produced a range of idealisations. For sure, many of these were again material in design. Commentaries on the Exhibition proclaimed that 'The Empire's greatest asset is its free and industrious populations ... as far as Africa is concerned, a concrete instance of this is to be found in the produce of the peasant farmers of the great Colonies and Dominions'.[14] This kind of idealising was part of the Federation of British Industries, Board of Trade and various other private commercial representative associations' attempts to hold up Nigeria and other large colonies as proof of the potential for market expansion and sources of raw materials that might prop up Britain's post-war economy.[15]

And yet, as with the anxieties driving the organisation of the Exhibition, the idealisations to emerge from these anxieties cannot be purely marked down as material. Indeed, as Stephen puts it, 'Imperial economics drew heavily on intuition, ideas of race, a view of empire as a moralizing force, and contained logical flaws and relied on intuitive leaps *bordering on mysticism*'.[16] Given the broad range of anxieties playing into idealisations of Africa, it is thus unsurprising that these idealisations should extend beyond the material. The Exhibition in general produced a multiplicity of orientalist tropes through its architecture and the feminised forms that many of the exhibits took on.[17] Furthermore, the idea of empire itself was being idealised; the interwar years were a time of great optimism in the British Imperial project, with no sense that within just a few decades the empire would be crumbling, and that African self-governing states would emerge. However, this optimism concerning the empire was not analogous with optimism about White civilisational vitality in the West. According to Stephen, the Exhibition itself was conceived to bring the empire into closer contact with Britain, acting 'as a panacea for alleged modern "problems" resulting from mass culture and class and gender conflict' that would 'cure British unemployment, secure the domestic standard of living, and halt the bullets of labor unrest, feminism, "national decline", and socialism'.[18]

---

[14] The African World, British Empire Exhibition Supplement, May 24th 1924, Empire Day, Brent Archives, British Empire Exhibition, WHS/0/1/0/6/9.

[15] Stephen, *The Empire of Progress*, p. 24.

[16] Ibid., at pp. 28–9, *emphasis added*.

[17] Ibid., at p. 3.

[18] Ibid., at pp. 31–2.

As a result, idealisations of Africa found at the Exhibition also drew on a number of supra-material anxieties. Many of the idealisations that resulted were constructed around aesthetic, as well as material concerns. While the African sections were full of 'primary products piled high',[19] it was 'the displays of native arts and crafts' and their 'artistic quality' that stimulated a strong demand for those products among the British public and the large London department stores, whose buyers purchased large amounts of stock.[20] Importantly, this was an aesthetic appreciation of an idealised 'native arts' Africa strongly conditioned by difference. Despite displays attempting to illustrate the civilising effect of colonial rule on Africans, a departure from previous metropolitan exhibitions of Africans as savages or sub-humans[21], public responses to the African exhibits 'suggest that the exhibition contributed to a growing pervasiveness, multiplicity, and arguably internationalization of languages of difference during the interwar years'.[22] This is apparent when we consider the words of the social and cultural critic Amelia Defries, who wrote of the native arts on display at the Exhibition that, 'Never before have we had such an opportunity to study the development of human nature and to revise our aesthetic theories and standards of taste' which had been in thrall to 'a theory of false aesthetics of their own'.[23] This was an 'epiphany of difference',[24] one which enabled British aesthetes to 'start our pilgrimage ... where we feel happy among the natural arts of mankind, as yet mercifully untouched by trade with the outside world'. Importantly, 'These are most valuable if we are to revise our aesthetic theory and base it on sound principles'.[25]

In these words, we find not simply an idealisation and objectification of African creative forms-as-different, but also a reflection of artistic anxiety; that British artisanal traditions had become 'too long in bondage to bad taste'. Indeed, rendering the products on display at the Exhibition as 'art' can itself be read as both a product of the desire to

---

[19] Woodham, 'Images of Africa', p. 15.

[20] Ibid., at p. 19.

[21] See, for one example, Phillips Verner Bradford, *Ota Benga: The Pygmy in the Zoo* (New York, NY: St Martin's Press, 1992).

[22] Stephen, '"The White Man's Grave"', p. 105.

[23] Amelia Defries, 'Craftsmen of the Empire: A Comparative Study of Decoration and Industrial Arts', *Architectural Review*, June 1924, p. 262.

[24] Mudimbe, *Idea of Africa*, p. 59.

[25] Defries, 'Craftsmen of the Empire', p. 262.

domesticate Africa into a White schema of distinct aesthetic and non-aesthetic categories – where the former are rendered as social objects and the latter are rendered with universalisable value and agency[26] – as well as part of a much broader relationship between White aesthetics and 'primitive' African culture. The Empire Exhibition occurred at a time not long after some of the mainstays of European counter-culture such as Picasso, Miro and Gauguin, had turned to so-called African 'primitive art' as a means by which to foment revolution in the staid world of European artistic production. For these artists, their work would bring joy to a decadent European culture, and be revealing of interior truths through a focus on symmetrical unity, clear stylisation and an emphasis of the surface.[27] This was however, a fundamentally ethnological enterprise, whereby the inspiration drawn from everyday and dynamic work-things, ritualistic tokens and communal pieces rendered these artefacts as static – ossified in some distant time – and did the same for the people and communities from which these pieces emerged. Indeed, ethnology and colonial power articulated themselves together in the work of artists such as these, for 'they had the same premises cohering in the same objective, that of converting overseas territories to the self and imagination of the West'.[28]

Thus, items invested with parochial meanings from the mundane to the spiritual were idealised to the status of art, and depoliticised, desocialised and ossified in the process, for this was a form of art that had to remain pristine and unchanging in order for it to rescue Western culture from a form of mundane decline and parochialism (summed up in Defries' attitudes towards the state of British artisanal traditions). What we see in these articulations of White colonial-aesthetics then is an idealisation of African 'culture' that is driven by anxieties concerning White aesthetic vitality, but which simultaneously objectifies African life-as-art, conforming it to Western aesthetic traditions that disdains and rejects 'other forms of aesthetic practices ... of sensing and perceiving'[29] – i.e., one which might understand these objects

---

[26] Walter Mignolo and Rolando Vasquez, 'Decolonial AestheSis: Colonial Wounds/Decolonial Healings', Social Text, 2013, available at: www.socialtextjournal.org/periscope_article/decolonial-aesthesis-colonial-woundsdecolonial-healings, accessed on 14 May 2015.

[27] Mudimbe, *Idea of Africa*, p. 56.

[28] Ibid., at p. 60.

[29] Mignolo and Vasquez, 'Decolonial AestheSis'.

as dynamic, multi-purposeful and part of an overarching sensory and meaningful set of practices. This was because these characteristics could only be attributed to phenotypically white people, and even then, given contemporaneous anxieties about working class and feminist militancy, not all of them.

As much as this perspective drew on a colonial genealogy, there was an important dimension that it took on in this period. Whereby artistic and literary representations of Africa had, for at least the prior century, rendered the continent as lacking in humanity or world-historical subjectivity, the interwar years were a period when we can begin to see subtle shifts in this regard. This is not to say that the historicisation of Africa came to an abrupt halt, either at the Empire Exhibition or more generally,[30] but simply that in this period we begin to see a shift. That shift involved seeing Africa as more than the sum of its resources and potential markets; as a place where White civilisational vitality might be saved from a degrading West. Population and demographic concerns were a central plank in this, as we saw in Figure 2.1, and perhaps best summed up by Leopold Amery prior to becoming Colonial Secretary in 1924, when he commented that 'there is no reason why, in the coming century, we should not grow to a population of 200 to 300 million white people in the Empire'.[31]

None of this suggests, however, that ideas about Whiteness in the 1920s cohered around a notion that an objectified Blackness could be on the same civilisational terrain as itself. Indeed, as this and the following chapter will show, Blackness became a powerful cultural commodity in this period precisely because it represented 'potent symbols of inversion, forbidden passions, the Freudian sub conscious, and white megalomania'.[32] Consuming Africa in ways that confirmed the phenotypical superiority of (some) whites, thus, necessitated maintaining Black Africa as constituted by a set of fundamental differences. In the world of art and aesthetics it was only because Africa's 'primitive' art was so starkly different from Western artistic traditions that it could

---

[30] See, for instance, the 108-page book *Nigeria: Its History and Products*, produced by the colonial government for the exhibition and which contains less than three pages on 'History', including sections on 'The People' and 'Religion', with the rest given over to 'Products'. See Brent Archive, British Empire Exhibition, 1924I/PRI/19/1.

[31] Amery in Stephen, *The Empire of Progress*, p. 11.

[32] Stephen, '"The White Man's Grave"', p. 127.

act to catalyse the latter from mundanity and decay. Similarly, it was Africa's challenging primitiveness that would foster a renewed White civilisation, but only *in* Africa itself. I will develop this point more comprehensively, for this need to produce an Africa-as-different in order to salve racial anxieties concerning Whiteness was widespread across various sectors of cultural production, and the generation of colonial knowledge more broadly. In particular, this chapter will build on the analysis of the British Empire Exhibition through an exploration of contemporaneous Afro-centric travel and exploration literature. In establishing this argument, the chapter will lay the historical and sociological groundwork for the case-specific events considered in Chapter 3.

Racial Confidence/Anxiety

The early-interwar years produced two complementary tracks of White self-regard. On the one hand, these years remained in many respects a period of White racial confidence. However, this confidence was pervaded by a sense of anxiety concerning White racial vitality in the West. As such, White racial confidence in this period was tinged, in some cases to an overwhelming extent, by anxieties concerning this vitality, and thus by a desire to locate idealised Africans, defined in terms of difference constructed around ideas of Blackness. In most instances, such idealisations rendered Africans mute, even while in the background their agency was being clearly demonstrated. Muting such agency required representations of Africans and Blackness to engage in a series of cognitive dissonances.

Confidence

Cognitive dissonances were most likely where White racial confidence was most pronounced, but also (and perhaps because it was) fragile. One area where this is most evident is within the range of travel and exploration literature that emerged in the 1920s. While it is certainly true that during this period the amount of literary fiction being published concerning Africa grew significantly,[33] it is the travellers and explorers of the period who, in attempting to faithfully represent their experiences, could not but escape from the dissonant agency of the

---

[33] Hammond and Jablow, *The Myth of Africa*, p. 118.

Africans who featured in their writings, even while simultaneously muting them. And so, even though at a general level, the books of travellers and explorers, which went through several rounds of editing and drafting, should not be taken to be much or any more 'authentic' than the work of novelists,[34] the pretensions of these authors to authenticity only makes more bare the cognitive dissonances involved in rendering and idealising Africans as different, not-yet-human, and mute.

There are some glaring examples of this kind of dynamic within the travel and exploration literature of the period. Captain W. T. Shorthouse's book on sport, 'adventure', big-game hunting and travel in the 'Wilds of Tropical Africa', seems from the outset designed to mute and relegate the human occupants of the continent to a sub-human level. This is achieved in several ways, most notably when the author thanks his friend for showing him 'the light in the dark of Africa'.[35] This is of course a completely unremarkable phrasing for the period, and yet despite the confidence with which Shorthouse implicitly depicts his own (and his comrade's) phenotypical and civilisational racial superiority, there are constant tensions between this sense of superiority, the agency denied to Africans in his rendition of them, and then the snippets of agency that shine through his account despite this. And so, for instance, appearing on the same page as each other we get the following statements:

Native gossip said a White Man had been shooting a number of buffalo in these districts ... as most native talk, however, it proved to be inaccurate information

Followed by:

Local natives complained bitterly of the depredations of lions in this vicinity, but I could scarcely believe that they would roam so near to our civilised cantonments. However, their stories proved to be true, and lions started roaring soon after dark, and kept up their music most of the night.[36]

---

[34] Dane Kennedy, 'Introduction: Reinterpreting Exploration, in D. Kennedy (ed.) *Reinterpreting Exploration: The West in the World* (Oxford: Oxford University Press, 2014), p. 8.

[35] Captain W. T. Shorthouse D.S.O., F.R.G.S., *Sport and Adventure in Africa: A Record of Twelve Years of Big Game Hunting, Campaigning and Travel in the Wilds of Tropical Africa* (London: Seeley, Service and Co. Limited, 1923), inner notes.

[36] Ibid., at p. 35.

'Native talk' here serves to be both reliable *and* unreliable. How can it be both? For Shorthouse, of course, 'Native talk' will almost always be unreliable. This is one way in which a schema of phenotypical white racial superiority is maintained. That, however, Shorthouse must admit an occasion where 'Native talk' has been reliable suggests that Africans might not be as inferior as otherwise presented. Of course, it is notable that such talk is only reliable in reference to animal behaviour (i.e., lions near to the camp) and was unreliable when reporting the actions of a 'White man' allegedly shooting buffalo. And so, even though this presentation of African sense seems to puncture the idealisation of Africans as without sense, it simultaneously confirms that Africans are able to understand better than white people – and might thus be on the same level as – animals. Taking place as it does in Africa, this serves to lay the groundwork for how White civilisation might perpetuate itself in the continent; by taking advantage of natural African capacities to commune with nature, in and of itself unthreatening to, and indeed facilitative of, the phenotypical white dominance necessary for the perpetuation of White civilisational vitality beyond the West.

In another former military man's account, Colonel Felix Shay writes of the Africans he encounters that 'the twentieth century AD rolled in on them unannounced and found them in the twentieth century BC. They have not yet recovered from it'.[37] The text of this piece is littered with such representations, and talk of 'savage boys',[38] as 'curious as children'.[39] And yet, being published in the *National Geographic Magazine*, the text is heavily interspersed on nearly every page with photographs of the colonel's trip. And there are many of these images; in total, the piece runs to 137 pages. What is so noticeable about these images is that so many of them display some aspect or other of remarkable local ingenuity, be that in engineering, agriculture, animal husbandry and so on. In Figure 2.3, the text tells us that the featured structure serves not simply as a bridge, but has also been explicitly designed to function as both a means by which fish can be caught *and* crocodiles warded off. And yet on the page immediately preceding the image, Shay writes about recruiting some maids for his expedition at

[37] Felix Shay, 'Cairo to Cape Town, Overland: An Adventurous Journey of 135 Days, Made by an American Man and His Wife, through the Length of the African Continent', *National Geographic Magazine*, 47:2, 1925, p. 187.
[38] Ibid., at p. 157.
[39] Ibid., at p. 158.

Figure 2.3 Sally Shay standing on a bridge in Uganda
Felix Shay, 'Cairo to Cape Town, Overland: An Adventurous Journey of 135
Days, Made by an American Man and His Wife, through the Length of the
African Continent', *National Geographic Magazine*, 47:2, 1925, p. 212.

Masindi in Uganda, writing that 'it is no easy task to pick four slightly
ones from a group of nearly naked savages'.[40]

Again, then, we can see the presence of a major cognitive dissonance. Presented on the one hand with evidence of African ingenuity and agency, the author nonetheless resides in a cognitive universe
whereby Africans remain fundamentally different, existing on a sub-
human level, and thus unable to challenge, or indeed inform the man-
ufacture and maintenance of White civilisational vitality in Africa.

Anxiety

It is difficult to talk about anxieties concerning White/white supremacy
in this period without talking about Lothrop Stoddard. Stoddard was,

---

[40] Ibid., at p. 211.

in the Anglosphere, a widely popular writer during the interwar years working on war and white racial power.[41] Stoddard was a eugenicist,[42] who believed in white racial purity and worked to avert the threat to that purity from the various other 'darker races'. He published prodigiously, with four books in the 1920s alone, as well as a large number of articles in respected scholarly journals such as *American Political Science Review*. So widespread and mainstream were his ideas that the newly elected US President Warren G. Harding could cite Stoddard's ideas on the race 'problem' to a crowd of 100,000 in Birmingham Alabama in October 1921.[43]

Evidently not a travel writer or explorer, it is nonetheless important to consider Stoddard here for two reasons. The first, general reason is that Stoddard's work illustrates perfectly the kinds of more implicitly stated anxieties to be found in cultural and traveller commentary of the period, with the public consumption of his ideas testament to their broad resonance with Anglospheric social attitudes at the time. Across the Atlantic, the influential British IR scholar Alfred Zimmern was for instance similarly and contemporaneously concerned with the rising power of 'nonwhite people'.[44] The second, more specific but related reason is that a dusty first edition of Stoddard's major work, *The Rising Tide of Color against White World Supremacy*, sits in the Kenya National Archive, sticking out like a figurative sore thumb. I will return to the political and social significance of this in Chapter 3, whereas for now we will focus in more closely on the anxieties very explicitly articulated in Stoddard's work, and in particular in *The Rising Tide of Color*, linked so closely as it is to events in the next chapter.

Stoddard saw World War I as a fundamental game-changer in the balance of racial power: 'I had hoped that the readjustments rendered inevitable by the renascence of the brown and yellow peoples of Asia would be a gradual, and in the main a pacific process' he wrote,

---

[41] Vitalis, *White World Order*, p. 64.
[42] Madison Grant, another notable eugenicist and trustee of the New York Metropolitan Zoo, wrote the foreword to Stoddard's *The Rising Tide of Color*.
[43] Vitalis, *White World Order*, p. 63.
[44] In Errol Henderson, 'Hidden in Plain Sight: Racism in International Relations Theory' in Robbie Shilliam, Alex Anievas, and Nivi Manchanda (eds.), *Race and Racism in International Relations* (Abingdon: Routledge, 2014), p. 22.

whereby the solidarity of 'the white race' would keep any other rising racial powers in check.[45] Stoddard continued, anxiously:

The subjugation of white lands by colored armies may, of course, occur, especially if the White world continues to rend itself with internecine wars. However, such colored triumphs of arms are less to be dreaded than more enduring conquests like migrations which would swamp whole populations and turn countries now White into colored man's lands irretrievably lost to the White world[46]

Similar tropes litter the book. Later on, for instance, Stoddard writes that 'If white civilization goes down, the white race is irretrievably ruined. It will be swamped by the triumphant colored races, who will obliterate the white man by elimination or absorption.'[47] These anxieties were not born simply from a geopolitical analysis of the relative military strength of Western and non-Western states, nations and empires. Rather, Stoddard believed that the White-West was in absolute decline, facing 'a demographically expanding white underclass and a shrinking white elite coupled with the dysfunctionalism of "socialist" state interventionism'.[48] And what of Africans in this vision of White civilisational decline? On the one hand, Stoddard was as dismissive of Africa as Samuel Huntington was to be in his influential, and not wholly dissimilar, 1994 book *Clash of Civilizations*.[49] Stoddard wrote that Black Africans lived in stasis, and thus posed no threat to White interests *except* as vessels for Asian imperial interests, who would take advantage of the emotional and vulgar character of the Black African.[50] Indeed, while Stoddard believed Western imperialism to have been a mistake, bringing incompatible races into close contact with each other and stoking anti-white grievances, he also believed that white control of Africa could serve as a bulwark against Asian imperial expansion.[51] As we will see in Chapter 3, this maps perfectly onto how white settlers in Kenya understood their historical

[45] Stoddard, *The Rising Tide of Color*, p. vi.
[46] Ibid.
[47] Ibid., at p. 303.
[48] In Hobson, *The Eurocentric Conception of World Politics*, p. 146.
[49] For Huntington's similar analysis, see Huntington, *The Clash of Civilizations*, pp. 40–6.
[50] Stoddard, *The Rising Tide of Color*, p. 90.
[51] Ibid., at p. 102.

mission. For now, though, it is relevant to note John Hobson's assertion that 'the label of "triumphalist white supremacy" as it applied to much of the eugenicist literature was an oxymoron'.[52]

Thinking about Whiteness as a universal civilisational marker was a relatively recent phenomenon, dating back only to the latter part of the nineteenth century, when advances in technology and communication began to shrink geographical distance and intensified spatially dispersed interactions in significant ways. Prior to this, civilisation had been thought about in more national or regional terms.[53] Right up to the early parts of the second half of the nineteenth century, mainstream political philosophy had maintained that Kantian transnational communities were impossible, unable to translate into communal homogeneity.[54] As we saw in Chapter 1, there is a long history of stratification that has gone on *within* notions of a white racial civilisation, whereby certain population groups with lighter skin pigmentation (i.e., Irish, Jews, Russians, Italians, and Boers, etc.) have nonetheless been construed racially and in inferior terms to 'true' whites.[55] Nonetheless, from the late-nineteenth century, ideas about a transnational White civilisation that traversed Great Britain, its settler colonies, and the United States, what Bell calls the 'Anglosphere', began to take hold as a means by which, initially at least, to sediment British global hegemony,[56] and witnessed increased communications and a heightened sense of comradeship among whites across several continents.[57] At the same time, W.E.B. Du Bois was famously declaring that the 'problem of the twentieth century' would be 'the problem of the color line'.[58] What was initially an elitist and intellectually driven project of British hegemony, thus, rapidly became a transnational socio-cultural phenomenon that united disparate socio-economic groups in fear of racial contamination, phenotypical white racial decrepitude and White civilisational decline. This was best expressed and evidenced through the popularity of Stoddard's books and the rise of eugenicism more broadly in the

---

[52] Hobson, *The Eurocentric Conception of World Politics*, p. 143.
[53] Bell, 'The Project for a New Anglo Century', p. 34.
[54] Ibid., at p. 37.
[55] Nederveen Pieterse, *White on Black*, pp. 212–24; Jeater, *Law, Language and Science*, pp. 192–3; Bell, 'The Project for a New Anglo Century', p. 34.
[56] Bell, 'The Project for a New Anglo Century', p. 39.
[57] Jack Temple Kirby, *Darkness and the Dawning: Race and Reform in the Progressive South* (Philadelphia, PA: Lippincott, 1972), p. 117.
[58] Du Bois, *The Souls of Black Folk*, p. vi.

United Kingdom and the United States during the immediate pre- and post-World War I period.[59]

In the British context, Stoddard's ideas were broadly reflected within the colonial establishment. Whether it was the shadowing of Lord Frederick Lugard's ideas about indirect rule in the 'Dual Mandate'[60] to be found in Stoddard's recommendations for 'separate but unequal development' in the US South,[61] or the sometime colonial administrator and explorer Harry Johnston arguing that 'it behoves us to see if the beginning of revolt against white supremacy is justified and if so how the thorn may be taken out of the wound',[62] this is apparent. Although less explicit, the travel, exploration and cultural commentary literature of the period similarly channelled many of Stoddard's anxieties concerning the absolute decline of White civilisation in the West.

The general tendency towards a Stoddardian perspective on White civilisational vitality was pervasive. In the midst of trumpeting the benefits to Africans of 'contact with Europeans' which was 'beyond argument', the peer and sometime amateur historian Hugh Archibald Wyndham, 4th Baron Leconfield, opined against the threat posed to both Africans and European settlers from 'poor Whites',[63] who in this sense represented the absolute decline of White civilisation, in the West itself, which Stoddard had similarly decried. Among travellers to the continent, Africa became a tableau for these concerns writ large.

C.V.A. Peel for instance wrote of his sojourn in Kenya (while engaging on a Cape-to-Cairo trip) that, 'Twenty one years ago ... one could roam all over the Athi Plains near Nairobi and shoot where one liked and what one wanted, but *with the advance of civilisation things have altered considerably*, with the result that when one's Safari appears on

[59] In Britain the Eugenics Education Society (later known as the British Eugenics Society) was founded by Francis Galton in 1907. For a useful overview of some of the main protagonists of this group and period, see: Michael G. Kenny 'Racial Science in Social Context: John R. Baker on Eugenics, Race, and the Public Role of the Scientist' *Isis: A Journal of the History of Science Society* 95:3, 2004: pp. 394–419.

[60] Lord Frederick D. Lugard, *The Dual Mandate in British Tropical Africa* (Fifth Edition. London: Frank Cass & Co. Ltd, 1965/1922).

[61] Lothrop Stoddard, *Reforging America: The Story of Our One Nationhood* (New York, NY: Scribners, 1927), pp. 46–50.

[62] Johnston, 'The Africa of the Immediate Future', p. 163.

[63] Hon. Hugh Wyndham, 'The Colour Problem in Africa', *Journal of the British Institute of International Affairs*, 4:4, 1925, p. 187.

the plains today it is met by native runners with instructions to warn one off so-and-so's farm'.[64] This reference to 'civilisation' is a common signifier among many of the travellers who wrote books about their time in Africa during this period. For Peel, the underlying factor is a negative attitude towards modernisation. He expresses this distaste through a story of his step-son being offered the steering wheel of a car by the owner of the farm they are staying on, and coming across a lion, who at first runs away, but then turns and behaves threateningly. The farm-owner jumps out of the car and shoots it dead. 'I suppose some people call that sport, and expect next we shall hear of shooting elephants from aeroplanes!'.[65] Indeed, while Peel's text barely mentions any Africans whatsoever, when it does it is to offer praise to those who conform more to his ideas of pre-modern, sub-human and animalistic life. In some instances, various groups of Africans are better because of how they look,[66] while in others it is related to how modern and civilised he perceives them to be. So, some Kikuyu guides Peel employs for his trip are 'far less trouble than the more civilised Swahili porters at the coast', because they are cheaper to employ and eat 'beans and bird seed', compared to the more expensive rice eaten by the coastal Swahili.[67]

Idealising Africans as simple, animal-like and free of the degradations of the contemporaneous 'civilised' West was a common trope of this kind of literature, and of the period more broadly, with the suspicions of more openly nationalistic and pan-African 'men in trousers' aroused among colonial administrators and settlers alike.[68] Ruminating on a campfire scene in another Cape-to-Cairo travelogue, Daisy Chown writes of the bright fires and watchful sentries that 'this was the real Africa – an Africa outside the narrow bounds of civilization'.[69] As with

---

[64] C. V. A. Peel, *Through the Length of Africa: Being an Account of a Journey from Cape Town to Alexandria and Sport in Kenya Colony* (London: Old Royalty Book Publishers, 1927), p. 97, *emphasis added*.

[65] Ibid., at p. 96.

[66] Ibid., at p. 42.

[67] Ibid., at p. 108.

[68] Joey Power, *Political Culture and Nationalism in Malawi: Building Kwacha* (Rochester, NY: University of Rochester Press, 2010), p. 20; Jean-Francois Bayart, *The State in Africa: The Politics of the Belly*, 2nd edn. (London: Polity Press, 2009), p. liii.

[69] Daisy M. Chown, *Wayfaring in Africa: A Woman's Wanderings from the Cape to Cairo* (London: Heath Cranton Limited, 1927), p. 131.

some of the authors noted in the previous section, however, the implicit critique of Western modernisation to be found here (which is debilitative of true White civilisational vitality) is conjoined with a cognitive dissonance regarding the 'out of time'[70] nature of the Africans Chown is observing. For, just two pages earlier, Chown praises a meal made for her by her porters in the middle of the bush, 'of such quality as to rival the best European kitchens'. Confronted by this, however, Chown does not seek to explore the other ways in which Africa might be thought of as being on equal terms with the West, but rather is driven to find and idealise the 'real' Africa, separated from the rest of the world by time and space. This maintains the calculation that while White civilisation might be in decline in the West, overwhelmed by modernising tendencies such as universal suffrage, Africa presents a potent opportunity for Whiteness to regroup among the idealised child-like and sub-human Africans who, because of these characteristics, pose no threat to White vitality and phenotypical (elite) white supremacy.

Shorthouse channels similar anxieties concerning White civilisational vitality in the West. He writes approvingly of the 'primitive peoples' he has met, and how they are 'in so many parts untainted by modern ideas of civilization',[71] and how being in Africa left him 'free now and far from troubles, away from civilization's roar and daily bustle [in] this land untrammelled and outside the City wall'.[72] Furthermore, this kind of lament for Western civilisation was not purely a right-wing aristocratic phenomenon; the Fabian eugenicist Julian Huxley, recording his thoughts of his time in Kenya, wrote of his dismay that the social divisions plaguing Europe were now finding themselves growing in Africa too, largely, in his view, at the hands of missionary agents who had left 'the converted African' feeling 'superior to his native brothers', and yet '[h]e was not educated enough to be enlightened as a European, but at the same time he had lost all his self-respect and pride in the native culture'.[73] We will see how this

---

[70] Stephen Ellis, *Season of Rains: Africa in the World* (London: C Hurst and Co, 2012), p. 1.
[71] Shorthouse, *Sport and Adventure in Africa*, p. 9.
[72] Ibid., at p. 63.
[73] In Krishna R. Dronamraju, *If I Am to Be Remembered: The Life and Work of Julian Huxley with Selected Correspondence* (Singapore, New Jersey, London, Hong Kong: World Scientific Publishing, 1993), p. 50.

lament transcends left/right/liberal divisions in a more concentrated fashion in Chapter 3.

To return momentarily to the 1924 British Empire Exhibition, this too was run through with a broad set of social and cultural anxieties. We have already seen how this related to Western aesthetic and artistic standards, but we can see these anxieties map out more broadly too. Jonathan Woodham suggests that the emphasis in the Africa section on sports and big-game hunting spoke to a desire for enjoyment 'away from the turmoil of 1920s Britain'.[74] Indeed, the chapters of some of the travelogues mentioned illustrate how important such activities were in the idealisation of Africa during this period.[75] Anxieties concerning labour struggles also informed an important backdrop to the idealisations of various African subjectivities during this period and at the Exhibition specifically,[76] contributing to installations that projected desires to find an unsullied and primitive landscape in which to escape the encroaching and militant depravations of Western modernisation in the metropole.[77] Ultimately then, the kinds of idealisations found at the Exhibition and in broader constructions of a place called 'Africa' at the time were based on a set of anxieties that sought to paint Africa as a place habitable for white (mainly aristocratic and military) people seeking to escape the depravations and declinist tendencies of metropolitan white power. Africa-as-territory is, thus, as much the subject of these kinds of anxious idealisations as Africans, who are idealised in such a way as to render them non-threatening (save some short-term savagery) to the prospects of safeguarding White civilisational standards.

In order to construct this notion of Africa as ideal for phenotypical white settlement and, thus, able to resolve anxieties concerning White civilisational vitality, a particular relationship had to be established between territorial Africa and the peoples who occupied it, whereby the latter were not only held to lack formal territorial claims, but also lacked formal claims of ownership over their bodies and personal property. Of course, this dates back to the emergence of the Atlantic slave trade, but its persistence into the 1920s is notable given the stirrings of African nationalism and pan-Africanism which

[74] Woodham, 'Images of Africa', p. 21.
[75] For an explicit example, see Peel's *Through the Length of Africa*.
[76] Woodham, 'Images of Africa', p. 21.
[77] Stephen, '"The White Man's Grave"', p. 103.

were beginning to make themselves heard within elite metropolitan circles.[78] So, for instance, Africans who feature in some of the travel and exploration literature of the period are rendered as objects to be described. Some are 'attractive'[79] while others have 'ugly protruding thick lips'.[80] When not simply to be looked at, they are there to chase animals away,[81] carry,[82] row boats,[83] or various other activities of a servile nature. Having no agency or voice of their own, they become servile objects, and as a result their personal possessions are not considered as such. So, for instance, upon seeing some women wearing some coveted earrings, Chown manages to get the master of an estate, 'after a little persuasion, to induce one of them to part with her earrings … paying in return for them a price sufficient to enable her to purchase a little copper wire and the few beads necessary to replace them'.[84] Similarly, Peel sees a small musical instrument people have been walking around with and which he is fascinated by, and which 'with great difficulty [he] persuaded a native to part with one'.[85] This objectification of Africans, whereby it is considered everyday to simply see something they want and lobby until the owner parts with it – without considering that such owners may have emotional attachment to such possessions – reflects the broader fascination with 'primitive' African objects seen at the British Empire Exhibition and in the turn to 'primitive' art more broadly in the Anglosphere and Europe at that time. And, as we shall see in subsequent chapters, this idealisation of Africans as objects, which simultaneously constructs an ossified idea of Africa, was to remain prominent in the ways in which the continent was consumed in Anglospheric culture for many more years.

[78] The Chilembwe Uprising, a short-lived armed insurrection in British Nyasaland, had erupted in 1915, and as Chapter 3 will illustrate, Marcus Garvey's United Negro Improvement Association had also begun to make inroads into urban African communities during this period. Stephen ('"The White Man's Grave"', p. 128) also notes that a large variety of nationalists from colonial territories were in attendance at the British Empire Exhibition, laying the groundwork, in some cases, for the struggles of the ensuing decades.

[79] Peel, *Through the Length of Africa*, p. 35.

[80] Ibid., at p. 42.

[81] Ibid., at p. 24.

[82] Ibid., at p. 25.

[83] Ibid., at p. 31.

[84] Chown, *Wayfaring in Africa*, p. 106.

[85] Peel, *Through the Length of Africa*, p. 23.

The exception to the kind of objectification that created the conditions for overlooking the emotional attachments, rights claims, ownership and humanity of the Africans they encounter is the figure of the African noble, in whom the aristocratic and military qualities associated with certain forms of Whiteness can be recognised. A meeting with a Banyoro King in Uganda, for example, is described as follows:

Their [Banyoro] organisation ... chain of responsibility being *correctly linked* from King (Mukama) through the Saza (district) and Gombolola (sub-district) Chiefs to the humble Omwami Wekyalo (village chief). I was introduced to the Mukama at Masindi. He is a very much respected man.[86]

David Cannadine has argued that, while race was an important way in which the British, for instance, viewed their imperial subjects, ideas about status trumped such considerations and that, as a result, agents of the British Empire (administrators, governors, explorers, etc.) were at least as much or perhaps more concerned with constructing affinities with imperial subjects than differences, 'on the presumption that society on the periphery was the same as, or even on occasions superior to, society in the metropolis'.[87] As such, the British sought to domesticate what was exotic, reordering the foreign in 'parallel, analogous, equivalent and resemblant terms'.[88] This meant seeking out imperial subjects that could confirm British aristocratic and governing class ideas about class hierarchy, hence Shorthouse's appreciation of the Banyoro King above.

There are two points to be made about this. The first is that whether seeking sameness or difference, in neither case did this translate into a belief that phenotypically white people, particularly white elites, should be displaced from positions of power in colonial African territories. As such, black Kings could never rise to the same status as white ones, making phenotypical presentation a still important, even predominant, marker of power and prestige. More broadly, then, it can be argued that phenotypical whiteness and civilisational vitality remained intrinsically tied together in this period, even if the morality and power of phenotypical whites and, thus, White civilisation in the West, were understood to be under threat. A second and related

---

[86] Shorthouse, *Sport and Adventure in Africa*, p. 179, *emphasis added*.
[87] Cannadine, *Ornamentalism*, p. xix.
[88] Ibid.

point to make here is that this desire to find affirmation of British class hierarchy was born out of anxieties concerning the reproduction of that hierarchy, which stood to represent the universality and sustenance of Western civilisation. This explains the regularity with which some of the authors we have considered bemoaned the characteristics of 'modern civilisation', which included for them Bolshevism, working-class agitation and suffragism. This led the governing classes in Britain to draw parallels between the overcrowded conditions and moral fecklessness of their metropolitan cities with the 'darkness' of their imperial possessions in Africa,[89] and at times even extended to identifying exceptions to these conditions in their possessions, all the while doing nothing to dispel their positions at the top of a class *and* racial hierarchy.

Concluding Remarks

This chapter has sought to establish the broad sociological and relevant historical terrain upon which the case study of Kenya Colony in the next chapter takes place. Taking elitist cultural representations of Africa and the empire in the British metropole as its starting point and focus of analysis, the chapter has argued that post-War Britain was marked by distinct confidence in the historical achievements of Western civilisation, as well as the place of phenotypical whiteness in a global racial hierarchy. At the same time, however, this confidence was marked by a series racial anxieties concerning civilisation in the West and its broader universality, based on what was seen as encroaching socialism, the moral fecklessness and depravity of modernisation and technology, and the nascent but growing spectre of race and class war.

As such, fascination with Africa during this period cannot be reduced to merely material or paternalistic impulses, but rather a simultaneous series of deep anxieties concerning Western civilisation and White vitality. Africa, idealised as a terra incognita, a land without people, history or society, became the ideal receptacle into which these anxieties could be poured. It was in Africa that Whiteness could be saved from the domestic depravities that threatened it in the West, and made wholesome again, away from Bolsheviks, Suffragists, various assorted abolitionists and humanitarians. All of these, in their own

---

[89] Ibid., at p. 5.

way, represented the erosion of a phenotypically white class and status hierarchy that had, in the privileged White telling of Western historical development, existed for centuries. As it eroded in the metropole, Africa would prove the place where it could be restored. Interestingly however, such a sensibility was not the sole preserve of the reactionary right. As we will see in Chapter 3, liberals and the Fabian left were also struck by anxieties concerning Whiteness and metropolitan Western civilisation and for them, too, Africa became analogous with their desire to preserve Whiteness, away from the degradations of phenotypically white people in Western metropoles.

3 | Native Rights in Colonial Kenya: The Symbolism of Harry Thuku

In July 1923 the British Government published the Devonshire White Paper, designed to resolve a rapidly growing conflict between European and Indian settler communities in Kenya Colony over representation and rights to land. The entire White Paper claimed to rest on one key principle, recorded thus: 'His Majesty's Government think it necessary to record their considered opinion that the interests of the African natives must be paramount'.[1] That the rest of the White Paper sought largely to protect settler interests – while keeping their more heady aspirations for self-rule under check – and placate the India Office, itself under pressure from the India National Congress to reach a more equitable deal for Indians in Kenya, betrayed the shallowness of this principle. Nonetheless, while not putting an end to the conflict completely, the White Paper became a progressive reference point for many stakeholders – some self-appointed – in the conflict, including British humanitarians and Fabians.

Ultimately, the conflicts in Kenya in the early 1920s had very little to do with 'native rights' or paramountcy, at least as far as the colonial administration and European settler bodies were concerned. That humanitarians and Fabians found themselves defending government policy is because they largely shared the Colonial Office's analysis that Africans might, one day, be ready for self-government, just not yet. In 1930 a letter appeared in *The Times* newspaper, signed by some of the leading lights of British humanitarian and Fabian circles, including John Hobbis Harris, Leonard and Virginia Woolf, Helena Swanick, H.G. Wells and Charles Roden Buxton. The letter defended British imperial policy in Africa from attacks by the South African Prime Minister General Barry Hertzog, arguing that political and legal equality should not be denied 'to certain persons on the ground of

[1] His Majesty's Government, *Indians in Kenya* (London: His Majesty's Stationary Office, 1923), p. 10.

72

their colour ... where a fixed standard of civilisation and education has been reached'.[2] And yet the Trinidadian activist and writer George Padmore argued not long after that the White Paper was merely a fig leaf to dampen down African aspirations,[3] while Robert Maxon has more recently argued that it was simply a way for the Colonial Office to reassert its control over an increasingly boisterous settler community in Kenya.[4] Why, then, were so many diverse groups so often at odds with each other – settlers, the British Government, humanitarians, Fabians – more or less at one on this issue? In keeping with other periods and events recounted in this book, and Western imaginaries of Africa more broadly and historically, material factors, or the paternalism of humanitarian and administrative bodies, are more normally foregrounded as explanatory factors in the coalescence around the White Paper. However, this chapter will argue that an additional and overlooked factor in this coalescence was anxiety concerning White racial vitality. The chapter will argue that each stakeholder reached their position concerning the White Paper driven by their own specific racial anxieties and the risks to White prestige from the failure to live up to Western civilisational standards by certain groups of phenotypical whites. This, in turn, produced idealisations about native Africans, and what was 'just' for them.

These anxieties included fears about metropolitan industrial exhaustion, weak central government, the decline of the power of the Church, and relatedly, growing working-class 'fecklessness' and political radicalism (mapping onto the concerns about 'civilisation' outlined in Chapter 2). As we will see, in these and other cases, anxieties about Whiteness produced idealisations about the universality and supremacy of the ideals and practices supposedly under threat, and the fulfilment of them was projected onto colonised subjects, under qualified, phenotypically white tutelage. An argument put forward in Chapter 1 was that such anxieties were not necessarily new. However, during the interwar years these anxieties became much more pronounced and

---

[2] Leonard Woolf et al., 'Natives in Africa, the Policy of Equal Rights: To the Editor of *The Times*', *The Times*, 12 November 1930, p. 19.

[3] G. Padmore, '"Left" Imperialism and the Negro Toilers', *Labour Monthly*, 14:5, 1932.

[4] Robert Maxon, *Struggle for Kenya: The Loss and Reassertion of Imperial Initiative, 1912–1923* (London and Toronto: Associated University Presses, 1993).

mainstream, as well as transnational (thanks largely to the eugenicist writings of figures such as Lothrup Stoddard – see Chapter 2). While colonial administrators and the British government thought in terms of the national interest, white settlers in Kenya were becoming more rabidly anti-government during this period and were just as likely to think in broader, racial-civilisational terms. This sensibility transcended Kenya and extended across the Anglosphere,[5] whereby white settlers were just as likely to hold only a conditional loyalty to the British imperial metropole in Whitehall and saw themselves acting as vanguards of a transnational race that transcended a now anaemic imperial centre.

Motivated by a different set of anxieties concerning the vitality of Christianity, many of the humanitarians we will meet in this chapter were driven by similarly transnational, civilisational anxieties. As such, the interwar period can be understood as a time when the kinds of tropes deployed about Africans ('good' versus 'bad'; 'savage' versus 'childlike') took on newer meanings and functions within colonial epistemologies. This chapter seeks to provide a snapshot into these anxieties and resultant idealisations, albeit that in some respects they pre- and post-dated the events recounted here.[6]

The story of the conflict that led to the Devonshire White Paper is, therefore, an instructive case about the relationship between anxieties about Whiteness and idealised representations of African economies and societies, where it will be seen that 'Kenya' came to stand for 'Africa' more broadly in the various imaginaries to be detailed in this chapter. That this case is so instructive is related to its temporal context, but also has to do with the broader significance of Kenya Colony in the 1920s, and as a result, the ways in which the events that unfolded there sparked crises and channelled anxieties concerning Whiteness that fed broader self-referential conceptions of Self and

---

[5] Donal Lowry, 'Ulster Resistance and Loyalist Rebellion in the Empire', in K. Jeffrey (ed.), *'An Irish Empire'? Aspects of Ireland and the British Empire* (Manchester: Manchester University Press, 1996), pp. 191–216.

[6] The events to be recounted here acted as a multiplier for local and transnational currents, but they did not, in and of themselves, create the anxieties and idealisations this chapter discusses. For an account of broader settler psychoses in Kenya see Shadle, *The Souls of White Folk*. For the broader concerns of colonial administrators in Kenya see Bruce Berman, *Control and Crisis in Colonial Kenya: The Dialectic of Domination* (Rochester, NY: James Currey, 1990).

Other in that period. The Devonshire White Paper, as well as the various responses to it, was simply one product of these anxieties.

There could, of course, be many different territories in the 1920s one could use to help isolate the relationship between anxieties concerning White civilisational vitality and idealised representations of African economies and societies. And yet for a number of reasons, Kenya, since its early European settlement, has 'held a special place in the hearts of Britons, Americans and others in the West'.[7] Perceived to be free of the controversial historical circumstances in which the Union of South Africa was formed, British East Africa Protectorate (changing its name to Kenya Colony in 1920) produced stories of 'brave men and women seeking adventure or escaping strait-laced Edwardian England'.[8] Indications of this special fascination can be found in the titles of travel literature of the period which featured Kenya heavily, even when the purview of such literature was pan-continental.[9] In addition to this general context of metropolitan fascination with Kenya, the specific events recounted here also made Kenya in the 1920s 'the central test case of British colonial trusteeship',[10] pitting, in the eyes of the Colonial Office, European settlers, Indian immigrants and different groups of native Africans against each other,[11] as well as incorporating the interests of the India Office and General Jan Smuts and allies in South Africa.[12]

To understand the background to the debate over paramount rights which rumbled on to the end of the decade we have to go back to the early-1920s. On 15 March 1922, a former Kenya Colony government

---

[7] Shadle, *The Souls of White Folk*, p. 2.

[8] Ibid.

[9] For instance: Peel, *Through the Length of Africa*.

[10] John W. Cell (ed.), *By Kenya Possessed: The Correspondence of Norman Leys and J. H. Oldham, 1918–1926* (Chicago, IL: University of Chicago Press, 1976), p. 3. See also Keith Clements, *Faith on the Frontier: A life of J. H. Oldham* (Edinburgh: T&T Clark/Geneva: WCC Publications, 1999), p. 214.

[11] The terms 'settler', 'immigrant' and 'native' are those of the Colonial Office and settler community. It is of course interesting to reflect that European 'settlers' were no less immigrants than the Indians who automatically earned that nomenclature. For a discussion of the positive connotations white immigrants associated with the nomenclature 'settler' see James Belich, *Replenishing the Earth: The Settler Revolution and the Rise of the Anglo World, 1783–1939* (Oxford: Oxford University Press, 2009), p. 150.

[12] Jeremy Murray-Brown, *Kenyatta* (London: George Allen and Unwin, 1972), p. 81.

telephone operator called Harry Thuku was arrested at his home in Nairobi and taken to the Nairobi Police Station (also known as Police Lines) where he was held for several days. Following a year of increasingly active and adversarial political activity, Thuku had left his job in government service when presented with an ultimatum; his job or his politics. He chose the latter. Thuku's politics, as we shall see, was interpreted in a number of ways by different stakeholders in the Colony at the time. We shall see that what was certainly true was that Thuku had been touring the countryside, provoking anti-settler and anti-government anger against the iniquities of post-war Kenya Colony, i.e., universal wage cuts of a third driven by the demands of a financially failing post-war settler agricultural project[13]; an increase in hut taxes; and, most hated of all perhaps, the Kipande, a form of pass system that distributed fines to any native African who did not have in their possession registration papers held in a small tin pot hung around their neck. More dangerously from a white settler and administration perspective, Thuku, a Kikuyu, had been forming alliances with Indians, Muslims, Luo and other groups who had historically been weak and divided (in line with British colonial policy).[14]

On the night of Thuku's arrest crowds began to gather at Police Lines as news spread of his incarceration. Over the following night and morning, the crowds grew, the odd scuffle broke out, some arrests were made, but the situation remained mostly peaceful. The crowds were swelled by a strike that had been called by Thuku's East Africa Association (EAA) – so named to distinguish itself from the tribally constituted associations administered by missionaries to act

---

[13] William McGregor Ross, *Kenya from Within: A Short Political History* (London: George Allen and Unwin, 1927), pp. 219–24.

[14] In the interests of retaining this book's focus on Whiteness, this chapter does not consider in great detail the actual politics of Harry Thuku, and his reception amongst Indian and African communities in Kenya. For an analysis of the latter, and especially Thuku's support from Indian activists, see: Bruce Berman and John Lonsdale, *Unhappy Valley: Violence and Ethnicity Book II: Conflict in Kenya and Africa* (Athens, OH: Ohio University Press, 1992), p. 370; Richard L. Tignor, *Colonial Transformation of Kenya: The Kamba, Kikuyu and Maasai from 1900–1939* (Princeton, NJ: Princeton University Press, 1976), p. 231; for an analysis of Thuku's pan-ethnic and pan-African politics, see Clive Gabay, 'Decolonising Interwar Anti-Colonial Solidarities: The Case of Harry Thuku', *Interventions: International Journal of Postcolonial Studies*: available at www.tandfonline.com/doi/full/10.1080/1369801X .2018.1487319, published online 04/07/2018.

as interlocutors with the colonial administration. The Kings African Rifles (KAR) was summoned to reinforce the police officers who were guarding Police Lines. The contemporaneous account of William McGregor Ross, Director of Public Works and one of two very vocal agitators against settler policy in the Colony (the other being Norman Leys[15]) reported that rumours circulated among the crowd that Thuku had been killed, that he had been removed from Police Lines or that the KAR were coming to charge the crowd.[16] As the crowd, now some 5,000–7,000 strong,[17] grew more febrile, shots emanated from the guns of the assembled police, killing at least 25 people – this was the conclusion of the official enquiry; tallies taken by members of the crowd in the aftermath led to estimations that the figure was closer to 200[18].

In the aftermath of these events, Thuku was rushed away, without trial, into enforced exile under British supervision, not to return to Nairobi until 1931 as a figure whose nationalist and pan-Africanist politics had shifted to a more collaborationist stance, splitting the early nationalist movement between his own wing of the now renamed Kikuyu Central Association – the EAA leadership had been arrested and dissipated in the aftermath of the 1922 protests – and the more oppositional wing led by people such as Jomo Kenyatta and James Beauttah, future leaders of the Kenyan African National Union (KANU). What is of interest for now, though, is how Thuku's symbolism was 'coloured-in' in during his pre-1922 presence in Kenya, and then in his absence, by a whole range of interested parties whose agendas drove their interpretation of him and subsequent idealisations about how different groups of Africans would relate/were relating to the colonial economy. On the one hand, then, Thuku came to represent a figure either through which, or against which, idealised tropes of African societies and economies were developed, all done in order to assuage anxieties about White civilisational vitality.

This chapter will proceed by taking each of the key white stakeholder groups in the Colony in turn, exploring their anxieties and resulting

---

[15] See Norman Leys, *Kenya* (London: Leonard and Virginia Woolf at the Hogarth Press, 1924).

[16] McGregor Ross, *Kenya from Within*, pp. 229–30.

[17] Murray-Brown, *Kenyatta*, p. 87.

[18] Parmenus Githendu Mockerie, *An African Speaks for his People* (London: Leonard and Virginia Woolf at the Hogarth Press, 1934), p. 49.

idealisations, and how these produced positive socio-economic representations of certain groups of Kenyans. Firstly, it will consider settler responses to and interpretations of Indian demands in the 1920s and the projected role and function of Thuku and his comrades in the EAA during this conflict. Next, I will consider the government and finally humanitarian and Fabian responses and interpretations. Throughout this chapter, a particular set of anxieties will be shown to have driven these idealisations, fitting into the broader period-specific, anti-modern anxious Whiteness identified in Chapter 2.

Settler Responses to Harry Thuku and Indian Claims for Equal Rights

Growing calls among Kenya's settler community for self-rule resulted in Kenya's status being changed in 1920 from the British East Africa Protectorate to Kenya Colony, complete with a new legislative council (otherwise known as LegCo). This high point for settler political aspirations was already being undermined, however, by Kenyan Indian demands for equal rights with white settlers. Arguing that like the white settlers they were immigrants to Kenya and subjects of the Crown, Indian leaders demanded equal voting and representation rights on a common electoral roll with whites. Importantly, the demand for equal rights extended to equal access to land and, in particular, the land of the 'White Highlands', Kenya's most fertile areas dominated entirely by white settlement (having expunged the land of its native population over successive years).

The core settler organisations responded to this apoplectically. Kenya's white settlers were a small group, not exceeding 20,000 through the 1920s. And yet they were immensely active, in both deed and vision, sustaining a huge array of organisations and associations,[19] all with the express aim of achieving self-government as soon as possible in order to pursue their commercial interests[20] and vision of White supremacy. This would also, of course, involve governing the Colony's two million African inhabitants.

The essence of the white settlers' position interwove several elements. Indian claims to equal rights were seen as a precursor to unchecked

---

[19] Cell, *By Kenya Possessed*, p. 6.
[20] Maxon, *Struggle for Kenya*, p. 7.

Indian immigration, in order to further the anti-British campaigning of the Indian National Congress (INC) and overwhelm white settler dominance in the colony. Settler anxiety in this regard had been stoked by Mahatma Gandhi's civil disobedience campaign which had been adopted by the INC at its December 1919 session. At a July 1921 meeting of the Convention of Associations, the main white settler representative body – distinct from the LegCo, which nominally at least was supposed to represent the interests of the Colony's whole population – delegates discussed how an 'influx of Indians would swamp both the Europeans and the natives'.[21] The advent of this 'Brown peril' was rendered even more dangerous by the projected character of Kenyan Indians. A fundraising circular issued by the Convention in 1921 warned of 'the cunning of the Oriental', who had established 'a network of intrigue … no attempt at cajolery, coercion or vilification has been spared which will succeed in spreading and strengthening the tentacles of this evil menace'.[22]

As a result of their seditious and cunning nature, Indians were also certain to retard African development. More importantly, this would also retard any prospects for White vitality in the Colony, making it impossible for the phenotypically white settlers to induct, even partially, Africans into civilised behaviour. 'So far the Indian has shown not the least interest in the welfare of the Natives, physical, mental or moral. His one interest is commercial and the bulk of the money he accumulates by trading with the Native is invariably sent to India' ran the argument of a pamphlet issued by the East Africa Women's League.[23] Elspeth Huxley, novelist, sympathetic contemporary of the settler leadership and retrospective documenter of events in the Colony at that time[24] wrote that:

[Indians were] an alien race … who occupied jobs as skilled workmen and traders that he [Africans] would otherwise be able to fill … The Africans

---

[21] McGregor Ross, *Kenya from Within*, p. 342.

[22] Ibid., at p. 342.

[23] The Indian Question in Kenya: The Kenya Women's Point of View (Nairobi: East Africa Women's League, undated), Anti-Slavery and Aborigines Protection Society Papers, Weston Library, Mss.Brit.Emp.s.22/G135.

[24] Prominent Kenyan novelist Ngugi Wa Thiong'o described Huxley as 'a scribbler of tourist guides and anaemic settler polemics blown up to the size of books'. See Ngugi Wa Thiong'O, *A Grain of Wheat* (Edinburgh: Pearson Education International, 1967/2008), p. 30.

were our responsibility; for good or for ill we had decided to impose our civilisation upon their savagery, and we had no right to share this responsibility
with an Asiatic race quite inexperienced in colonisation, and unqualified for
the task of ruling a less enlightened people ... we could not leave the job half
done ... it would leave the native far worse off than before.[25]

While talking of Africans as being 'less enlightened', Huxley also talks
of a 'job half done' in imposing 'our civilisation upon their savagery',
implying that Africans might one day reach Western civilisational
standards, but only under phenotypically white tutelage. Settlers were
driven by the belief that they were creating a new Eden in Kenya,
escaping a British metropole in civilisational decline.[26] As such, and in
addition confronted by the devastation of World War I, it is possible to
read in the settler campaign a maniacal attempt to 'save' Whiteness –
which for them was expressed by the civilisational norms historically
associated with phenotypically white elites, i.e., rationality, stoicism,
command over the natural environment, and so on – by creating, in
the unspecified long term, a group of civilised Africans who could act,
certainly not in the stead of, but perhaps as equal partners with, white
settlers, all of them conjoined in their ability to reproduce the universalisable norms of Western civilisation. This is the implicit message in
the passage from Huxley above. Furthermore, this sensibility is intimately tied into a positive idealisation concerning the future vitality
of Whiteness. This is because civilising a people of such 'savagery' (in
Huxley's words) would represent the culmination, universalisation
and unmatched superiority of Western civilisation (even if that project
was failing in Europe and the West) brought to Africa and legated to
the continent by phenotypical whites, and under their tutelage.

Being cunning, seditious and unscrupulous in the pursuit of their
own interests to the detriment of native interests (which of course, as
Huxley explains, whites had solemnly taken on as their own responsibility); Indians were subsequently blamed for flare-ups in native agitation. As well-attended meetings Harry Thuku was organising in and
around Nairobi through 1921 began to come to the attention of the
colonial authorities and settler establishment, attacks he made on both
the settlers and compliant Kikuyu chiefs and headmen were attributed

[25] Elspeth Huxley, *White Man's Country: Lord Delamere and the Making of
Kenya* (London: Macmillan and Co, 1935), pp. 117–18.
[26] Shadle, *The Souls of White Folk*.

to Indian meddling in native affairs. Thuku was essentially portrayed as a puppet of Indian activists, unrepresentative of the majority of loyal, docile, albeit savage, Africans who were the key to the settlers' vision of a future prosperous Kenya of which they would be in control, and which, some day, civilised Africans might also play a part in. This is the first stage at which it becomes clear that, in the settler imagination, Thuku *had* to be acting alone at the behest of Indians. If he were believed to be broadly representative of significant sections of African opinion in any way, then the fantastically idealised edifice of African behaviour (as savage, but largely docile and compliant, and in need of protection from Indian designs) constructed by settlers to justify their presence and power in the colony, in turn, linked to their belief in the sustainability of White vitality, would begin to crumble. Furthermore, the only way by which the settlers could eventually assent to the Devonshire White Paper – which they did, by virtue of shelving secret plans to kidnap the Governor and deport all Indians to Mombasa should their demands not be met[27] – was to deny that significant numbers of Africans were making political demands to be met more or less instantaneously. There was no other way that they could support a policy that, formally at least, claimed to hold African rights as paramount over their own, as to do so would have been to recognise the instability and unsustainability of white settler power in the Colony and would, thus, threaten what they saw as the perpetuity Whiteness and its greatest bequeathment, Western civilisation.

At this juncture it is instructive to consider the place of the colonial administration in Kenya, and particularly Governor Sir Edward Northey. Although ostensibly a part of the British government apparatus (addressed in the following section) Northey and his immediate circle are more helpfully treated as a part of the white settler movement, deeply involved as they were in reproducing settler narratives of Indian demands and African agency within the conflict (the settler leadership had even requested Northey's appointment[28]). Even though many of the Governor's recommendations concerning the Indian conflict to the Colonial Office resonated with attitudes in London,[29] on the main sticking point between the white settlers and the Imperial

---

[27] Elspeth Huxley, *White Man's Country: Lord Delamere and the Making of Kenya* (London: Macmillan and Co., 1935), p. 135.

[28] Murray-Brown, *Kenyatta*, p. 77.

[29] Maxon, *Struggle for Kenya*, p. 163.

government – i.e., reducing or preventing further Indian immigration – Northey was so loyal to the settler side of the argument that in a power-play the Colonial Office saw it as necessary to release him of his duties in the aftermath of the Thuku demonstrations in 1922, a year prior to the formal expiration of his governorship.[30]

And so it was Northey, as much as any settler association, who reproduced this idea of Thuku and the EAA as puppets of Indian agitation. Northey commented of an EAA public meeting that 'a mass meeting of natives in Nairobi like this means nothing: it does not represent the views of responsible natives, in fact this particular business is clearly engineered by the Indians'.[31] This position was echoed by the white settler representative body, the Convention of Associations, which, in an official publication claimed that African 'agitators' were being 'directed by the seditionist party in India'.[32] Asserting the puppet-like status of Thuku and his associates meant that somewhere there was an 'authentic' body of native African opinion that could, and should, be tapped into. And of course, the seditious Indians were not the ones to locate it. This task fell to the settlers themselves, missionaries, and compliant chiefs and headmen.[33] Around Nairobi, the base of Thuku's operations, this was to be the Kikuyu Association.[34]

It is in speaking for sanctioned native African opinion that the colonial administration and white settler opinion converged around positive and idealised socio-economic and civilisational tropes about Africans. In a letter to Winston Churchill, then Secretary of State for the Colonies, Acting Governor W. K. Notley wrote that:

The African values highly the increase of self-government to which he is attaining under British rule; the more educated are aware that British policy

---

[30] Ibid., at p. 213.

[31] 'Native Grievances': Memo from Purly, 22/071921, TNA, CO533/267.

[32] Memorandum on the Case Against the Claims of Indians in Kenya, Nairobi, 09/1921, Weston Library, C.K. Archer papers, MSS Afr.s.594, Box 1, File 12, p. 3.

[33] Although this latter group were constantly subject to the administration's suspicions and doubts about their ability to reinforce government hegemony in the colony.

[34] Rosberg and Nottingham suggest that the Kikuyu Association sought only the 'modification and reform' of colonial governance, whereas the EAA 'tended to reject the fundamental premises of white rule'. See Carl G. Rosberg and John Nottingham, *The Myth of Mau Mau: Nationalism in Kenya* (New York, NY, Washington, DC: Frederick A. Praeger, 1966), pp. 42–3.

is to allow the African in an increasing degree to share the reins of his own government as his progress towards civilization warrants, and he would view the interposition of the Indian as postponing that ideal.[35]

The self-deception contained within this statement was stark. For it was precisely these 'more educated' Africans, such as Thuku and his EAA associates, who were rejecting British colonial policy, and who saw Indian activists as collaborators, not enemies.[36] Nonetheless, and as we have already seen, this divide-and-rule strategy was a very common trope deployed by the colonial administration and settler rhetoric. In doing so, however, we find the kind of African that is idealised, with a share in the colony's future – i.e., those who assent to participate in the colonial administration of the territory, rather than fight it, and who might one day 'progress towards civilization',[37] all the while buttressing White and white settler supremacy in the Colony. This, of course, can be considered obvious; the point, however, is that this positive idealisation about who was considered qualified and desirous to participate in the Colony's political and economic affairs, tightly cohered to shifts in anxieties about the white settler project in the Colony, and thus White civilisational vitality. The fact that this idealisation of African support for the settler project could be expressed at a time when conventional dismissive racial attitudes towards Africans, and as we have seen Indians too, were still prevalent and primary reinforces the instrumental nature of this positive idealism. We will return to these relationships between racial anxiety and fantastical idealism about Africans in white settler discourse during this period towards the end of this section.

Settler organisations also deployed divide-and-rule rhetoric to sanction the behaviour of some Africans, on whose behalf they spoke, as against those whose behaviour could not be sanctioned. A Convention of Associations memorandum talked of the 'contempt and distrust with which the Indian is regarded by the native', whereby ordained 'sub-chiefs and headmen and all influential Kikuyus' rejected Thuku's campaign

---

[35] Letter from W. K. Notley to Secretary of State for the Colonies, 16/08/1921, TNA, CO533/267.

[36] Letter to M Desai, 2 May 1922, in Harry Thuku, *Harry Thuku: An Autobiography* (Nairobi, Lusaka, Dar Es Salaam, Addis Ababa: Oxford University Press, 1970), p. 91.

[37] Letter from Notley, 16 August 1921.

against the iniquities of colonial rule and settler racism.[38] Indeed, Thuku had been dismissed from his post as secretary to the Kikuyu Association (KA), the missionary-administered and officially sanctioned consultative group of Kikuyu chiefs and headmen.[39] This perspective, which divided Africans into sanctioned and unsanctioned groups, extended to visiting sympathisers too. Noel Lytton, later Earl Lytton, recollected of his time with the Kings African Rifles, stationed in Kenya, that he 'shared in the distaste the settler community, most of it, Africans too, felt for the Indians ... everybody thought they were diddling the African. The African certainly thought it'. Unlike many of his contemporaries however, who sought in Africa a pre-modern terrain upon which to salvage White vitality, Lytton goes on to draw a distinction between those Africans who are part of the colonial-modern project, about whom he is positive, and those who are wilfully not. In these terms he describes 'those who want to go on with all their tribal ways and all their handicaps ... [and those who] wanted to change ... they're all after Western civilisation!'.[40] Given that these words were uttered more than fifty years after the events they relate to, it is hard to know how Lytton might have felt about this at the time. Nonetheless, we see that optimism about the sustenance of Whiteness and Western civilisation remains invested in 'good', idealised and sanctioned African behaviour, even if the day when this idealism is fulfilled is far off and unspecified – thus necessitating the continuing presence of, and governance by, white settlers.

Thus far it has been argued that idealisations about African participation in the white settler colonial project were expressed according to the willingness of the native population of Kenya to commit to white settler tutelage and dominance in the territory. Those who did not were labelled as 'uncivilised', or only 'semi' educated.[41] But

---

[38] Memorandum on the Case against the Claims of Indians in Kenya, Nairobi, 09/1921, C.K. Archer Papers, Weston Library, MSS Afr.s.594, Box 1, File 12, p. 10.

[39] Thuku had nearly been sentenced to death by the KA for publicly undermining and humiliating the association by going over their heads and sending a set of resolutions agreed at a KA meeting at which Thuku was in attendance, directly to the Colonial Office in London, rather than through the usual channels (i.e., the District Commissioner and then Governor). See Rosberg and Nottingham, *The Myth of Mau Mau*, pp. 46–7.

[40] Noel Anthony Scawen Lytton, 28/11/1978, IWM Oral History Collection, Interview 3972, Reel 5.

[41] For use of this term to delineate between the 'more educated' compliant Chiefs, and the 'uneducated' mass of the native population, see, for instance Letter

there were also those who, in speaking for African opinion, simply launched into a far more unmoored and fantastical set of idealisations. These included the East African Women's League, which proclaimed that, 'The native on the whole has taken very kindly to the rule of the white woman [and] has learned to look on the British Woman as his friend'.[42] Indeed, such detached idealisation concerning African feelings towards the settler community led to a serious case of over-reach by the Convention of Associations, when its leader, Lord Delamere, visited London in February 1923 to present settler opinion at talks between Northey and Winston Churchill. In seeking to portray the white settlers as the true trustees of native welfare, and natives as willing and welcoming recipients of settler largesse, Delamere and his associates 'over-stressed their interest in the affairs of the native. There have never been heard, inside or outside Kenya, more outspoken advocacy of the welfare of the African'.[43] The degree to which this informed the Devonshire White Paper is certainly questionable, and yet having set out their stall as the defenders of native interests, the Convention and other assorted groups could do little but to acquiesce to the solution set out in the White Paper, which fell far short of the full self-rule they were hoping for.

Settler discourse about Africans at this time was influenced by contemporaneous, racist eugenicist thinking, as outlined in Chapter 2. It is in this influence that we can draw out the relationship between the fantastical idealisations of white settler organisations concerning Africans in the colony, and broader Anglospheric racial anxieties amongst white elites. This is because, as outlined in the previous chapter, influential eugenicist accounts of international order at the time were deeply embedded in anxious and pessimistic accounts of White vitality (under threat as it was from 'unclean', 'darker' races). The Convention of Associations chair throughout the Thuku affair

---

from W. K. Notley to Secretary of State for the Colonies, 16 August 1921, TNA, CO533/267; Letter from C.W. Guy Eden, Provincial Commissioner, Eastern Province, Uganda, to Eric Dutton, Private Secretary to Sir Robert Coryndon, Governor of Kenya, about the Indian and the African in Uganda, 15 March 1923, Sir Robert Coryndon Papers, Weston Library, MSS.Afr.s.633 Box 3, File 1, Ff118–120.

[42] *The Indian Question in Kenya: The Kenya Women's Point of View* (Nairobi: East Africa Women's League, undated), Anti-Slavery and Aborigines Protection Society Papers, Weston Library, Mss.Brit.Emp.s.22/G135.

[43] McGregor Ross, *Kenya*, p. 380.

and subsequent developments in Colonial Office policy, C.K. Archer, delivered a speech around this time where he extensively referenced the two most well-known contemporaneous proponents of white-supremacist eugenics, Madison Grant and Lothrup Stoddard, and quoted the latter's central argument that 'the basic factor in human affairs is not politics, but race'.[44] Indeed, the very title of this address, 'The Thermopylae of Africa', speaks to the anxieties settlers enveloped themselves in concerning the perpetuation of the settler enterprise and, thus, White civilisational vitality more broadly.[45] Seeing themselves as final defenders of Western civilisation and, thus, Whiteness, did two things. First, it established phenotypically white settlers as the flame-carriers of Western civilisation in Africa, thus cementing ethnocentric ideas about phenotypical white exclusivity into a calculation of White supremacy (i.e., that only phenotypical whites could reproduce White historical genius); and second, it created the conditions in which loyal (mainly tribal) Africans had to be identified and then optimistically idealised as fellow travellers in holding back the hordes of 'semi-educated' Africans and nefarious Indians.

Although we can only speculate on who deposited it there, the fact that a copy of Stoddard's 1920 book, *The Rising Tide of Color Against White World Supremacy*, is still held in the Kenya National Archive is at the very least symbolic of prevailing attitudes to questions of race and racial conflict among settlers around the time of its publication. Nonetheless, in this section I have tried to illustrate that even among this implacably racist community[46] there were times when white settlers resorted to positive idealisations of the native Africans whose land and livelihoods they had stolen. That those producing this rhetoric *were* so obviously racist makes the reasons for their idealisations more obviously self-interested. Were it not for their attempts to wrest control of the colony away from both the Colonial Office and (in their eyes) the India National Congress, then there is little doubt that they would not have felt the white settler project so insecure, and not gone

---

[44] C. K. Archer, The Thermopylae of Africa. Kenya Colony's Responsibility in the Conflict between the Primary Races. Undated speech, MSS Afr.s.594, Box 1 (C.K. Archer papers), File 16.

[45] Thermopylae is the narrow Greek coastal passage where in 480 BC an alliance of Greek City States fought and lost a rear-guard battle with the invading Persian armies of Xerxes.

[46] The depth and breadth of these attitudes are illustrated in Shadle, *The Souls of White Folk*.

to such great lengths to praise those 'good' Africans who complied with white settler writ in the territory. But as we have seen, white settlers were also deeply invested in the project of furthering White vitality and Western civilisational standards, as a result of anxieties about metropolitan malaise evidenced by their belief that their own government was no longer acting in their own interests and that it was they, and not the metropole, who stood as Western civilisation's most effective defenders. As such, white settlers *had* to be fantastically optimistic about the outcomes of that project, which, if it were to succeed, would necessitate fellow civilised African travellers, living according to self-defined White logics of individualism and self-sufficiency,[47] at some unspecified point in the future.

It is because other stakeholders at the time, and indeed other groups who we will consider in later chapters, were *not* so explicitly racist that makes the settler community in 1920s Kenya an instructive case for beginning to map out why certain people at certain times have positively idealised the functions and capabilities of various groups of Africans. In the next section, we shall stay with Kenya in the 1920s, but consider the next stakeholder group relevant to the Thuku affair and the paramountcy debate – the British Government.

British Government Responses to Thuku and Paramountcy

In some ways it might not make much sense to divorce settler from British Government narrations of, and responses to, the Thuku affair and subsequent policy developments. Colonial Office (CO) officials also initially put the EAA's grievances down to 'Indian influence'.[48] And again, these same officials created a version of events that pitted Africans against Indians more so than against white settlers. The following is indicative: 'the native, speaking generally, distinguishes very sharply between "White men", and "Indians", and ... he puts the latter in a much lower category'.[49] And yet, at the same time, debates within the CO reveal a tension between the view of Thuku and the

---

[47] The degree to which white settlers themselves could live according to these idealised logics was continuously undermined by the daily reality of the failing agricultural economy in the Colony, which required regular Government subsidies and bail outs.

[48] Memo from Purly, 23 July 1921, TNA, CO533/267.

[49] Memo from M. Grindle, 'Relations between Indians and Natives', 16 August 1921, TNA, CO 533/262.

EAA as insignificant Indian puppets and a view of Thuku and the EAA as potentially threatening to the future of British rule in Kenya. 'We shall do no good by combatting the suggestion that there is any community of thought between Indian and Native', declares another official in response to Grindle's comment concerning African attitudes to Indians.[50] This comment reveals the threat that some in the CO perceived Thuku to represent, in terms of the possibility of African and Indian activists successfully provoking a collaborative anti-colonial movement. This was an insight that went far beyond anything that most settlers seemed capable of admitting.

Such tensions no doubt represented the transition the CO itself had been undergoing over the previous fifteen years. When Churchill, as parliamentary under-secretary, toured East Africa in 1907, he was accompanied by the one CO civil servant to have visited sub-Saharan Africa prior to 1914.[51] As these numbers grew after the war, and administrators began to return to the UK to take up roles within the metropolitan civil service, divisions emerged between these men depending on their pre-civil service lives. Recruits to the colonial civil service had not been drawn primarily from what was considered to be the highest and most-talented managerial class.[52] Furthermore, military and civilian officials often had different conceptions of Africa. Whereas the latter were comfortable with academic study, and often saw themselves as amateur anthropologists, officials with a military background often thought that force was the best way to govern, and experienced Africa primarily as a place not of difference and heterogeneity, but of homogeneity, 'the only real source of differentiation being whether an African society was hostile or not'.[53]

Once the Devonshire White Paper had been published in 1923 and anti-Indian pressure from the Convention had abated a touch, the opinion that Thuku and Indian agitation represented a threat to Britain's interests in the Colony prevailed, not simply within the CO,

[50] Memo from Bottomley, 'Relations between Indians and Natives', 16 August 1921, TNA, CO 533/262.
[51] Andrew Roberts, 'The Imperial Mind', in Andrew Roberts (ed.) *The Colonial Moment in Africa: Essays on the Movement of Minds and Materials, 1900–1940* (Cambridge: Cambridge University Press, 1986), p. 27.
[52] Ibid., at p. 28.
[53] Prior, *Exporting Empire*, pp. 100–1.

but within the colonial administration in Kenya also, facilitated perhaps by the replacement of Northey by Sir Robert Coryndon in 1922.
Coryndon was formerly Governor of Uganda, and a far less aggressive figure in his relations with the CO than Northey had been. This
transition from seeing Thuku as insignificant to being significant produced of a series of myths about Thuku, his appeal to other native
Kenyans, and the lines between those idealised as 'good' Africans and
those rendered as 'bad'. It is probably not coincidental that such myths
grew more pervasive in the *aftermath* of Thuku's arrest and exile – i.e.,
when he was no longer present and his actions could neither support
nor disprove such ideas.

The aftermath of the Thuku protests in March 1922 were rich in
cynical attempts to discredit Thuku, his followers and the protestors,
and thus set out clear lines of distinction between those Africans wor-
thy of being a part of the forward motion of historical time implicit
in ideas about Whiteness and civilisation, and those who were not, or
who refused to be a part of it by dint of their actions. The degree of
myth-making about Thuku at this point reflected the concern of the
colonial administration and the CO at his potential for disruption, or
instigating disruption among his followers, and what this might represent in terms of the vitality of British imperial rule in Kenya. That
a version of Thuku-as-troublemaker continued to haunt the colonial
imagination for some years thereafter testifies to the anxieties of that
imagination, rather than the realities of Thuku's personal political
development during this period, which eventually saw him collabo-
rating with the colonial administration and pledging himself to the
British Crown upon his return from exile in 1931.

These anxieties became clear in the midst of the crisis involving the
protestors' deaths. The day after the shootings, on 17 March 1922, a
pamphlet written in Kikuyu and signed by Chief Native Commissioner
G.V. Maxwell was circulated in Nairobi and its rural environs. The
pamphlet proclaimed the following:

Wisdom cannot be found in the young ones only in the elders. The Black
people do not know anything because they have not been taught, the White
people are the ones who know because they were taught ... The Black people who might want to talk to their friends about their country, should be
told to first speak to their leaders and elders before taking the matter to the
D[istrict] C[ommissioner] ... The Black people at home who would like to

emphasise issues happening in their communities or within their households should go to the district commissioner for him to tell them what to do.[54]

Here we see that any gradations of 'civilisation' that might have been adopted previously concerning 'educated', 'semi-educated' or uneducated natives was jettisoned. In its place came a strict reassertion of the colonial bureaucratic order, and a racialised civilisational hierarchy. A 'good' (Black) African very rapidly became those who consented to this bureaucratic and epistemological ordering. Maxwell laid out in fine detail this bureaucratic ordering to a group of assembled Kikuyu chiefs in an address a couple of weeks after the protests in Nairobi. After detailing the organisation of the colonial administration, through Assistant District, District, Senior and Chief Commissioners, Maxwell dubbed those who made use of this system to air their grievances as 'honest and loyal'.[55] There are obvious reasons for this reinforcing of the colonial epistemological and bureaucratic order, namely CO and colonial administration anxiety concerning the meaning of the Thuku protests and what the response from local people might have been to the gunning down of at least 25, and probably many more, of the protestors. Nonetheless, it is clear that at some of its most anxious moments, the colonial governmental imagination and bureaucracy reacted quickly to mark out those Africans idealised as loyal and who could, thus, be treated as part of, and invested in, the ordered functioning of the Colony, and those who could not.

Of course, such civilisational gradations and distinctions were not unusual for the period. At a similar time to these events in Kenya, Sir Donald Cameron, Governor of Tanganyika, wrote of the 'duty ... to do everything in our power to develop the native on lines which will not Westernize him and turn him into a bad imitation of a European'.[56] Similarly, such a conception formed the basis of Smuts' infamous Rhodes Lectures at Oxford in 1929 (dealt with in more detail the next section) which became one of the key intellectual planks for what would later become Apartheid. As such, imperial and metropolitan governing elites were perhaps less likely to be quite as keen as settlers,

[54] Choro Wa Thirikari (Trans: Government News), 17 March 1922, Weston Library, Papers of Canon Harry Leakey and Charles Richards, MSS.Afr.s.633, Box 17/2.

[55] CNCo address at Kyambu, 03/04/1922, Papers of Canon Harry Leakey and Charles Richards, MSS.Afr.s.633, Box 17/2.

[56] Sir Donald Cameron in Mamdani, *Citizen and Subject*, p. 80.

with their distrust of metropolitan government, to make a pretence of wanting to 'civilise' Africans. Nonetheless, like settlers, what the events surrounding Thuku reveal is the manner by which governmental attitudes were driven not simply by the arrogant paternalism often cited by historical scholarship as the basis for such developments, but also by an increasingly insecure notion of racial superiority. Ideas about the supremacy of Western modes of bureaucratic ordering, therefore, functioned at least in part as a sticking-plaster for anxieties concerning White vitality and Black and Brown racial revenge.

The anxious nature of this civilisational and bureaucratic ordering is underlined by the temporality of CO efforts to discredit Thuku. While one might expect these efforts to be prevalent in the immediate aftermath of his arrest and to reappear upon his return from exile in 1931 – which they did, briefly, until he proved himself loyal to the colonial administration[57] – it was the persistence of these efforts for the *duration* of his exile that reveals the degree to which Thuku haunted the government's imagination and forced the colonial administration to engage in exercises of self-deception. At a meeting with the Kikuyu Central Association (KCA)[58] held at the Fort Hall District Commissioner's office in 1927, a question put by a KCA representative, Henry Mwangi, concerning the likelihood of Thuku's return from exile, quickly devolved into a discussion of the legitimacy and representative appropriateness of the native councils through which official administration–native consultation and business was conducted.

It is worth reproducing the full transcript of the dialogue between Mwangi, his KCA colleagues and the District Commissioner here to illustrate the rapidity of this move on the DC's part:

HENRY MWANGI: Harry Thuku was taken by Government and deported to a place far away, just because he criticised the Government's boundaries. Every time we ask when he will be allowed to return, Government puts us off and we are told that his return is a matter for Government to decide.

[57] See Political and other deportees, 1929–41, KNA, PC/CP.18/3/2, Files 15a, 20 and 27.
[58] The KCA was the successor organisation to Thuku's EAA. A year after this meeting Jomo Kenyatta, future president of Kenya, would become the KCA's General Secretary.

DC: When have you approached Government?

HENRY MWANGI: In Mr Stone's time. We have also approached H.E. the Governor.

DC: If you approach his Excellency other than through the proper channels, you merely annoy him. You may bring the matter before the Local Native Council and should the other members wish to approach Government on the subject the minute will be forwarded.

MATTHEW MAGUTA: As the Association[59] only has 2 members on the Council and most of the remaining 23 are paid Government servants, is it likely that Council will move in the matter? 8 of the 12 elected members are Government officials. Why is this?

DC: They were elected by Akikuyu themselves and therefore represent the will of the people. Do you wish the Council to consist merely of Association members? ... Had the Akikuyu wanted more Association members, they would have elected more. Don't you think the Council helps the people?

LOWI MWANGI: No, because our people do not get a fair hearing.[60]

This is the full minute of the discussion. It is not impossible that the substance of the question – i.e., Thuku's release – was also discussed, but there is no record of it. As such the impression we are left with is that the CO and its agents in the colonial administration were fully bent on using the Thuku affair, some five years after he was arrested, to continually reassert the colonial bureaucracy and to condone particular and idealised forms of African political behaviour – i.e., behaviour that accorded with the proper ways of making grievances known in the colony. In this calculation, it is the Native Councils, such as the Kikuyu Association, which are idealised as loyal and obedient, reinforcing an epistemology that equates a parochial political and bureaucratic order

---

[59] Presumably here referring to the KCA.
[60] Meeting of the Kikuyu Central Association held at the District Commissioner's Office at Fort Hall, at 9.30am on 25/07/1927, KNA, Kikuyu Central Association Papers 1925–27, PC/CP/8/5/2, File 3.

with universal democratic and governing norms, a universalism that equates with White supremacy. For as long as the Native Councils were construed as representing 'the will of the people' any complaints about their composition could be painted as sectarian and according to pre-modern, non-democratic logics incompatible with the supposed universalism of Western democratic traditions.[61]

However, there was a dissonance at play in the discussion between the DC and the KCA members. Despite concerns about Thuku's continued role in driving African anti-colonial militancy,[62] a note attached to the minute of the meeting with the KCA written by the DC, asserted that 'for the majority of the Kikuyu rank and file, Harry Thuku is but a shadowy memory'.[63] Although contradicting some of the official correspondence of the time, this was nonetheless an important argument for the CO to digest, for without it the brittleness of British legitimacy and imperial hegemony in Kenya would have been laid bare before it. Anxieties about this brittleness were evident when in 1921 CO officials had debated the efficacy of playing up Indian manipulation of African demands and decided against it for fear of stoking further anti-colonial sentiment. Placating that anxiety was, thus, one function of maintaining Thuku as a ghostly yet unpopular threat on the horizon of the colony's affairs, and for the success of that strategy, and the well-being of British rule in Kenya and elsewhere, the native councils had to, therefore, be consistently idealised as functional and popular in colonial administrative discourse, while Thuku could only be the opposite.

Humanitarian and Fabian Responses to Thuku, Paramountcy and Indian Demands

Just as events in Kenya in the early 1920s distilled anxieties and attitudes among British colonial officials and administrators and were an

---

[61] For a more extended discussion of this kind of dynamic see Jean Comaroff and John Comaroff, 'Introduction', in John Comaroff and Jean Comaroff (eds.), *Civil Society and the Political Imagination in Africa: Critical Perspectives* (Chicago, IL, London: University of Chicago Press, 1999), p. 28.

[62] Various letters between colonial administrators in Kenya and officials in London justifying Thuku's continued exile through the rest of the decade attest to this. See folder marked 'Deportation of Harry Thuku', TNA, FCO 141/6441.

[63] Meeting of the Kikuyu Central Association, KNA, PC/CP/8/5/2, File 3.

early high-watermark for settler agitation against the metropolitan imperial government, so this time was also a significant period for British humanitarian networks, which in this instance formed principally around issues pertinent to Africa more broadly, but with a particular and keen interest in events taking place in Kenya. All of the key humanitarians of the period were in contact with at least one if not all other members of the core activist group at that time. John Harris, secretary of the Anti-Slavery Society was a key figure here, keeping up a regular correspondence with William MacGregor Ross and Norman Leys, both of whom had resided in Kenya and were excoriatingly critical of British rule in the colony. Another figure central to this group was Charles Roden Buxton. Along with Leys, Buxton was probably the most radical in his views among this entire group. Buxton, also a member of the ASS, wrote prodigiously on Africa in general and Kenya in particular, as well as other questions of the empire. He was in regular correspondence with Leys and Harris, as well as the Woolfs (novelist Virginia and her husband and publisher Leonard[64]). Leys, although occupying some very different political ground, kept up an ongoing correspondence with Joseph Houldsworth Oldham,[65] secretary of the International Missionary Council and subsequently member of the 1927 Hilton Young Commission into the possibility of closer union between the British East African territories, and a member of the Permanent Advisory Committee on Native Education in Tropical Africa chaired by the Conservative Under-Secretary of State for the Colonies William Ormsby-Gore. Oldham was a prodigious writer on African affairs and, perhaps more than any of this group, was the individual most embedded in government thinking and practice, although his influence on colonial policy – which has been acclaimed in some quarters, particularly the policy of native rights and paramouncty[66] – has been questioned.[67]

The following analysis will proceed through a deeper consideration of a select few of these individuals, their writing on Africa more broadly and how the perspectives that emerge from these writings were embedded in racial anxieties and resultant idealisations of 'Africans', which

---

[64] Emily Buxton, Some Colonial Papers of Charles Roden Buxton, Weston Library, Papers of Charles Roden Buxton, Mss Brit.Emp.s.405, Box 5.
[65] Serialised in Cell, *By Kenya Possessed*.
[66] See Clements, *Faith on the Frontier*, p. 452.
[67] Maxon, *Kenya*, p. 27.

subsequently shaped their attitudes towards the Kenya conflict. These anxieties were essentially concerned with the following: (i) in keeping with the anti-modernisation trend identified in the previous chapter, that industrial capitalist modernity had created moral and political decay in the West; (ii) that this represented an aberration of White genius, variously held to be more or less analogous to Christianity; and (iii) that true Western civilisational vitality could be nurtured in Africa, among Africans, but only under politically progressive white tutelage (i.e., not white settlers).

The latter of these three points is already well-established. The oft-thought of as anti-imperial political economist John Hobson, for example, actually distinguished between a number of different imperialisms, including a normatively valid 'sane' imperialism 'devoted to the protection, education, and self-development of a "lower race,"' and an invalid '"insane" Imperialism, which hands over these races to the economic exploitation of white colonists'.[68] Indeed, this attitude was characteristic of liberal humanitarians and Fabians in the interwar period who were mainly focussed on improving or purifying Imperial governance rather than replacing it with native independence.[69] Scholars of this acquiescence of liberal humanitarians and Fabians to a reformed imperialism, however, tend to locate its drivers in progressive moralising and/or economic determinism.[70] In addition to these drivers, however, and in keeping with the argument of this book, as this section unfolds we will find that an important component of the humanitarian and Fabian attachment to reforming imperial governance was a set of deep anxieties concerning the Western civilisational project, a powerfully affective component in interwar humanitarian/Fabian epistemology that drove many of the positions undertaken by these groups during this period.

---

[68] John A. Hobson, *Imperialism, A Study* (London: George Allen and Unwin, 1938/1968), p. 231; for an extensive analysis see: Hobson, *The Eurocentric Conception of World Politics*, pp. 45–52.

[69] Keith Robinson, *The Dilemmas of Trusteeship: Aspects of British Colonial Policy between the Wars* (London: Oxford University Press, 1965), p. 7.

[70] See for instance, Alan Lester, *Imperial Networks: Creating Identities in Nineteenth-Century South Africa and Britain* (Abingdon: Routledge, 2001), p. 4; Barbara Bush, *Imperialism Race and Resistance* (Abingdon: Routledge, 1999), p. 21; Hobson, *The Eurocentric Conception of World Politics*, pp. 45–52.

Table 3.1. *A heuristic typology of British humanitarian and Fabian thinking in the 1920s*

	Imperial-sympathetic	Imperial-agitational	Imperial-antagonistic
Emblematic Figure	Joseph Houldsworth Oldham	John Hobbis Harris	Norman Leys

In Table 3.1 I have selected three figures emblematic of what I consider to be different strains of British humanitarian/Fabian thinking in the 1920s.

Imperial sympathisers, such as Oldham, were essentially supportive of British imperial policy – particularly in light of attacks on it by white settlers in Kenya and South Africa – and saw it as their role to better it through gentle persuasion and engagement. Imperial-agitators, like Harris and the ASS campaigning and advocacy material he authored/sanctioned, saw British imperial policy as failing to live up to the promise of what the British should be doing in its colonies. As such, agitators were not anti-imperialist or anti-British, but were disappointed at the direction of British imperial policy, particularly as it wavered under assault by Kenya's white settlers. Lastly, imperial-antagonists like Leys, faced with the evidence before them of brutality and/or incompetence, were broadly dismissive of the whole imperial enterprise. Importantly though, antagonists, as much as the other categories on this spectrum, were not *anti*-imperial. All of them, to different degrees, had their doubts about the ability of Africans to govern themselves – which, bar Leys, involved them idealising Africans as capable, just not yet, of self-government[71] – and thus for the necessity of continued British rule in some sense, even if, in the case of Leys in particular, this took the form of a rudimentary dialectical account of the inevitability of British rule in East Africa.[72]

---

[71] The 'not yet' part of this formulation is important – see Chakrabarty's discussion of how the non-West remains locked in the 'waiting room of history' – *Provincializing Europe*, p. 8.

[72] See Leys' discussion of the 1915 Chilembwe Uprising in Nyasaland in Cell, *Kenya*, p. 21.

Imperial-Sympathiser: Joseph H. Oldham

It is clear that, despite the at times hagiographic account of his biographer,[73] which portrays him as a central figure in fighting racism and challenging British imperial policy in the 1920s, Joseph Houldsworth Oldham was an enabler of British imperialism as well as being committed to the Christianisation of Africa. He also fore-shadowed some of the self-interested proclamations that accompany contemporary fascination with the 'African Middle Class' (see Chapter 7). For Oldham, too, was a breathless advocate of what he called Africa's 'chief significance ... its human inhabitants'. They were, he proclaimed, 'a great potential market', who 'will become increasingly the purchasers of the products of the industry of other lands'.[74] Of course, this focus on the moral value of opening Africa up to trade and instilling entrepreneurial practices was always integral to missionary endeavours on the continent,[75] and it should, thus, be no great surprise to hear Oldham channelling them. In this material sense, then, his idealisation of Africa's inhabitants served both as a historical echo, as well as a premonition of contemporary 'Africa Rising' narratives. And again, like many contemporary commentators who recognise the abuses of capitalist modernity, this does not mean they, or Oldham, are/were against capitalist modernity per se.[76] In an article in 1925, Oldham wrote of the negative consequences of uncontrolled economic forces in Africa for Africans. But his solution was not to remove such forces; the problem was rather one of 'reconciling the obligation resting on the ruling Western nations to develop its [Africa's] potential resources for the good of humanity as a whole with the discharge of their responsibilities as trustees for the welfare of the native inhabitants'.[77] This is evidence of how Oldham was broadly sympathetic with, and facilitative of, the imperial project and also of what he envisaged the 'welfare of the native inhabitants' to be – i.e., a process that would make

---

[73] Clements, *Faith on the Frontier.*

[74] Joseph H. Oldham, *White and Black in Africa: A Critical Examination of the Rhodes Lectures of General Smuts* (London, New York, NY, Toronto: Longmans, Green and Co, 1930), p. 3.

[75] Curtin, *The Image of Africa*, p. xii; Mudimbe, *Idea of Africa*, p. 142.

[76] For a contemporary example see: Severino and Ray, *Africa's Moment*, pp. 64–82.

[77] Joseph H. Oldham, A Landmark in Imperial Policy, Weston Library, J. H. Oldham Papers, MSS.Afr.s.1829, Box 7, Ff12-18, 28 May 1925.

them more productive. Oldham, thus, idealised Africans in the sense that they were expected to gradually become more productive, civilised, intelligent and, thus, able to self-govern according to capitalistic and Christian ethics. Indeed, in another premonition of contemporary debates about Africa's 'rise', Oldham exhibited how a material interest in African productivity and resources easily segued into a concern with African minds and bodies in the following statement: 'If the resources of this new continent are to be developed, the first essential is the physical, intellectual and social advancement of its peoples. Their too scanty numbers must be increased. Their physique must be improved. Their intelligence must be raised'.[78]

Oldham's idealisation of Africans and their function in a global economy remained embedded in an ossified representation of Africanicity. Although still in a primitive stage, Oldham argued that 'the African' had 'gifts of perception, wisdom, and imagination ... express[ed] in an inexhaustible store of proverbs and folk-lore'.[79] Oldham's idealisations of Africans, thus far, appear embedded in both moralistic and economistic drivers. However, problematically super-historicised and romanticised as these idealisations were, Oldham's moral and economic idealisations of Africans and his sympathy with the imperial project were underpinned by his affective anxieties concerning the missionary movement to which he was central, as well as the broader metropolitan societies from which they emerged. Indeed, it was these anxieties that provided the context for his ossified idealisations of Africans. So, for instance, Oldham's principle problem with the course that imperialism had taken in some of the continent, most notably in South Africa, but also in Kenya, was not merely that an overly economistic approach had debased African societies, but Western societies too. In what can be read as both a warning and commentary on the contemporaneous record of white rule in settler colonies, Oldham wrote that, 'The whole of our civilization must feel the effects of contact with a new continent ... If through our action or our neglect we allow the peoples of Africa to be debased, they will inevitably drag down with them our standards and ideals'. His solution was to push for an aggressive effort at helping to raise Africans up 'into a world

---

[78] Oldham, *White and Black in Africa*, p. 3. See Chapter 7 for a discussion of the contemporary fascination with African bodies and minds that pervades recent 'Africa Rising' debates.

[79] Oldham, *White and Black*, p. 43.

of wider horizons and expanding moral energies, of increasing justice and fair play, compassion and generosity, helpfulness and co-operation'.[80] In order to qualify for this kind of moral, social and economic upliftment Africans simply had to be imagined as a kind of *tabula rasa* upon which Western civilisation could be saved from its own deprivations among white people in the West and in the colonies.

Those best placed to engage in this project were not Africans, but whites, specifically missionaries. While this maintained the hierarchy of phenotypically white superiority identified by critical scholars of Western imaginaries of Africa, this was not simply driven by ethnocentric racial arrogance, but also a genuine anxiety about the ability of phenotypically white people to perpetuate White genius, the apogee of which for Oldham was Christian morality. For Oldham this, therefore, boiled down to the relationship between White vitality and Christian vitality, a relationship with a long historical provenance, for as Henry Goldschmidt and Elizabeth McAlister argue, the originary 'boundaries of Christendom shaped the boundaries of Whiteness, and longstanding perceptions of heathenism shaped emerging perceptions of racial difference',[81] whereby institutionalised and bureaucratised religion – in particular official Christianity – has, thus, long-acted to consolidate racial hierarchy.[82]

This relationship between religious morality and appropriate (white) racial behaviour can be seen in Oldham's reaction to contemporaneous developments in South Africa. When the South African politician Jan Smuts delivered his infamous 1929 Rhodes lectures at the University of Oxford, his justification for the policy of European/African segregation that he set out was in part based on the notion that Africans had educationally and morally benefitted from European policies and would only continue to do so if they were kept separate from whites.[83] Oldham's *White and Black in Africa* was explicitly written as a rebuttal to many of Smuts' arguments. And yet, on

[80] Oldham, *White and Black*, p. 71.
[81] Henry Goldschmidt and Elizabeth McAlister, 'Introduction', in Henry Goldschmidt and Elizabeth McAlister (eds.), *Race, Nation, and Religion in the Americas* (New York, NY: Oxford University Press, 2004), pp. 12–13.
[82] Mustapha Kamal Pasha, 'Religion and the Fabrication of Race', *Millennium: Journal of International Studies*, 45:3, , 2017, pp. 312–34.
[83] Jan Smuts, *Africa and Some World Problems, Including the Rhodes Memorial Lectures Delivered in Michaelmas Term 1929 by General J.C. Smuts* (Oxford: The Clarendon Press, 1929), p. 76.

this latter point, Oldham was in full agreement, writing that 'We can heartily agree ... with General Smuts that where the two races have to live together in the same territory it is desirable to create homogeneous native and non-native areas of sufficient size to enable each to develop its own distinctive institutions'.[84] In this sense Oldham's views were evocative of a contemporaneous form of Cape Liberalism that combined a Victorian-era sense of moral uplift refracted through a very South African prism of racial categorisation and prejudice.[85] The source of Oldham's disagreement with Smuts, therefore, was not over the content of the policy, but the driver, writing that 'what education advance there has been in South Africa has been due entirely to the devotion of the missionaries; the keenness of officials and the enthusiasm of the natives themselves ... white settlement has done nothing to further native education'.[86] To fully understand the anxiety that drove Oldham to engage in this kind of battle with Smuts, one has to comprehend how Oldham understood the broader context of the world missionary movement in the 1920s. As Oldham saw it, the movement was at a crossroads. Failing to retain its support in Europe, where it was beset by materialism, urban industrial and moral decay, ideological conflict and failing to attract support in Asia because the movement had been too late to recognise the significance of the rise of regional nationalisms, Africa was for Oldham the 'last continent' where Christianity could make its mark. Oldham's concern, then, was not so much for Africa and his idealisations of Africans simply served to allay his anxieties concerning the ecumenical missionary movement. Africa became a Petri dish whereby the great challenges facing the Christianity – modern decline, materialism, race, etc. – could be put to the test. Oldham himself put it thus: 'Africa is a single battlefield in a conflict that is being waged on a world-wide front' between Christian morality and secular vanity.[87]

It can, therefore, be argued that Oldham's belief in the reception Christianity would receive among the 'wise' and 'perceptive'

---

[84] Oldham, *White and Black*, p. 36.

[85] Paul B. Rich, *White Power and the Liberal Conscience: Racial Segregation and South African Liberalism, 1921–60* (Manchester: Manchester University Press, 1984), p. 3.

[86] Oldham, *White and Black*, p. 10.

[87] Joseph H. Oldham and Betty Gibson, *The Remaking of Man in Africa* (London: Oxford University Press, 1931), p. 18.

Africans,[88] a manifestation of his idealisations, existed as a result of his anxieties concerning the state of the global missionary movement and its reception in other, non-white parts of the world. Being broadly positive in his prognosis for their moral, educational and economic development was, therefore, not simply a result of a vacuous moralising bent towards 'civilising the savages', but was intrinsically related to his concern for the continuing vitality and centrality of Christianity in the world, including in the West. Whiteness was, thus, for Oldham deeply intertwined with the successes of the missionary movement. A threat to the latter was a threat to the former, and thus the 'raising up' of Africans would signal the perpetuation of both the missionary project *and* the products of White genius – i.e., Christianity.

Oldham's anxieties about the sustainability of Christianity as a mass religion and his fantastical idealisations concerning certain forms of ossified African subjectivity came together in his pronouncements on Kenya and the 'native question', particularly as it pertained to the EAA/KCA and EAINC campaigns. In a letter to the Atheist scholar C. Delisle Burns written in 1927 when agitation over native rights and representation persisted thanks to a more effective and internationally networked KCA, Oldham wrote that:

The real difficulty in giving effect to this ... policy [i.e., paramountcy] does not lie in the reluctance of any party in Great Britain to provide safeguards for the natives, but to the unalterable fact of the present backwardness of the native races. The native cannot pull his oar in the boat ... I should favour the adequate representation of natives on the Legislative Council by Europeans. There are ... at present no natives who could hold their own in the Legislative Council and their point of view can be much more effectively presented by Europeans ... the principle of the representation of native interests has been conceded in the appointment of Dr. Arthur as a member of the Legislative Council.[89]

In this passage we can see the limits of Oldham's positive idealisations of Africans. While they were telling stories or practicing other 'folk' traditions they were deserving of praise, but it was exactly this form of temporal and social ossification that prevented them from

---

[88] Oldham, *White and Black*, p. 43.
[89] Joseph. H. Oldham, Letter to C. Delisle Burns Esq. 05/05/1927, Weston Library, J.H. Oldham Papers, MSS.Afr.s.1829, Box 7, Ff19–27.

representing their own interests in the 'modern' arena of representative legislative politics. Oldham simply could not recognise that Africans might be able to articulate themselves; to do so would be to invalidate the missionary project in Africa which itself was so central in Oldham's understanding of the global battle between Christianity and secular immorality. Given Oldham's broader anxieties, who better to represent native opinion then than a missionary, Dr. John William Arthur, Church of Scotland medical missionary and appointed expert on 'native affairs' in Kenya, where he had been stationed since 1907? Arthur was popular with the settler community, having broadly sided with them – as other church groups had done, in the conflict with the East Africa INC – and the settler leader Lord Delamere had consented to Arthur representing native interests at the 1923 conference in London at which paramountcy was first mooted as a solution to the conflict. Arthur was, thus, not an uncontroversial figure as far as the EAA, EAINC and, indeed, other humanitarians and Fabians were concerned.

Nonetheless, by invoking Arthur, Oldham here maintains white-Europe as a source of civilisational genius and qualified phenotypical whites (missionaries) as tutors of this genius. Africans here are, thus, imagined as in need of phenotypical white tutelage, but White vitality is similarly in need of Africans in a relationship of self-validation. As such, it is impossible to view Oldham's relationship to Africa purely through a material or paternalistic lens. These factors were certainly at play, but underpinned by a set of racial and religious anxieties that were also at play among other strands of 1920s liberal humanitarian activism.

Imperial-Agitator: John Hobbis Harris

As we move away from the imperial-sympathetic Oldham to the more imperial-agitational John Harris, general secretary of the Anti-Slavery Society (ASS), Arthur proves a useful figure in illustrating the distinction between the former and the latter, even though Oldham and Harris were regularly in friendly correspondence with each other concerning Kenya and a range of other humanitarian issues of the period. On the issue of Arthur, however, they were not in step. In a letter to Oldham prior to the 1923 London conference on paramountcy, Harris met the announcement of Arthur's appointment by proclaiming it as a 'disastrous suggestion'.[90] Harris's own disquiet concerning Arthur mapped onto Oldham's reasons for liking him. As a former missionary himself, Harris was concerned about the bad name being accrued by the Church across the British Empire, and particularly in Kenya, due to Arthur's closeness with the Convention of Associations. Arthur's reputation with Harris had been solidified by the former's actions at a special meeting held by the ASS in London in June 1923 when a vote was put to support native rights in Kenya. Arthur had left the meeting prior to the vote. Harris viewed this as a convenient measure taken by Arthur to avoid having to vote for the motion, thus, upsetting his settler allies, or against the motion and upsetting his humanitarian contemporaries. Arthur protested his innocence in a letter to Harris. Writing to the British advocate for Indian rights Henry Polak, Harris made his feelings on the matter, and Arthur's correspondence, clear: 'Here is a slippery fellow for you! ... I rather gather he left the meeting purposely, as the weakest way out of a difficult dilemma.'[91]

Harris marked himself out as an imperial-agitator in the years preceding the Thuku crisis. He was a member of the circle – including E.D. Morel and Roger Casement – which helped bring to light in Europe the crimes of Belgium's King Leopold in the Congo as part of the Congo Reform Association.[92] This experience did not however turn him into an *anti*-imperialist. Rather, Harris agitated to enable the European imperial mission to fulfil what he saw as its potential; the raising up of Africans. It was not that Harris thought that Africans per se were necessarily uncivilised or incapable of auto-development –unlike Oldham– more that imperialism could assist Africans to develop in a more proper and orderly manner. Thus, it was that for Harris, European Imperialism should deliver unto Africa the 'gift of sovereignty',[93] in order to overcome the damaging inroads made by 'the influx of white men and the over-hasty introduction of European land laws' that had 'made the retention of the native system almost,

---

[90] John H. Harris, Letter to Joseph H. Oldham, 16 May 1923, Weston Library, J.H. Oldham Papers, Mss.Brit.Emp.s.22/G135.
[91] John H. Harris, Letter to H.S.L. Polack, 14 June 1923, Weston Library, H.S.L. Polack Papers, Mss.Brit.Emp.s.22/G135.
[92] See Adam Hochschild, *King Leopold's Ghost* (New York, NY: Mariner Books, 1998).
[93] John H. Harris, *Africa: Slave or Free?* (London: Student Christian Movement, 1919), p. 232.

although not quite, impossible'.[94] The answer to the damages of what Harris saw as a particularly pernicious form of European Imperialism (rather than imperialism per se) was, thus, to impose on Africa (or 'gift' to it) a system of sovereign territorial areas, under title (based on an ideal-typical view of that system, derived from the parochial and mythologised experience of Europe[95]). At first, this would have to be instigated by some kind of trustee power – i.e., European trustee power. Harris was, thus, no anti-imperialist, but agitated for an improved form of internationalised imperial trusteeship.

As a leading figure in the ASS and broader international humanitarian networks, Harris exemplified the kind of 'sane imperialism' positively identified by the political economist John Hobson in his 1902 book, *Imperialism: A Study*. While critical of the existing record of white settlement in Africa, this was a position that nonetheless maintained a hierarchical relationship between those deemed 'White' and those deemed 'Black' – which at this stage normally fell along phenotypical distinctions. We see Harris's belief in this hierarchical relationship continue in his discussion with colleagues about the issues raised by the EAA and EAINC campaigns in the early 1920s. In a letter to a correspondent about to visit Kenya, Harris writes: 'The African should be developed as far as possible along African lines ... and that in his relationship with the white man we should lay the emphasis upon the native producer and *white tuition*.'[96] White knowledge, carried by phenotypically white people, is deemed central to African/Black development and necessitates the imperial relationship. In relation to the special meeting on the paramountcy debate, different drafts of the resolution to be voted on illustrate the manner in which Harris's beliefs in this regard were detailed and specific. An earlier draft of the resolution reads as follows:

That until such time as an adequate proportion of the native community attains to the franchise, native interests shall be served on the legislative body by men and women, selected for their interest in native affairs.

This draft is overlaid with Harris's notes and crossings-out. One such crossing out occurs in this passage, which Harris has overlaid with a

[94] Ibid., at p. 234.
[95] Grovogui, 'Regimes of Sovereignty'.
[96] John H. Harris, Letter to Oliver Baldwin, 29 May 1923, Weston Library, Anti-Slavery and Aborigines Protection Society Papers, Mss.Brit.Emp.s.22/G135, *emphasis added.*

replacement text, which formed the final resolution members of the ASS voted on at the 5 June 1923 meeting at Westminster Central Hall, London. The key revision reads: 'That until such time as an adequate proportion of the native community *shall be deemed capable* of exercising the franchise'.[97]

The words 'attains to the franchise' have thus been replaced with 'shall be deemed capable of exercising the franchise'. The change has obvious and important ramifications. No longer does the exercise of the franchise become something organic and endogenous to the 'native community', but is now something that is an ability, to be judged exogenously by, one can only assume, phenotypically white people. That this change may not have simply reflected Harris's own beliefs about Africans in Kenya, but his beliefs about what the ASS membership would have been willing to support, only serves to further illustrate the degree to which imperial-agitation was an important stream in British humanitarianism during the early 1920s. This is brought into focus in this instance through the EAINC campaign for equality and the related Thuku/EAA campaign and protests.

A year after the protests against Thuku's arrest and after the publication of the Devonshire White Paper, Harris wrote that: 'We felt that the interests of the natives ought to be paramount, and we think it is satisfactory that in the decision which the Colonial Office has reached ... that the British are trustees for the natives.'[98] This suggests that for Harris, and indeed the ASS more broadly – Harris is explicitly reporting the position of the whole society in this letter, as published in the *Anti-Slavery Reporter* – the Thuku affair was embedded in a form of imperial-agitation that sought to internationalise the imperial relationship with Africa, by taking the continent's future out of the hands of settlers, rather than oppose or replace it.

And so, although Thuku was viewed more sympathetically and positively by Harris and the ASS, it was impossible for Harris to channel his sympathy about him into anything that recognised the broad-based,

---

[97] Both of these excerpts are taken from: Resolutions, Annual Meeting, 05 June 1923, Anti-Slavery and Aborigines Protection Society Papers, Weston Library, Mss.Brit.Emp.s.22/G135, Point II.3, *emphasis added*.

[98] John H. Harris, Letter to G. Gordon Dennis, 22 August 1923, Anti-Slavery and Aborigines Protection Society Papers, Weston Library, Mss.Brit.Emp.s.22/ G135.

multi-ethnic nature of the support for the EAA campaign,[99] thus producing an idealised narrative of African subjectivity – as largely content to wait, indefinitely, for self-government and/or political representation – that reinforced imperial rule. For instance, Harris got concerned for a period about rumours of a prior conviction Thuku had been given for a petty case of forgery. The story was being reported in the East African settler press as a means to discredit Thuku. There are several letters over a period of weeks pertaining to this, and the following is indicative: 'I am sure you would not like him to rest under any stigma', Harris wrote to the editor of a South African newspaper, 'moreover there is the very practical consideration of the unemployed Indian lawyer looking for a "case", and I should not be at all surprised if one of these rather astute individuals did not think he could work up a case for libel, and they would not hesitate to undertake a job which would not only mean political prestige amongst the natives, but the hope of financial advantage'.[100] And so even though Harris was seeking to prevent the besmirching of Thuku's character, his projection of Thuku had the effect of idealising him as a romanticised native, incapable of criminality – Thuku did indeed have the conviction. But this still led Harris to the same conclusions about Thuku as the settlers and colonial administration – i.e., that Harry Thuku and the EAA were in reality fairly insignificant, naïve lone wolves, manipulated by slippery Indian political agitators and completely unrepresentative of broader African opinion, which would, idealised as docile and pre-modern, ultimately require the nursing and tending of white trusteeship and 'white tuition',[101] as laid down in the Devonshire White Paper.

As with Oldham, however, it would be a mistake to view Harris's idealisations of Thuku and native Africans more broadly as simply the product of a civilising and moralising imperative. We have already seen how Harris was driven, in part, by his concerns over the reputation of the Church. Furthermore, to recognise that Thuku was (a) capable of criminality, however minor and (b) capable of inspiring anti-imperial agitation, would have been to dismantle Harris's own conceptions of

---

[99] On this, see, Berman and Lonsdale *Unhappy Valley*; Gabay, 'Decolonising Interwar Anti-Colonial Solidarities'.

[100] John H. Harris, Letter to Leo Weinthal, 27 April 1922, Anti-Slavery and Aborigines Protection Society Papers, Weston Library, Mss.Brit.Emp.s.22/ G142.

[101] Harris to Baldwin, 1923.

civilisation and the function of Africa as a saviour of White vitality. In 1919 Harris recorded three components of civilisation that Africans should meet before being accorded rights of representation and legislative oversight: education, income and freedom from criminal conviction. If an African could meet these standards 'he is not merely capable of expressing an opinion upon legislation, but evinces a higher level of civilization than thousands of white men who control to-day the destinies of the African'.[102] In this way Harris was again falling back on the sane/insane imperialism identified by Hobson. But with 'insane' imperialism dominant, in the form of the 'thousands of white men' controlling 'the destinies of the African', such a manifestation of White power, driven by 'insane' white men, represented, for figures like Harris, its greatest threat. Harris's attraction to ideas of phenotypical white tutelage, then, cannot be understood simply as a function of his desire to uplift Africans, but also whites. This is because the depiction of contemporaneous imperialism as manifestly 'insane' rested on racial anxieties concerning White morality as a vulnerable construct and a certainty that the agents of 'sane' imperialism (Hobson, Harris, etc.) would govern better and in doing so resuscitate White vitality suffering from the fecklessness and violence of its primary contemporaneous manifestations. As such, while both Oldham and Harris represented different strands of humanitarian thinking – the former seeking to facilitate imperial rule, the latter seeking to reform it – both idealised Africans to the degree that the latter were ossified, viewed as in need of protection, out of historical time and requiring the assistance of 'sane' phenotypical white Europeans to develop along lines that would assuage their anxieties concerning White racial decay at the hands of the West's own developing a moralism and violence. Importantly then (sane) white people (like Harris and Oldham) rather than Africans *or* (insane) white settlers, remained central to African and world development, as at this stage it was still a central principle that phenotypically white people would figure in safeguarding Whiteness and Western civilisation from the deprivations of white society in the West and in settler colonies. This would change after World War II at a general sociological level, as well as specifically for Oldham, as we will see in Chapters 4 and 5. For now, though, these attitudes informed both

---

[102] Harris, *Slave or Free?* pp. 240–1.

Oldham's and Harris's responses to Thuku's arrest and deportation and the related – as they saw it – EAINC campaign for equal property and representation rights in Kenya.

Imperial-Antagonist: Norman Leys

The final category of humanitarian and Fabian thinking we need to consider sits apart from the sympathising of Oldham and agitation of Harris, being quite antagonistic towards, and at times even contingently opposed to, the project of European Imperialism and white settlement. It sits apart also because in many ways, at least through the vessel of Norman Leys, it does not leave us with very much evidence of positive idealisations about anyone or anything. It *is* anxious, but much more pessimistic about any forms of both African agency *and* White civilisational vitality than either of the other two categories of humanitarian thinking discussed. I include an analysis of it here because imperial-antagonism is an important precursor to the forms of anxiety-driven idealisations concerning Africa that emerged in the 1950s and which will be discussed in Chapters 4 and 5.

In terms of the Thuku affair we find this imperial-antagonism best expressed through the attitudes of Leys, a former colonial medical officer in Southern and Eastern Africa and by the 1920s a general commentator on African and Kenya affairs. Leys wasn't alone in channelling the opinions we are about to consider; both William MacGregor Ross[103] and Charles Roden Buxton were also broadly in this camp, although it is Leys we shall consider most closely here, writing in more depth and for longer about Kenya than either of the other two, although Buxton will be briefly considered.

Leys' anti-imperialism was ambiguous, which is why it is best to think of his position on imperialism as antagonistic rather than full-throatedly oppositional. For instance, reflecting back on events that had occurred in Kenya over the preceding years – i.e., the emergence of Harry Thuku, the EAINC campaign and so on – Leys wrote in 1924 that '[some] Africans realise that their servitude need not last forever … some day, they may win back both their country and their liberty'.[104] Indeed, although inducted into the Colonial Service in Kenya

---

[103] See in particular MacGregor Ross, *Kenya*.
[104] Leys, *Kenya*, p. 63.

as a medical officer, Leys' own understanding of his role was instructive of his impression of British Imperialism. At the time of his arrival in Kenya in 1904 he wrote: 'What I imagine the black and yellow people need most is not so much treatment for dyspepsia or rheumatism as something to make them stand up to the circumstances of the new civilization that is coming to them',[105] a civilisation he understood as co-terminus with the overpowering and morally deleterious forces of Western industrialisation which he saw it as his function to help Africans come to terms with[106] (again repeating a trope we encountered in Chapter 2, albeit from a different and more radical political foundation). Already, therefore, we can see that Ley's outlook was shaped by anxieties concerning the condition of Western civilisation. Indeed, one implication of this perspective was a distinction between 'Africa' on the one hand, and 'modernity' on the other, with the latter being ascribed violent tendencies – it is clear that Leys holds this view in his 1924 book *Kenya*, which details the damage and suffering inflicted by settler-colonialism in Kenya to the native population. As such, for Leys, imperialism becomes something with which he is distinctly uncomfortable with and antagonistic towards.

Leys was distinctive in another important respect too. While many of his contemporaries in humanitarian and Fabian circles, as well as in government and colonial service, were suspicious of the actually emerging urban educated African elite – all the while simultaneously idealising its emergence at some future point – Leys was excoriatingly critical of the tribal and customary Africa that many of his contemporaries sought to perpetuate as a storm-breaker against rising urban African agitation, or in the case of humanitarians like Oldham and Harris, because this latter group signified the failure of missionary/White supremacism and embodied the decay of contemporaneous Western industrial society. Leys saw tribalism as a source of weakness that Europeans could exploit to divide Africans politically. In this sense Leys' position foreshadowed the anti-tribalism that was to take hold of anxiety-driven idealisations of Africans in the 1950s, to be found particularly among modernisation theorists of the period (to be discussed in Chapter 4).

---

[105] Norman Leys, in Cell, 'Introduction', p. 8.
[106] Cell, 'Introduction', p. 19.

Despite his critique of existing imperialism and white settlement, Leys' anti-imperialism was ambiguous. He did not simply recommend that white settlers should pack up and leave, but rather that they should stay to help Africans to modernise correctly, along recognisably White lines, for 'there is nothing to do but wait till Africans prove themselves men, as they certainly will. But what kind of men will a generation of commercialism produce?'.[107] It was this question, underpinned by an anxiety about how Africa would evolve, which phenotypical whites could help address. Of course, in posing the question this way, Leys placed Africa as history-less – what were Africans precisely before they were 'men'? – sharing the 'waiting room' perspective on global development intrinsic to Eurocentric and White ethnocentric historiography.[108] Additionally, these kinds of questions reflected the anxiety that drove Leys' imperial-antagonism. Fundamentally this was an anxiety not simply about the dangers and damages of imperialism, but of the dangers and damages of Western modernity more broadly and, in particular, the conditions modern industrialism had created that had, in his view, fomented unwieldly and potentially dangerous revolutionary movements. Leys' pessimistic account of the 1915 Chilembwe uprising in Nyasaland for instance, where he argued that to shoot the participants of a rising led by a man, John Chilembwe, who had travelled to the United States to receive a 'Western education', was 'the kindest way of dealing with native risings',[109] indicated his moroseness concerning the nature of the colonial-modern, as well as the dialectical approach inherent to his analysis – whereby shooting the agitators was a necessary by-product of the uprising itself. In this same vein it is also interesting to note that Leys did not just think that industrialisation would overpower African society, but had already done so to rural British society too. According to his daughter, Agnes Avery, Leys felt that the low-income patients he saw when a general practitioner in Derbyshire at the end of Wold War I 'were very like Africans, both being at that time a deprived and inarticulate people with their potential abilities stunted and discouraged' by a runaway industrial policy that had taken their livelihoods and undermined their communal traditions.[110]

---

[107] Leys, in Cell, 'Introduction', p. 16.
[108] Chakrabarty, *Provincializing Europe*, p. 8.
[109] Leys in Cell, 'Introduction', p. 21.
[110] Cell, 'Introduction', p. 17.

Leys' ambiguity vis-à-vis imperialism and African history and agency coloured his views on how positive he could be about Thuku and the EAA. While settlers and the government took a very clear view on Thuku as a negative counter to the 'loyal' tribal Africans in whom they invested their optimism and positivity, one might expect that Leys, opposed as he was to any policy that differentiated Africans on tribal lines, would be positive about what Thuku represented. However, even though Thuku worked with and mobilised Indians, Luo and African Muslims and had noticeably named his organisation the East African Association to emphasise its trans-tribal aims, Leys nonetheless viewed the EAA as a tribally-based movement.[111] This led Leys to occupy an ambiguous position, for while Thuku and the EAA were clearly artic- ulating political positions that went well beyond parochial Kikuyu or even Kenya Colony concerns – Thuku was for instance in correspond- ence with pan-Africanists across Africa and in the United States[112] – Leys could not but help to view the EAA as serving Indian interests, largely because he could not ascribe politics to any movement based in part in tribal tradition – Thuku was, ultimately a Kikuyu, and his initial attempts at recruiting followers were most successful among his fellow Kikuyu. This explains Leys' attitude towards the emerging conflict between the EAINC and the settlers in 1921, prior to Thuku's arrest and the shooting of the protestors in March 1922:

The Indians were not slow to take advantage of the introduction of native interests into the controversy by their opponents ... I feel certain that hith- erto the average Indian has been more disliked and mistrusted than the aver- age European. But I am equally certain that now that Indians offer, however vaguely, means for redress of African grievances, articulate native opinion

---

[111] Leys, in Cell, *By Kenya Possessed*, p. 28.
[112] Marcus Garvey spoke out about Thuku's incarceration in a letter cabled to Prime Minister David Lloyd George four days after Thuku's arrest. See Robert A. Hill (ed.), *The Marcus Garvey and Universal Negro Improvement Association Papers, Volume IX, Africa for the Africans 1921–1922* (Berkeley, Los Angeles, London: University of California Press, 1995), p. 382. For correspondence between Thuku and a number of pan-Africanists in Uganda, see: TNA, FCO 141/6440, 'Office of the Chief Native Commissioner, Nairobi, A.1 Administration', Files 3a, 3b, and 3c. See also, Gabay, 'Decolonising Interwar Solidarities'.

must swing round to the side of the Indians in the political controversy ... we don't want exploiter-Jeevanjee[113] to step into exploiter-Grogan's[114] shoes.[115]

Indeed, Leys continued to deny political agency to the nascent Kenyan nationalist movement later on, when Jomo Kenyatta emerged more fully as a major figure in the late-1920s, along with his more obvious internationally networked anti-colonial politics.[116] What is also interesting in the quote is that Leys, along with all the white protagonists in this story, held that the EAA and 'articulate native opinion' was merely subject to EAINC machinations. This is once more revealing of Leys' ambiguity concerning African agency and his distrust of metropolitan movements, in Africa as much as Britain, based on his anxieties concerning Western modernity and phenotypical white depravity more broadly.

In summary, the imperial-antagonism of Norman Leys could not extend to recognising the political nature of EAA demands and the subsequent March 1922 protests. Leys was not alone in this. Coming from a similar political perspective to the left of mainstream Fabianism, Charles Roden Buxton[117] wrote that the protests were a 'wild gesture of despair by ignorant unarmed men'.[118] Both Leys and Buxton wrote in what for the time were very admonishing terms about the imperial project. Buxton for instance wrote of the 'new slavery' and of how 'the black man is sweated'.[119] And yet it was because this perspective emerged from a set of anxieties about Western civilisational respectability and the deleterious social effects of industrialisation that this

[113] Abhilai Jeevanjee, President of the East African Indian National Congress.
[114] Ewart Grogan, British settler with large commercial interests.
[115] Letter from Norman Leys to Joseph Oldham, 22 August 1921, in Cell, *By Kenya Possessed*, pp. 189–90.
[116] Cell, 'Introduction', p. 28.
[117] Buxton regularly cited Leys' work, and compiled reports on the iniquities of colonial rule that shared a great deal with Leys' analysis. See, for instance: R. Buxton Charles, *The Exploitation of the Coloured Man* (London: Anti-Slavery Society/Aborigines Protection Society, 1925), Weston Library, Charles Roden Buxton Papers, Mss.Brit.Emp.s.405, Box 7, Item 13.
[118] Charles R. Buxton, *British Land Policy in Tropical Africa, memo for Executive Committee Labour Party* (London: Joint Research and Information Department, Advisory Committee on International Questions, ND), Charles Roden Buxton Papers, Weston Library, Mss.Brit.Emp.s.405, Box 5.
[119] Charles R. Buxton, *The Black Man's Rights* (London: International Labour Party, ND), Charles Roden Buxton Papers, Weston Library, Mss.Brit.Emp.s.405, Box 7, Item 12.

radical critique of imperialism could not be transformed into a recognition of the distinctly political and modern claims of Thuku and the EAA, precisely because, perhaps, they reaffirmed everything that Leys and Buxton understood was wrong with White vitality and Western civilisation.

While Leys' anxieties played out in his structural analysis of both 'downtrodden' Africans *and* Europeans, Buxton deployed the narrative of the pre-slavery 'noble savage', blaming what he saw as the degradation of African societies on systems of slavery imposed by European states: 'For three hundred years the gap in civilisation has been widening. It is mainly our fault that Africans still have the fears, the hatreds, the cruelties, the vices, the mental inertia of slaves'.[120] In both cases (of Leys and Buxton) the main reference point here is not Africa, but Europe, and the emergence of a Western modernity based on dispossession and the violent erosion of tradition. Of course, this shares a great deal with contemporary critical arguments about the colonial nature of modernity.[121] The major and central difference is that while critical of Western modernity, Buxton maintains the West as the apogee of progress and civilisation. Africans here are still held to be 'behind' in terms of progress and civilisation, even if that is the fault of white European programmes of slavery and Imperialism.

And so, while positive idealisations are not a feature of imperial-antagonism, anxiety about White vitality in the West is and furthermore lays the ground for the kind of positive idealisations about selected African subjectivities that were to emerge in the 1950s which rebounded off the imperial-antagonist belief that tribe was incommensurate with political agency. This is something we will return to in Chapters 4 and 5.

For now, however, the central point is that it is impossible to understand the broad range of humanitarian and Fabian interwar attitudes to race and Africa without reference to the anxieties about modernity and White Christian vitality detailed thus far. As such, commitments to 'sane' imperialism cannot be reduced purely to material or moralising drivers. All of the key stakeholders in the debates around paramount rights, Thuku and Indian claims for equal property and representation

---

[120] Buxton, *British Land Policy*.
[121] See, for instance, Walter Mignolo, *The Darker Side of Western Modernity: Global Futures, Decolonial Options* (Durham, NC: Duke University Press, 2011).

rights in Kenya Colony in the early-1920s engaged in forms of fantastical idealisations of African subjectivity as the basis by which to undermine and contest the political agency of Thuku and the EAA, creating a narrative of events that enabled them, in their own ways, to support the policy of British imperial trusteeship of native interests, even when confronted by 'natives' willing and able to define their interests for themselves. In that sense, even though imperial-antagonists like Leys and Buxton did not channel very much idealisation of anything, they nonetheless existed on the same spectrum as settlers, the imperial government and administration, and humanitarian imperial-sympathisers and agitators concerning the degree to which they all portrayed Thuku as a puppet of Indian demands – thus denying the validity of the EAA's own demands. The only difference on this spectrum was the degree to which these stakeholders 'talked-up' other groups of Africans in order to carry out this denial. Centrally, all of the key phenotypical white stakeholders/stakeholders in Whiteness were driven in their analyses by anxieties concerning White genius – i.e., Christianity and governance – that made their narratives of the conflict partial, and fantastical, in the sense of producing positive idealisations about the place of certain groups of Africans in the social and political affairs of the colony pertaining to White vitality and the compliance of those groups of Africans in performing these roles. As we move into the period following World War II, the following two chapters will suggest that racial anxieties concerning Whiteness and the relationship between phenotypical whiteness and Western civilisational prowess deteriorated further, to the degree that after WWII a belief emerged that phenotypical whiteness may no longer be a necessary precondition in the safeguarding of White vitality in Africa and beyond.

4 | 'Exploding Africa'
Of Post-War Modernisers and Travellers

[Africa] is springing in a step from black magic to white civilization[1]

... liberalism manifests its own version of the Gramscian
motto, 'Pessimism of the intellect, optimism of the will'[2]

An important transition in race-thinking took place in the wake of
World War II, one that overwhelmed the scientific racism and eugenicism characteristic of the pre-War period at a governmental, administrative and policy level. In the wake of the war, phenotypical whiteness
was increasingly no longer seen as a necessary prerequisite for White
genius and Western civilisational prowess. This did not, however,
mean that the White standards of civilisational genius had been jettisoned, or that the fight to protect them in the West did not continue.[3]
Nonetheless, attaining civilisational genius and meeting the standards
of White morality had become a more meritocratic exercise, whereby
any racial group could become civilised in a way recognisable to a set
of moral and ethical optics that cohered around Whiteness – albeit

---

[1] John Gunther, *Inside Africa* (London: Hamish Hamilton, 1955), p. 3.
[2] Amanda Anderson, *Bleak Liberalism* (Chicago, IL: University of Chicago Press, 2016), p. 13.
[3] This came down to how civilisational standards were defined. While post-war Keynesianism was dominant in this period, producing a sense of civilisation-as-bureaucratic modernism, this was also a time when advocates of the free market libertarianism later to become popularised through the economically neoliberal governments of Margaret Thatcher and Ronald Reagan began to seriously mobilise, seeing in Keynsianism a threat to White civilisational order. This mobilisation, led by key figures like Friedrich Hayek, or the Koch family in the United States, was explicitly driven by a desire to protect Western civilisation from socialist and morally feckless decline. For an overview of this period, its main protagonists and intellectual context see, for the United Kingdom: Richard Cockett, *Thinking the Unthinkable: Think Tanks and the Economic Counter Revolution, 1931–1983* (London: Harper Collins, 1994); and for the USA, Jane Mayer, *Dark Money: The Hidden History of the Billionaires behind the Rise of the Radical Right* (New York, NY: DoubleDay, 2016), Section One.

that this remained a highly monitored process. The apogee of civilisational progress, i.e., something which looked like industrial modernity, therefore, remained the same, and dissenting voices – i.e., those
such as Leys – were now far fewer. As a result, the post-war decades
were a time resonating with ideas and theories about how 'backwards'
people could be best tooled to take advantage of this new meritocratic international social order, most notably a loose conglomeration
of economic and political science known as 'Modernisation Theory'.
This chapter will explore in some detail the contours of this post-war
transition in race-thinking, before outlining the relationship between
Modernisation Theory and Whiteness, its idealisations of Africans
and how pervasive it was in shaping cultural, literary and artistic representations of Africa in the 1950s and 1960s. These representations
will be shown to have important consequences for how groups of liberal and other assorted settlers managed British decline and decolonisation in Southern and Eastern Africa in Chapter 5. Importantly, the
transition in race-thinking was underpinned by a raft of geopolitical,
economic and fundamentally civilisational and racial anxieties.

The aftermath of World War II bore witness to several changes in
the governance of international order. The drafting of the Universal
Declaration of Human Rights and the subsequent engineering of the
United Nations and associated architecture represented a rupture
with the loose confederalism that had defined the interwar years. The
deterioration in relations between the USA and USSR in many ways
served to buttress the nascent UN system, by locking the machinations of the organisation into the very heart of the new balance of
power. At the same time, the geopolitics of the Cold War necessitated
alliances. With or without the perceived global threat of the USSR,
domestic Jim Crow laws were unsustainable in a world where the
USA sought to emerge as a global leader, (self) defined by a strain of
anti-imperialism designed to set itself apart from its competitors – i.e.,
European empires.[4] In other words, if the USA wanted to be a global
leader and appear morally superior to the empire builders of Europe
and the USSR, then all this would be undercut by the continuation
of racial segregation within the USA itself. This was the implication

---

[4] American progressives and liberals appeared to genuinely believe this too,
    seeing in Africa a test case for post-war American anti-imperialism – see
    Staniland, *American Intellectuals*, p. 31.

of the major study conducted by Swedish economist and sociologist Gunnar Myrdal in 1944, *An American Dilemma: The Negro Problem and Modern Democracy*, where, aided by the future UN diplomat and civil rights campaigner Ralph Bunche,[5] Myrdal argued that the USA was living a contradiction between its, as he put it, democratic 'creed' and the realities of racial oppression and segregation.

Similarly, American criticisms of the empire were deflected in Europe with recourse to counter-accusations against hypocrisy on the part of segregationist USA, with its wartime internment camps for Japanese-Americans.[6] Nonetheless, American criticisms did hit home and led to a reformulation of justifications for European Empire away from naked beliefs in racial hierarchy and phenotypical white dominance.[7] Such a transition, driven by nascent Cold War geopolitics, struggles against empire and racism within the USA and from within various European colonies, resulted in a rapid change in the ways in which governments and policy-makers framed the challenges of the post-war world. Lothrup Stoddard's widely popular scientific racism rapidly disappeared from public political discourse, delegitimised by the racist violence empire brought home to the European heartland through the genocidal conduct of the Nazi regime during World War II. Indeed, explicit ideas about racial hierarchy even disappeared from the scholarly discipline that had been funded and constructed to study and direct international order, namely International Relations, where Robert Vitalis argues that 'while arguments about imperialism proliferated across the globe after 1945, they completely disappeared from scholarship in a discipline that ten years earlier considered it to be the fundamental problem of world order'.[8]

Instead of informing a policy debate that sought to justify continued imperial expansion and domination, the discipline of International Relations – and international diplomacy and policy-making more broadly – turned to debates over how to ensure cooperation under conditions of an anarchic world system. In such a system, explicit

---

[5] Himself undergoing somewhat of a transition from Marxist class warrior to UN diplomat and civil rights campaigner – Vitalis, *White World Order*, pp. 97–100.
[6] Ibid., at p. 116.
[7] Suke Wolton, *Lord Hailey, the Colonial Office and Politics of Race and Empire in the Second World War* (London: Palgrave, 2000).
[8] Vitalis, *White World Order*, p. 120.

racial hierarchy could no longer operate; all polities were now as open to the threat of violence and invasion as any other, and it was only through forms of contingent alliance-building (from a Realist perspective) or collective security (from a Liberal perspective) that such violence could be averted. Of course, all those staking out these positions worked within a White milieu, reproducing and universalising the anxieties of a parochial set of concerns relating to the history of warfare and violence in Europe and the Anglosphere – and the prospect of anti-imperial and anti-segregationist violence in the post-war decades to come. This was the implicit message of Myrdal's study, as well as of the growing independence movements in colonial territories around the world. This all led to 'threat inflation' concerning the likelihood of the peoples of territories as diverse as Saudi Arabia, Pakistan, Ghana and so on, rising up as one to strike against international and domestic white power, egged on by Jim Crow segregation in the US South. This leads Vitalis to argue that the primary threat to world order was in fact 'the quite natural, albeit tragic, resistance whites exhibited to the notion of relinquishing power'.[9] This chapter and the next, however, aims to illustrate that many people identifying as White were more than willing to cede power from what they saw as a diminished West, as long as those who were taking up the mantle committed themselves to White logics of social, economic and political order.

This operated as an unacknowledged impulse, however, for as has been argued in previous chapters, for those who inhabit it, Whiteness does not tend to function out in the open.[10] Nonetheless, for those who see Whiteness, its operation can be very clear, and necessitates the outcome that bodies marked by their non-whiteness must conform to logics of White sociability, which derive from the privileges that accumulate by being phenotypically white and passing relatively frictionlessly through a White world.[11]

---

[9] Ibid., at p. 124.

[10] Ahmed, 'Phenomenology', p. 157.

[11] A personal example: at a recent conference I attended, an African American scholar was asked on two separate occasions by members of an adjoining conference session to speak more quietly (i.e., more calmly) when talking about institutional and societal racism on a panel about racism in the academy. Being viscerally angry about racism, *especially* when you have been the victim of racism, does not cohere to logics of Whiteness, which holds calmness and rationality as signifiers of civilised behaviour, and are much more easily practised by those who have had little reason to feel existentially challenged by

While race became a less invoked component of international hierarchy after World War II, this does not mean that race did not continue to operate as an ordering principle of international order. The replacement of race with 'culture' or 'tradition' did not displace the sense in which Whiteness was held to be the normative referent against which all other social manifestations would be judged. As such, culture or tradition 'explained all the same phenomena, but it did so in strictly non-biological terms ... For "race" read "culture" or "civilisation", for "racial hierarchy" read "cultural heritage", and the change had taken place'.[12]

Hobson suggests that this transition from race to culture was a product of what he calls 'colonial-racist guilt syndrome'.[13] However, as this and the following chapter unfold, it will become clear that guilt was not a primary factor in explaining the transition. Very few policy-making, policy-informing or humanitarian elites evinced guilt in their proclamations on imperialism and decolonisation. Indeed, many of the protagonists considered in these two chapters expressed pride in the historical imperial record in Africa, even if the self-same was becoming to be seen as anachronistic. Rather, the belief that international order, social progress and modernisation was actually a meritocratic exercise was driven by deep anxieties concerning the vitality of White genius and Western civilisation following World War II.

The anxieties concerning Whiteness bred by World War II led to a new discipline and policy industry, that of 'Race Relations', which was based on 'apprehensions about Western global decline' and that 'regarded racial tension as not merely dangerous but specifically a threat to Western interests'.[14] This was ultimately a process of pre-emption, censoring overt White racism in an attempt to contain reactions to it, all the while maintaining the centrality of White logics to

---

institutional and societal racism. Trying to close down the anger of those who suffer from racism is one of the products of 'White fragility'; the sense in which confrontations between Whiteness and the racism perpetuated by Whiteness are only reconcilable through an act of denial – see DiAngelo, 'White Fragility'.

[12] George W. Stocking, *Race, Culture, and Evolution* (Chicago, IL: Chicago University Press, 1982), p. 265.

[13] John H. Hobson, 'Re-embedding the Global Colour Line within post-1945 International Theory', in Alexander Anievas, Nivi Manchanda, and Robbie Shilliam (eds.), *Race and Racism in International Relations* (Abingdon: Routledge, 2014), p. 83.

[14] Furedi, *The Silent War*, p. 2.

the management of world order. As we have seen in earlier chapters, the anxieties about White civilisational decline that drove these post-war dynamics were not new; what was new was the manner by which in this period these anxieties began to manifest themselves as a retreat from the notion that phenotypical whiteness was a necessary prerequisite for contemporaneous White genius and Western civilisational practice.

All of this was a necessary move in order to reassure anxieties concerning racial revenge against international 'white power'. Indeed, far from being confined to Blacks and Africans, such a shift also applied to one of Europe's internal persecuted Others, Jews, who, having been subjected to centuries of anti-Semitic persecution, violence and genocide, were very swiftly re-constructed as epitomes of good racial relations and as loyal and well-integrated citizens of the countries in which they had settled.[15] As such, claims to victimisation within what remained an imperial world order, especially if and when they became violent and conflictual, could be painted as irrational or intensely destructive.[16]

Indeed, good 'race relations' was premised on an idea of fundamental racial compatibility. This did not, however, translate into a notion that what were seen as distinct cultural practices could be reconciled with each other. Rather, non-whites had to engage in a process of 'becoming-White' – like the figure of the post-war European Jew. That this process was perceived to be legitimate was distinct from pre-war conceptions of racial hierarchy. Nonetheless, in effect, the colour bar had merely been replaced by a cultural one. The proliferation of Modernisation Theory in the post-war period exemplifies the White anxieties that drove this transition from colour to culture, and the resulting shift in African objects of White idealisation that emerged as a result, from tribal to urban, traditional to bureaucratic-modern.

The Anxieties and Idealisations of Modernisation Theory

Modernisation Theory was a set of ideas about economic and political development rooted in Weberian schematics concerning the

---

[15] Santiago Slabodsky, *Decolonial Judaism: Triumphal Failures of Barbaric Thinking* (New York, NY: Palgrave MacMillan, 2014), p. 17.
[16] Furedi, *The Silent War*, p. 3.

relationship between entrepreneurial economic practices and social and civic maturity. It is important to note that although this section will refer to a singular Modernisation Theory, and indeed Modernisation *theorists*, it would be inaccurate to suggest that Modernisation Theory was anything more than a loose schematic developed to explain how development had historically occurred in the West and would do so in the future for post-colonial states. Coalescing under this rubric came geographers, historians, economists, former colonial officials, journalists, film-makers, literary authors, post-colonial elites and others.

Modernisation Theory was embraced by many post-colonial elites, although its initial intellectual development was distinctly Anglospheric. There were broader differences in the USA and British approaches to Africa during this period, not least that decolonisation in Africa served as a significant blow to British prestige and international hegemony, whereas it served the inverse function for the USA, underlining its anti-imperial credentials and hegemonic aspirations.[17] Nonetheless, in this section we will see that there were also important similarities of approach between scholars and travel writers working across both national contexts, not least that on both sides of the Atlantic there was, with reference to Africa, 'a great deal of leaping, bursting, emerging and straining, as well as much metaphorical movement of mighty and irresistible forces'.[18]

A further transatlantic backdrop to the emergence of Modernisation Theory was the predilection in this period for what Amanda Anderson calls Bleak Liberalism, 'a dialectic of skepticism and hope' that channelled 'bleak sociologies, sober psychologies, historical pessimism' with more necessarily hopeful commitments to 'freedom and equality, to individual and collective self-actualization, to democratic process and the rule of law'.[19] In the context of decolonisation and post-war recovery (or lack thereof), one might well expect British liberals to be bleak, but this applied to North Americans too, and particularly regarding Africa – a continent where North American liberals had very little experience – and where the function of Africa as a mirror of US exceptionalism soon ran aground among the messy realities of African decolonisation. It is within this crevice of liberal sensibilities that most Modernisation

---

[17] Staniland, *American Intellectuals and African Nationalists*, p. 76.
[18] Ibid., at p. 66.
[19] Anderson, *Bleak Liberalism*, p. 22.

theorists sit and Anderson notes the historical conjuncture of the post-War period as a singularly important one in the development of Liberal 'bleakness',[20] reinforcing the importance of the post-War period in the broadening out of anxieties concerning Whiteness.[21]

Modernisation Theory was most famously exemplified within the works of the economist and US National Security Advisor Walt Whitman Rostow, specifically his 'non-communist manifesto' of 1953, in which he wrote of the five stages that all societies must go through in order to reach 'take-off' into a mature, democratic, consumerist society.[22] Importantly, Modernisation Theory and its associated off-shoots provide an interesting staging post in the evolution of the contours of White anxieties in the twentieth century, bridging earlier, more overtly racial theories such as those discussed in Chapters 2 and 3, to some of the idealisations of Africa that can be found in contemporary political, economic and cultural representations of the continent (discussed in Chapters 6 and 7).

As a first step, it was central to key Modernisation theorists that what they held to be African tribal societies were inimical to – and outside of – modern civilised time. Indeed, Rostow's 'five stages' saw history as a progressive march away from tradition, the latter understood as pre-scientific and prone to 'long-run fatalism', both of which were inimical to the individual and collective self-maximisation necessary for the final stage of mass consumerism.[23] Similarly, in Gabriel Almond and Sidney Verba's seminal The Civic Culture, where they explore the components of what they take to be the cultural bedrocks of liberal participatory democracy, African culture is held to be 'parochial' – as against the 'subject' populations of the Eastern Bloc and the 'participant' cultures of the Anglo-Saxon world. In the 'parochial' world, there are no political movements, offices, nor even expectations of political change.[24] Taking a similar position, Rostow argued that the reason

---

[20] Ibid., at p. 23.

[21] For the relationship between aspects of political and social Liberalism and Whiteness, see Mills, Racial Contract.

[22] Walt W. Rostow, The Stages of Economic Growth: A Non-Communist Manifesto (Cambridge: Cambridge University Press, Third Edition, 1990/1953).

[23] Ibid., at pp. 4–6.

[24] Gabriel Almond and Sidney Verba, The Civic Culture: Political Attitudes and Democracy in Five Nations (London, New York, NY: Sage Publications, 1963), pp. 17–20.

why so many African countries had not 'taken off' into modernisation was that 'The African heritage ... was likely to make the interval between independence and take-off protracted'.[25] In a book redolent of contemporary titles considered in Chapter 7, *Africa Emergent*, the historian and colonial administrator William Miller Macmillan wrote of the hold that tribal custom and psychology held over Africa's development. This was an obvious reversal of general attitudes towards the subject of African development as expressed in the 1920s, where tradition was seen as a marker of 'equal but different' development. By now, however, such difference was seen as inimical to development, with 'detribalised' Africans becoming the idealised objects of anxious White idealisation. MacMillan argued that:

In almost every community today there are individuals ... wholly or in part cut loose from the old tribal life. *The ferment of ideas is hopeful* in so far as it promises to undermine the passive submissiveness which has certainly helped to keep Africa backward.[26]

Channelling the mythologised *homo economicus*, with its choice-maximising and rational outlook,[27] MacMillan went on to assert that, 'The [tribal] African is the helpless victim of spirits ... the future depends on the new individualists rather than on the old groups'.[28] Modernisation Theory, thus, sought to extract the individual from the grip of tribal culture, and, when concerned with Africa, painted an idealised vision of Africa's future based on this move. Other Afrocentric modernisation writers of the period similarly sought to idealise the subject of the 'detribalised African'. Laurence Dudley-Stamp wrote of the 'crop of problems' that had arisen from the clash of cultures between African tribal organisations and 'western concepts of democracy and European law'. Increasing the rate of modernisation through training and educational programmes was central to diffusing

---

[25] Rostow, *The Stages of Economic Growth*, p. xxiii.

[26] MacMillan, *Africa Emergent*, p. 65, *emphasis added*.

[27] Jason Read, 'A Genealogy of Homo-Economicus: Neoliberalism and the Production of Subjectivity', in Sam Binkley and Jorge Capetillo (eds.), *A Foucault for the 21st Century: Governmentality, Biopolitics and Discipline in the New Millennium* (Cambridge: Cambridge Scholars Publishing, 2010), pp. 2–15.

[28] MacMillan, *Africa Emergent*, p. 69.

this tension and creating 'world-ready' Africans.[29] Similarly, a book
by the pseudonymous Scipio included chapters such as 'Opportunities
for individual existence – freedom from tribal restraints', and 'Towns
as the most active agents of emancipation'.[30] In summary, all of these
ideas about what modernisation entailed were clearly inflected with
parochial-as-universal ethnocentric logics pertaining to the primacy of
individual economic agency, 'progressive' versus 'regressive' cultural
practices, electoral representative democracy and so on. Any forms
of practice that did not conform to these standards were immediately tagged as pre-modern, backward, fundamentally uncivilised and
implicitly un-White.

Of course, in this sense, modernisation tropes of the period simultaneously shadowed *and* contradicted the earlier overtly racial theories
of Jan Smuts, Joseph Houldsworth Oldham and others, which asserted
absolute differences between native and white European populations
in Africa and elsewhere. In particular, the docility and Otherness
through which Modernisation Theory construed 'tribal' Africa was a
clear shadowing of these earlier attitudes. As such, at this stage, the
idealisations of Modernisation Theory still placed most of Africa in
'the waiting room of history'.[31] However, significantly, tribal Africans
were no longer being idealised as they had been in the pre-war period,
and 'detribalised', 'modern' exceptions were beginning to be noticed
and idealised as Africa's potential saviours – again, in marked difference to the ways in which 'detribalised' Africans such as Harry Thuku
were conceived of in the 1920s. Despite the ambiguities, then, this
nonetheless represents a significant shift; no longer are whites seen
to be the only, or even favoured saviours of Africa. Now Africans are
placed with this responsibility, but only those who meet the idealised
standards of a universalised individualistic rationality, or put differ-
ently, only those who can show that they are becoming White.[32]

[29] Laurence Dudley Stamp, *Africa: A Study in Tropical Development* (New York,
   NY: John Wiley and Sons Inc., 1953), p. 7.
[30] Scipio, *Emergent Africa* (London: Chattum and Windus, 1965).
[31] Chakrabarty, *Provincializing Europe*, p. 8.
[32] There are obvious parallels here then with Franz Fanon's analysis in *Black
   Skin, White Masks* (New York, NY: Grove Press, 1952), the main difference
   being that whereby Fanon locates this notion of becoming White in the
   psychological impact of colonialism on the colonised, here I argue that this
   was at least matched by the psycho-social impact of decolonisation on the
   colonisers.

This transition begins to occur for two main reasons. Firstly, World War II shifts the ground upon which the old confidence in phenotypically white tutelage of African historical development stands. Secondly, growing and articulate calls for decolonisation across the continent presents imperial power with a dilemma, the outcome of which might pose an existential threat to imperial dominance in the international order – in line with contemporaneous discussions concerning 'race relations'. In this context, key Modernisation theorists began to present much more optimistically idealised visions of Africa in particular and the developing world in general, which were partnered by more pessimistic visions of the West. One finds this shift clearly present when Sidney Almond, co-author of *The Civic Culture*, writes a quarter of a century later that 'we had assumed that other nations might move in the "civic" direction of the United States and Britain', before going on to admit that 'in fact, the latter two nations moved away from that position'.[33] Rostow more fully embodies this simultaneous pessimism and optimism, when, nearly twenty years after the publication of *The Stages of Economic Growth*, he writes of the decline of the USA, particularly its inability to continue its global policing function,[34] while also proclaiming that:

My temperately optimistic judgement emerges not merely from faith but from knowledge of how men and women have voted, with dignity and conviction – and sometimes at risk of their lives – in honest elections of Latin America and Asia, when given a chance; by having looked often – and in many countries – into the shrewd and passionate faces of men and women who have grasped the possibilities offered them for making, through their own responsible efforts, a better life for their children than the life they and their parents knew in the villages of the developing world.[35]

It is this simultaneous pessimism towards the self/idealisation of the Other that Modernisation Theory represents during this juncture in the twentieth century. Indeed, in many respects Modernisation theorists such as Rostow or MacMillan are the missionaries of the

---

[33] Gabriel A. Almond, 'On Revisiting the Civic Culture: A Personal Postscript', in Gabriel A. Almond and Sidney Verba (eds.), *The Civic Culture Revisited* (London, New Delhi: Sage Publications, 1989), p. 399.

[34] Walt W. Rostow, *Politics and the Stages of Growth* (Cambridge: Cambridge University Press, 1971), p. 308.

[35] Ibid., at p. 301.

post-war era, seeking to convert the heathen (proto-socialist and/ or tribal) world to state-capitalism and secularism. And like the nineteenth-century missionary societies, Modernisation Theory was emerging from a social and political context that embedded a series of anxieties concerning White vitality at the heart of its prospectus,[36] rocked as it was by the savagery of war and the intransigence of the Soviet Union. Indeed, actual missionaries were posing similar questions in the same period, whereby the key problem revolved around the fact that 'they' (Africans) might have to continue 'our' (Christian) mission. In that case, 'what do we do to ensure an orthodox path? ...how can we survive? How can we maintain the legitimacy of our presence?'[37] The answer to these questions in a modernisation context was that those not already on the path to modernisation had to be brought into line, something that was essential for the continued survival of the White genius that was Western civilisation. Again, this was a fundamentally different outlook when set next to the 1920s, when phenotypically white leadership was still seen as the only means by which Western civilisation could flourish and Africans were held to be incapable of developing into civilised subjects – thus necessitating the idealisation of 'tribal' and 'traditional' Africans as objects, rather than acting subjects. Questions of how the potentially wayward could be brought into line lay behind the position of University of Indiana development geographer George Herbert Tinley Kimble, who wrote with some relief in 1963 that 'to their credit, many [African] countries show a growing realization' that they 'just don't really have what it takes to flourish independently' and that it was important that their 'friends should help [them] as much as possible'.[38]

In addition to Kimble and MacMillan, Modernisation Theory had many disciples among development economists, urban planners and a variety of other disciplinarians. For many, Africa was a burning cauldron of possibilities. The American geographer and State Department adviser William A. Hance (Columbia University) proclaimed that the

---

[36] Richard Price asserts that missionary endeavours in Africa was driven as much by anxieties concerning the vitality of Christianity in the West as it was with optimism about the potential conversion of millions of Africans in the missions – See Price, *Making Empire*, p. 57.

[37] Mudimbe, *The Idea of Africa*, p. 126.

[38] George H. T. Kimble, 'How Free are the New Countries?', 1963, p. 171.

'adjective awakening is passé. Africa has awakened'.[39] Similarly, the highly respected British geographer Dudley-Stamp wrote that 'There is perhaps no part of the world where rapid change is so apparent in the middle of the twentieth century as throughout Africa … the changes which are taking place are so marked, so fundamental. And so rapid that we may properly use the word kaleidoscopic'.[40] As we saw with Rostow, such breathless excitement could be a key attribute of Modernisation Theory more generally, but also penetrated deeply into travel and other cultural forms of representation of Africa during this period, something the next section will return to.

Not all Modernisation disciples expressed fully idealised tropes about Africans, however. Where some of the above rhetoric might be considered as emerging from a liberal epistemology of social order – one that is embedded in the idea and indispensability of social progress wedded to scientific rationalism – more conservative accounts were also apparent. W.J. Jarvis, city planner for Salisbury in Southern Rhodesia, wrote for instance that ideas about racial hierarchy (with Africans the least civilised) were not only true, but also drove human progress and competition. Nonetheless, channelling the optimism of Modernisation Theory, Jarvis went on to argue that, 'If the African is given a reasonable chance under improved economic and social conditions, it is likely that he will advance in civilization and culture and contribute his quota to general development.'[41] To achieve this, Africans would have to be trained, for 'it is by training the African and race minorities to do the obvious and possible things to improve their living conditions that it will be possible later to solve the economic, social and political problems inherent in a multi-racial structure'.[42] There are a number of ideas here worth extrapolating. Africans are racially inferior, and yet they cannot be allowed to simply persist in their irrational tribal enclaves. With training (and, thus, a degree of 'detribalisation') Africans will be able to contribute their 'quota to general development', but only within a perpetuated 'multi-racial structure' – i.e., a social order predicated on hierarchical racial

---

[39] William A. Hance, 'Economic Change in Africa', *Journal of Geography*, 58, 1959, p. 180.
[40] Dudley Stamp, *Africa*, p. 517.
[41] W. J. Jarvis, *Planning from a Multi Racial Aspect in Africa* (Salisbury: Government House Publications, 1951), p. 255.
[42] Ibid., at p. 259.

differences. While conservatives of this period, particularly in the USA,[43] looked at social order in far more strictly hierarchical terms than their liberal counterparts – the latter of which dominated the broad collective that constituted Modernisation Theory – and conversely were intrigued by 'African tradition', this was only a prop for their fundamental belief in racial hierarchy and phenotypical white supremacy.[44]

Nonetheless, inflected by a conservative or liberal bent, Modernisation Theory of the period created an inversion of the pre-war idea that Africans were too backward to be entrusted with their own historical development and thus required indefinite phenotypical white tutelage, even though Western civilisation was already deemed to be under threat in the imperial metropoles. With this threat, then, came a withdrawal (albeit uneven depending on different political outlooks) from the belief in the necessity or, perhaps more importantly, efficacy of white tutelage, although the foundational belief in the unique civilisational genius of Whiteness – that this should act as a developmental milestone for the rest of the world – and be simultaneously defended in the West, persisted. This was the period more broadly, then, when supreme efforts were made on the part of Western governing elites to ensure that decolonisation resulted not in rupture or some other kind of political awakening divorced from White logics of enlightenment and Modernity, but 'the socialization of newcomers into the established norms and practices of the international'.[45] As we will see, this was a driving impulse during this period, shaping much of the cultural and social landscaping of Africa in Western imaginaries.

[43] There was a slightly different slant given to this by the British context. This is explored in subsequent sections.
[44] Staniland, *American Intellectuals and African Nationalists*, pp. 214–5.
[45] Mustapha Kamal Pasha 'The "Bandung Impulse" and International Relations', in Sanjay Seth (ed.), *Postcolonial Theory and International Relations: A Critical Introduction* (Abingdon: Routledge, 2013), p. 146. See also Jan Vansina's discussion of the Catholic Sisters in Congo who sought to create a foreign market for the weaved textiles of Kuba women, but in doing so 'destroyed the dynamic rhythms that turned each piece into its own work of art' by 'requiring exact reproductions of the geometrical motifs used' and then 'began to invent their own Kuba-like motifs and imposed them on their vendors' (Vansina, *Being Colonized*, p. 275). This is an Africa produced to be palatable to Western mores and a denial of difference in the name of White power-logics.

Africa in Travelogue, Literature and Film
in the Immediate Post-War Period

In the Victorian version, civilisation equalled the positive good and savagery its abhorrent negation. Modern writers often reverse the equation as an expression of their uncertainties[46]

Modernisation Theory was symptomatic of broader post-war socio-political trends and anxieties in Western societies. As such, we can see parallels of the kinds of anxious idealisations we found in Modernisation Theory across a whole array of equivalent social and cultural epiphenomena produced during this period. An analysis of these other epiphenomena helps to furnish some of the arguments made in the previous section. Specifically, Dorothy Hammond and Alta Jablow's comments regarding the literary imagination of Africa and the transition it underwent in the middle of the twentieth century opens up a set of questions about this imagination that this chapter has so far only partially addressed. Crudely, these questions revolve around the 'how' and 'why' of this transition. This section seeks to put more flesh on the arguments already made, and illustrate how anxieties about Western civilisation and White vitality played out in socio-cultural terms, all the while that a new discursive alignment pertaining to ideas about Africa in this period remained far from settled and consistent.

This section draws on a range of literature, films and travelogues concerning Africa that proliferated in the post-War era especially, a period that, for instance, saw more than four times as many novels pertaining to Africa published than had been produced in the preceding 350 years.[47] In particular, it will become clear that ideas about Africa very much depended on the relative liberalism or conservatism of the author in question. What united the different approaches, however, was the ways in which they were both embedded in racial anxieties about Whiteness.[48] The liberalism and conservatism of the various authors considered here can be deduced from the differences between

---

[46] Hammond and Jablow, *The Myth of Africa*, p. 121.
[47] Ibid., at p. 118.
[48] In a more strictly North American context this was more complicated; many US conservatives for instance were strongly invested in the notion of American exceptionalism. See Staniland, *American Intellectuals and African Nationalists*, pp. 216–24.

them concerning the degree to which Africa and Africans were viewed
as potential saviours of White vitality, with liberals more likely to see
Africans as capable of contemporaneous auto-development according
to White rationalities – thus saving Western civilisation from phenotypical white decline – whereas conservative thinkers and writers were
not, seeing a Western civilisation in decline and increasingly beyond
the reach of both white people and, it went almost without saying,
other peoples of colour.

Liberal Anxieties and Idealisations

Within liberal writing on the continent, there was a consistent desire
to see a particular kind of Africa that would conform to White standards of civilisation. This became particularly prominent when faced
by information that contradicted liberal expectations of modernity –
ideas of progress, individualism, etc., all found in Modernisation
Theory. So, for instance, Frederick Spencer Chapman, the author of a
travelogue called *Lightest Africa*, writes that 'Durban is like Sydney',
and that the Zulus are 'a magnificent and colourful native people'.
In so doing, Spencer Chapman asserts a sameness in the urban cosmopolitanism of Durban and a difference in the tribalism of the
Zulu, thus, upholding core Modernisation Theory tropes of urban-
progress and tribal-difference/backwardness. In both cases there is a
degree of idealisation occurring that seeks to iron out any problematic
features that might disrupt Spencer Chapman's depictions. Indeed,
Spencer Chapman makes this process of ironing out explicit, when
he states that 'Admittedly ... there is an Indian problem and a Native
problem and the ever present political problem – but this is *Lightest
Africa* and although we were aware of these darker matters and often
heard them discussed, I do not intend ... to write about them'.[49] And
indeed, he doesn't. He doesn't write about the inter-communal riots
that left nearly 150 dead in Durban in 1949, nor does he write about
the decade-long simmering tensions around beer production – pitting
state production against artisanal native beer producers in the Durban
townships – that contributed subsequently to anti-government riots in
the city in 1959, the Cato Manor riots. All of this is necessary because
of the fact that Durban offers the reader a much more luxurious life

---

[49] F. Spencer Chapman, *Lightest Africa* (London: Chatto & Windus, 1955), p. 58.

than that commonly available in the United Kingdom,[50] an impossible assertion to make if the inequalities that pervaded daily life for most people in South Africa in the 1950s were fully acknowledged.

The paths Africans are deemed to have taken on their journey to become more White is rendered clearly in an article by Elsie May Bell-Grosvenor, an instrumental figure in establishing the *National Geographic Magazine*. In an article entitled 'Safari through *Changing Africa*' (emphasis added). Bell-Grosvenor records her impressions of the mineworkers in Johannesburg who, 'forgetting they are civilised', 'dance to the primitive rhythms of their old tribal life'.[51] Tribal life is 'old', and revived when the new, urban, civilised life is momentarily forgotten. Again, both versions of Africa are idealised, but only one can be entrusted with the vitality of Western civilisation, for 'the long range objective is to teach Africans to govern themselves',[52] which presumably cannot be achieved if Africans keep on forgetting how to be civilised.

While Bell-Grosvenor still invokes phenotypical white tutelage in the brief passage above, it is also clear that there is a sense of trying to bridge backwardness to modernisation, a feature characteristic of liberal idealisations of Africa during the 1950s. It is prevalent in the film as well as literature. *Daybreak in Udi* was a short feature film produced by the Crown Film Unit, a Central Office of Information unit accountable to the British Cabinet Office.[53] Set in what was then the village of Udi, now part of Enugu State in Nigeria, the film was populated by locals performing a dramatised script – this included the local British District Commissioner, E.R. Chadwick, performing a version of himself. The film was entered into the Academy Awards and won an Oscar and BAFTA for best documentary feature in 1950. The plot of the film perfectly sets out what was commonly understood as the tensions between old and new in the 'detribalising' societies of Africa.

The film opens with a text that perfectly combines idealisations of African commitment to White norms concerning the Weberian work ethic, with tropes consistent with Modernisation Theory: 'With few

---

[50] Ibid.
[51] Elsie May Bell-Grosvenor, 'Safari through Changing Africa' *National Geographic Magazine*, 104, 1953, p. 158.
[52] Ibid., at p. 198.
[53] More information is available at the British Film Institute. See www .screenonline.org.uk/film/id/469778/, accessed on 16 July 2017.

resources but their strength and spirit ... [t]hey are starting to bridge the centuries that divide their way of life from ours'.[54] In the opening scenes this statement is made literal. Rows of traditionally dressed men, women and children sit in a large outdoors area where they are being taught English by rote. The three teachers are also Nigerian and presumably local given that they speak the same dialect as the people they are teaching, but wear the clothes of colonial officialdom – Khaki shirts and shorts. These three teachers prove to be the main interlocutors between colonial officialdom and subject populations, always appearing at opportune moments to translate the District Commissioner's (DC) words at communal events and consultations, but also acting as the film's main agents of modernisation.

The plot of the film revolves around the teachers' attempts to convince the DC and resistant 'tribal' elements within the local community of the benefit of building a new maternity clinic in the area. The real stars of the film are the teachers, in particular the one female teacher who is repeatedly shown speaking disparagingly of superstition and other 'nonsense' – her gender is arguably significant in foregrounding the particular entrapment women are seen to experience in tribal society by way of comparison[55]. In one scene in particular, after the clinic has been built – to the annoyance of one of the village elders, who has consistently been trying to block the project by threatening builders with vengeful spirits – the female teacher visits the newly appointed midwife who is tending to a patient. From a different area, the midwife has been scared by the stories of vengeful spirits. Darkness has fallen, mood music is playing and every unusual sound from outside jolts the midwife. When the teacher approaches we are not sure who it is, seeing only a hooded and vaguely threatening figure walking out of the darkness and over to the clinic. When she arrives and unhoods herself, the music changes and the midwife is swept with relief. The teacher meets the concerns of the midwife by admonishing

---

[54] All subsequent references to this film are: *Daybreak in Udi*, Crown Film Unit Production, in collaboration with SDO ED Chadwick, and Nigerian Government, 1949, Directed by Terry Bishop. Held at the British Film Institute archive.

[55] As is the case today, women were seen during this period as central to Africa's modernisation. For one example see the otherwise pessimistic and conservative account of Stuart Cloete, *The African Giant: The Story of a Journey* (London: Collins, 1957), p. 417. Cloete's book will be explored in more detail in the following section.

her for not tending to her patient properly and by asking her, with incredulity: 'you don't believe in that superstitious nonsense, do you?' Suddenly the audience sees, unbeknown to the three women inside the centre, figures dressed in masks and cloaks quietly approaching, clearly posing as vengeful spirits. As they approach the windows the teacher spies one peering in and chucks a pot of hot water in its face. The afflicted 'spirit' retreats screaming, as do the others, but silently. Thus, a great victory is won for modernity, exemplified by the female teacher, over tradition, exemplified by the tribal men.

The film is replete with these kinds of motifs and the teachers are the idealised vision of White vitality in African-as-human form. Other Africans in the film are also idealised, however. If not as 'modern' as the teachers, then the 'traditional' villagers nonetheless are shown – bar the elder and his followers who resist the clinic – embracing what the DC calls in one encounter with a villager 'progress and civilisation'. At every available opportunity, the villagers are shown applauding or dancing to the progress of the clinic. This is quite literal: the building of the centre, taken on by the villagers, is done by everyone dancing as they lay the bricks, cement and so on. For the presumed audience of Anglospheric white society – and perhaps the growing Nigerian bureaucratic elite – scenes like these are supposed to convey the old-becoming-new, and of tradition being thrown aside in embracing modernity. This kind of idealisation is fundamental, especially for phenotypically white elites, in placating anxieties concerning the perpetuation of White genius in the West and the definitional relationship between Whiteness and civilisational prowess. Even if civilisational decay is apparent in the West, then here in Udi we find Africans increasingly able to take the mantle up. Of course, another interpretation of the scenes in the film might hold that precisely because the villagers embrace the clinic through an expressive demonstration of dynamic tradition, that technological advance does not necessarily equate with civilisation as understood in the liberal-secular (White) terms of Modernisation Theory – i.e., the adoption of individualism and rational self-maximisation, which, in the figures of the teachers and their rejection of traditional cosmology, is precisely the message that the film seeks to convey.

Nonetheless, coming as they do at the height of decolonisation, these idealisations of African progress combined with 'old-to-new' tropes are also highly embedded in narcissism and geopolitical insecurities, which fit with Mustapha Kamal Pasha's characterisation of this period as one whereby the major powers sought to socialise the newly independent states into White racial logics of economic cooperation/ appropriation and social organisation, rather than recognise what was happening as a form of rupture[56] with that self-same system.

As an indicator of public reception to such tropes, trade press responses to *Daybreak in Udi* reinforce the impression that such tropes of old-to-new idealisation-as-socialisation were popular. For instance, in its review of the film, *Variety* magazine reported that 'In emphasizing the social change in the natives, the British producers have a picture which is considerably above stereotyped travelogs',[57] presumably referring to those stereotypes of previous periods that held that Africans were an unchanging, and unchangeable brute mass. However, in asserting this process as a 'change', the subjects of the film were clearly changing from something into something else. The *New York Times* in one of its reviews made this clear when it reported that the film tracked 'the social revolution that is slowly overcoming the ancient superstitions and savagery of the Abaja Ibos people, living for the most part as their ancestors did'.[58] And so, the idealisation is of something becoming more recognisably White (in its liberal iteration) – i.e., more rational, more materialistic and so on. But the dichotomous rationality on which such characterisation rests, where

---

[56] The point here is not to homogenise or romanticise the various nationalist movements that emerged and/or solidified during this period as being universally anti-colonial and, thus, uniformly signifying rupture with colonial order. Clearly, there were many movement figureheads more comfortable with the role of comprador. In Africa these included people like Félix Houphouët-Boigny in the Cote D'Ivoire, or Mbuto Sese Seko in Zaire. Equally, there were those who occupied more ambivalent ground, and those who seemed genuinely committed to the idea of decolonisation as some form of rupture from neo-imperial control, although in many cases these people were assassinated (Congo's Patrice Lumumba) or ejected by coup (Ghana's Kwame Nkrumah) before a more informed judgement could be made. Nonetheless, and regardless of this diversity, it remains the case that socialisation rather than rupture, where necessary by force (as in the case of Lumumba, whose assassination was allegedly carried out with the active and logistical support of the Belgian secret service and the CIA) became the strategic preference of the former imperial states and Cold War super-powers.

[57] *Variety*, 07 June 1950, Core Collection Production Files, Margaret Herrick Library, Academy of Motion Picture Arts and Sciences.

[58] *New York Times*, 02 June 1950, Core Collection Production Files, Margaret Herrick Library, Academy of Motion Picture Arts and Sciences.

Africans are either superstitious and savage *or*, as the same *New York Times* report put it, 'enlightened' and 'civilised' is rendered unsustainable when we discover that the maternity clinic constructed in the film was real and was demanded by the villagers in return for their cooperation. In other words, for all of their 'ancestral ways', a facility that promises that more women and children will survive childbirth was, unsurprisingly, not a point of consternation within the community. Furthermore, we also learn that while women are traditionally not allowed to look at the masks worn by the elders during the night-scene at the clinic, a special dispensation was granted by the village elders in this case.[59] This is indicative of the ways in which Africa was being publicly consumed during this period in ways that reinforced certain kinds of idealisations at the expense of other more problematising accounts. For instance, an alternative way of reading the demands for the maternity clinic and the special dispensation given by the village elders is that the cultural practices of this community were clearly far more dynamic and flexible than a dualistic old-to-new form of idealisation allows for. Such nuances however serve to directly challenge the kinds of modernisation-inflected accounts of African history and agency that dominate liberal cultural and political representations of the continent during this post-war period – which were themselves becoming increasingly dominant. As such, these kinds of nuances are rendered invisible in the drive to see Africa as a place where White racial logics, coded under the term 'civilisation', might be in a position to thrive.

This kind of drive to see Africans embodying White racial logics was widespread during this period. Commenting on the 1959 documentary *Giant in the Sun*, which explored provinces of Northern Nigeria as they prepared for self-government, the Educational Film Library Association in America's house journal commented that:

[I]t is a fine thing about this film that, though made by the British as a report of accomplishment over the years of Britain's protectorate, its approach is not 'see what we have done', but rather, 'the Nigerians have done this to prepare themselves for independence and membership in the Commonwealth'.[60]

[59] *New York Times*, 09 June 1950, Core Collection Production Files, Margaret Herrick Library, Academy of Motion Picture Arts and Sciences.
[60] *Film News* (New York, NY: Educational Film Library Association in America, 1960), p. 18.

There is a very strong material and geopolitical element to these liberal 'from old-to-new' idealisations of Africa and Africans. In another revealingly titled book, *Remaking Africa*, the British travel writer and agronomist Nigel Heseltine writes a typically liberal critique of Western military over-spending, asserting that it is incorrect to see the 'underdeveloped world' as a separate entity from the 'developed world'[61] and calling for government spending to be diverted from military to developmental priorities. The geopolitics of this assertion is apparent when Heseltine retains a duality in international order, between the West and the East; the challenge then is to redirect military spending into the newly independent states so that they may contribute to building a 'new world' (implicitly a non-Soviet new world), itself a result of emerging from the 'separateness of colonial thinking'.[62]

Similarly, the US travel writer John Gunther reports that 'Africa lies open like a vacuum ... it pants for development. If we do not help it to develop, somebody else will'.[63] Gunther continues and lays open the deep self-regarding anxieties underpinning the geopolitical statements made in these texts when he writes that 'some will turn to Communism in our place. It will be a bad joke for them, *but a worse joke for us*'.[64]

There is a further challenge here that is biopolitical, which again correlates with the micro-social and cultural project characteristic of Modernisation Theory. For a true socialisation into White rationality requires Africans to change and to stop 'forgetting' they are civilised (or trying to be so) as reported by Bell-Grosvenor. Thus, Heseltine states that 'In the Koran it is written that Allah cannot change the country until every man in that country changes. When we examine the human resources of Africa, we must also think of the changes which the men must bring about in themselves to bring them fully into the life of the twentieth century'.[65]

---

[61] Nigel Heseltine, *Remaking Africa* (London: Museum Press Ltd, 1961), p. 10.
[62] Ibid., at p. 17.
[63] Gunther, *Inside Africa*, p. 4. As a sign of the coverage Gunther's book received (itself a part of a popular series of *Inside* titles Gunther authored) *Inside Africa* was one of only two books the soon-to-be-renowned British scholar of African history Terence Ranger had read about Africa prior to him taking up a post at the University College of Rhodesia and Nyasaland in 1956. See Terence Ranger, *Writing Revolt: An Engagement with African Nationalism, 1957–1967* (Woodbridge, Suffolk, UK: James Currey, 2013), p. 7.
[64] Gunther, *Inside Africa*, p. 18, *emphasis added*.
[65] Heseltine, *Remaking Africa*, p. 17.

We can see here the unevenness, even within liberal perspectives, with which Africa and Africans are deemed capable of saving White genius in the form of Western civilisation from phenotypical white decline. There is still a clear 'not-yet' component here, characteristic of White civilisational supremacy more broadly, whereby Africans are not yet deemed ready to take the mantle on. Nonetheless, there is also a very enthusiastic desire to see Africans step up and fulfil their historical role as carriers of Western civilisational norms. Thus, it is that one author writes that, 'The old signposts of African civilisation are being torn down ... in the crucible of social change, new human foundations are beginning to take shape ... signifying the end of an age of innocence ... Africa is fashioning new values, identities and orientations'.[66] Similarly, Gunther writes that Africa is 'flashing with vivid light'. Again, there are biopolitical implications whereby 'Africa is like an exploding mass of yeast; its fermentations are not merely political and economic, but social, cultural, religious'.[67]

Attempts to socialise Africans, based on anxieties concerning racial conflict and phenotypical white decline can also be found in more left-liberal circles. Oden Meeker, a freelance journalist and former executive director of the aid NGO CARE International, wrote a book, *Report on Africa,* in which he claimed to be convinced that 'the most important problem of our times was that of race', and, comparing Africa to China, that the 'the West ... can ill afford to lose another continent'.[68] Heseltine worried too about 'a class war between the rich and the poor nations'.[69] Indeed, the tide was already running against the West as far as Meeker seemed concerned, labelling the ANC leader Walter Sisulu's 1953 visit to Moscow and Beijing as a 'sad straw in the wind', especially because Sisulu was 'not a communist' and, thus, should have been 'winnable' for the West.[70] Turning his attention to the composition of the soon-to-be independent states that would proliferate across the continent, Meeker expressed opinions familiar from the policy-sphere in which Myrdal and other 'threat inflaters'[71] were

---

[66] William H. Lewis, *Emerging Africa* (Washington, DC: Public Affairs Press, 1963), p. v.
[67] Gunther, *Inside Africa*, p. 3.
[68] Oden Meeker, *Report on Africa* (London: Chatto and Windus, 1955), p. 2.
[69] Heseltine, *Remaking Africa*, p. 9.
[70] Meeker, *Report on Africa*, p. 324.
[71] Vitalis, *White World Order*, p. 124.

operating. Once again, and driven by implicit anxieties concerning racial revenge, Meeker argued that:

It is evident that self-government can mean government by only one race, in a society where there are several of them, with conflicting interests ... the classical "one man one vote" ... is an ineffective safeguard for democracy in some of the countries with strong Indian and European minorities.[72]

The post-war period brought perspectives that idealised 'modernised'/'detribalised' Africans to the fore in ways that would have been unimaginable prior to the war, due to the dominance of scientific racism in how Africa was imagined in Western public and even liberal imaginations. It would, however, be overstating the case to suggest that these Modernisation Theory-inflected narratives were the only narratives of Africa to resonate during this period. It was certainly the case that more conventional narratives that posed Africa as backward and primordial continued to circulate in some very prominent places. As we will see, while these latter narratives shared a great deal with both the liberal and illiberal attitudes towards Africa of the 1920s (considered in Chapters 2 and 3) they were also distinct from these in one very significant way that placed them in a discursive relationship with the more liberal attitudes in the 1950s, namely the way that they too were embedded in anxieties concerning White vitality.

Scientific Racism

Scientific racism persisted in the ways in which Africa was imagined and narrated in some quarters. Returning to Hammond and Jablow and their exploration of fiction-writing about Africa, they argue that the canon almost in its totality remained locked into conventional tropes that stressed 'the futility of the attempt to civilize savages'.[73] As we have already seen, this was not uniformly the case, but even where it was so, this was partnered with a new set of anxieties (in a British context at least) concerning 'the whole notion of British competence to rule'.[74] As such, the scientific racism of this period was characterised by a deep and overwhelming set of anxieties concerning phenotypical

[72] Meeker, *Report on Africa*, p. 321.
[73] Hammond and Jablow, *Myth of Africa*, p. 118.
[74] Ibid.

white tutelage that was far less prominent thirty years earlier – and relatedly White vitality – while at the same time holding that Africa was a barbaric continent of barbaric peoples. While the latter part of this calculation was distinct from the more liberal and modernisation-inflected narratives with their idealisation of detribalised/detribalising Africans, the former part of the calculation concerning deep anxieties about the perpetuation of White historical genius, shared much in common with more liberal narratives.

Not all of the scientific racists of the period were as explicitly pessimistic about Whiteness as others. While retaining ideas about Africans that held them to be inferior, with, for instance, a lack of 'retentive brains',[75] some were in fact positively breezy about White vitality in those places in Africa where white European settlement was thriving, namely South Africa.[76] In this sense, such authors were similar in tone and outlook to the 1920s authors considered in Chapter 2 and the Kenya settlers in Chapter 3. Significantly however, those figures *saw* Africans, even if they only saw them adults as children or happy and trusting lapdogs. Those who saw in post-war South Africa a place where phenotypically white people could make a home away from the post-war decline of the West, had a much more obvious and pernicious fact to face – Apartheid. So undermining of their breezy optimism was Apartheid, that these authors simply couldn't write about it. This was, after all, 'Lightest Africa'.[77] Where Spencer Chapman (who, as we have seen was more liberal in some of his views) simply refused to engage with Apartheid, the travel writer Katherine Courlander took a different approach:

One of the first things I was asked by a stranger when I had been in Cape Town only a few days was: 'what do you think about the Native question?' I was startled: the fact was I had not considered it. I had been to the United States and had seen the negroes at work so that the sight of Africans performing humble duties did not seem unfamiliar. But soon I became aware of the implications of the question; that it indicated a shadow which darkened the lovely land, caused unhappiness to kind-hearted Europeans – the tragedy of Africa.[78]

[75] Katherine Courlander, *I Speak of Africa* (London: Robert Hale Ltd, 1956), p. 24.
[76] i.e. Spencer Chapman, *Lightest Africa*; Courlander, *I Speak of Africa*.
[77] Spencer Chapman, *Lightest Africa*.
[78] Courlander, *I Speak of Africa*, p. 22.

One cannot dismiss the notion that such ignorance was not perhaps at least partially the product of artistic license on the part of the author. Nonetheless, this (wilful?) ignorance of the racism embedded into South African society speaks to the impossibility of explicitly recognising it as such if South Africa was going to function as a place where (white) women could, for instance, live a life 'far more fortunate than her contemporaries in the other parts of the British Commonwealth, and, indeed, in the United States, in that she has obtained a reasonable supply of domestic help ... it has left the housewife free to follow an unhampered social life'.[79]

These attitudes are outliers relative to the majority of scientifically racist travel literature in the post-war period, which for the most part rages against phenotypical white decline as much as it projects overtly racist ideas about Africans. Examples of persistent scientific racism in the travel writing of the period include S.R. Cleland Scott's analysis that detribalisation was equivalent with deterioration, and that Africans were best-off remaining in a 'savage' state, where racial differentials in education and manners could be best inoculated from each other.[80] A notable exponent of this kind of position was the author Evelyn Waugh. Recounting a tour through East Africa, he noted how Africans were gluttonous and wasteful,[81] drunk and lazy[82] and lacking in significant historical features – i.e. nationhood – saying of Zanzibaris that 'they have no nationalism; part Aryan, part Indian, part Swahili ... No doubt we shall soon read in the papers about "Zanzibar nationalism" and "colonial tyranny"'.[83] And yet a heightened strain of anxiety concerning White vitality ran its way through Waugh's work, writing for instance that while white settlers might fret over the urban dangers of Nairobi, 'why should not this equatorial Arcadia, so lately and lightly colonised, go the way of Europe?'.[84]

'The way of Europe' was down. We can find an eloquent and lengthy exposition of this perspective in the work of another author who had turned his hand to travelogue, the British-South African Stuart Cloete.

[79] Ibid., at p. 19.
[80] S. R. Cleland Scott, 'Travelling through Africa', *The Fortnightly*, 1951, pp. 100–2.
[81] Evelyn Waugh, *A Tourist in Africa* (London: Chapman and Hall Ltd, 1960), p. 55.
[82] Ibid., at p. 60.
[83] Ibid., at p. 63.
[84] Ibid., at p. 41.

Again, the author emphatically channels scientific racism in his depictions of Africans, who, fired by foreign notions of nationalism and pan-Africanism, 'ran like ants about a broken nest'.[85] Searching for an 'African giant' Cloete writes that:

[E]ach part was against every other part. His hands were at his own throat, his feet tripped each other up whenever he took a step, his internal organs were out of order, his brain deranged, fevered by a dream. His ears could not understand the thousand languages of his tongue. But his blood pounded in his veins as the tom-toms throbbed, the adrenalin loosed into its stream envenomed him. Hatred enveloped him like a cloak. Hatred of the white man who had betrayed him.[86]

The familiar tropes of African irrationality, savagery and immaturity resonate through this passage. And yet, as with Waugh, Cloete is far from convinced that white tutelage is even a possibility, let alone an answer to the problems posed by Africa's too-soon insertion into modernity, which had shattered 'the pattern of ten thousand years'.[87] Although Cloete deems Africans to be not yet ready to enter into modernity (thanks to 'white direction ... they know so much more than they did [but] they think they know it all, and are not ready to wait and learn the rest'[88]) he is adamant that white tutelage is actually not really an option, given the endemic decrepitude of White vitality among phenotypically white people. He writes:

But are we absolutely convinced of the success of our own experiment? Our science whose ultimate achievement seems to be bombs of greater destructive powers? Of populations which appear to suffer from increasing neuroses? Of publishers who find endless sales for books explaining how a man should make love to his wife? There is no doubt that ritual murder continues in Africa, that there are still slaves. But how many of us are free? And how many hundreds of thousands of lives do we sacrifice to the god of speed on the highways of our land? One more world war and our complex civilisation may go down and the African, nearer to the earth in his plains and forests, may survive.[89]

---

[85] Cloete, *African Giant*, p. 417.
[86] Ibid.
[87] Ibid.
[88] Ibid., at p. 422.
[89] Ibid., at p. 433.

These kinds of anxieties in some ways marked out British conservatives from their American Anglospheric relations, with their certainties
about American exceptionalism.[90] They too, however, were beset by
anxieties concerning runaway modernity in the West, with the influential conservative commentator William F. Buckley writing in the mission statement of the conservative periodical *National Review* that
'[this magazine] stands athwart history, yelling "Stop"'.[91] It is nonetheless telling that while these post-war scientific racists, where they
did so at all, idealised the same 'tribal Africans' that had been the
subject of most forms of 1920s popular idealisation, the more telling
attribute of this post-war iteration is its extreme anxiety concerning
the perpetuation of Whiteness. Where this distinguishes itself from the
scientific racism of the 1920s is where it fails to see any chink of hope
in the record of phenotypically white people in Africa in safeguarding
White historical genius, an optimism that carried settlers to Africa in
the hope that the continent might help them save Western civilisation
from decline in the West. The pessimism of the scientific racists of the
1950s seeps into more liberal narratives of Africa during this period,
which, as we have seen, shaves some of the rough edges off but nonetheless remains in a discursive relationship with scientific racism concerning the threats to, and decline of, White vitality.

As we will see in Chapter 5, settler inter-racial associations established during this period to fend off both overt settler scientific racism
and what they labelled as the anti-white racism of African nationalism, channelled the more and less extreme versions of these anxieties
concerning Whiteness. In the process, they constructed modernisation-
inflected idealisations of Africans as saviours of Western civilisation
from declining White supremacy. If anyone embodied the countervail-
ing impulses of seeking out new agents of Western civilisation in Africa
while simultaneously seeking to fight a battle against the enemies of
that self-same product of White genius in the West, it was Colonel
David Stirling, founder of the British Army Special Air Service (SAS),
facilitator of UK–Saudi arms deals, anti-communist counter-revolution
in Yemen in the 1960s and union-busting agent provocateur in the
United Kingdom in the 1970s. Among all of these efforts to stem the

[90] Staniland, *American Intellectuals and African Nationalists*, pp. 216–24.
[91] Our Mission Statement, *National Review*, New York, NY, 19 November 1955,
available at: www.nationalreview.com/article/223549/our-mission-statement-
william-f-buckley-jr, accessed on 27 June 2017.

tide of leftist class and identity politics, to defend White genius, as he defined it, in the West, Stirling was also the founder of the Capricorn Africa Society, the largest and most significant of the settler inter-racial associations established in British Southern Africa in the 1950s, and an explicit attempt to construct a body of Africans that could act to secure Whiteness in Africa, in the face of declining White vitality in the West. It is to Stirling and his fellow travellers that the next chapter turns.

5 | The Age of Capricorn
Bridging the Past to the Present

[A]n opportunity for men and women of goodwill and liberal outlook to come together ... on the assumption that this vital and initial problem of race relations can be solved.[1]

Less than thirty years had passed since supporters of Harry Thuku had been gunned down in Nairobi in 1922, and yet, as we explored in Chapter 4, political, economic and geopolitical landscapes in Africa, and globally, had shifted monumentally with the passing of World War II, the increasing popularity of Keynesian economic policies and social democratic parties in Europe and the advent of the Cold War. Idealised notions about Africa and Africans had also, as a result of these changes, evolved, although not always in straightforward ways. This chapter will present the various continuities and discontinuities in anxieties concerning White vitality, and subsequent idealisations of Africa and Africans through an exploration of broadly liberal,[2] -settler, inter-racial associations in British Southern and Eastern Africa.

The Liberal-Settler, Inter-Racial Societies of British Southern and Eastern Africa: Capricorn, the Inter-Racial Association of Southern Rhodesia and the New Kenya Party

In the 1950s there emerged in British Southern and Eastern Africa a range of associations and groups dedicated to rejecting the overt racism of the right-wing of the settler movement through the projection of

---

[1] Sir Robert Tregold's Address at the Inaugural Meeting of the Inter-Racial Association of Southern Rhodesia (IRASR), 26 May 1952, CRL, Eileen Haddon Collection of Southern Rhodesia, MF2811, REEL 1

[2] Only broadly liberal because the protagonists of these movements were often politically ambiguous, expressing more liberal sentiments concerning Africa and Africans than they did concerning white socialists or working-class activists in the UK.

a vision of a series of independent African states where all races would live together harmoniously and society would be ordered according to a meritocracy. The significance of these associations has often been overlooked, both more generally as well as in terms of what they have to tell us about anxieties concerning White vitality during this period and the subsequent, and often fantastical, idealisations of Africans that emerged as a result. None of these groups have prominently featured in the conventional historiography of the period which can, in part, be justified by the fact that in terms of membership they were small and that, beyond 1960, they were gradually overcome by the power and reach of the African nationalist movements to which they were opposed. And yet, as we will see, associations like the Capricorn Africa Society, the Inter-Racial Association of Southern Rhodesia and the New Kenya Party became, for a brief period, key players in British imperial policy. They were also consistent exponents of a more liberal form of white-settler politics, seeking to position themselves between the archly conservative racism of right-wing settler movements and the (equally dangerous and racist, in their eyes) radical, probably communist, movements of African nationalism. In this they had ground in common with South African liberal inter-racialists, who wanted to show 'the blacks ... that there were white fellow South Africans who shared their aspirations and did not do so mainly in the interests of an alien political creed, Marxism Leninism, which liberals found totally repugnant'.[3] This chapter will argue that this kind of positioning reflected a particular form of anxiety-driven Whiteness that coheres in many respects to Amanda Anderson's notion of 'bleak liberalism' (see Chapter 4); most notably the way in which such a sensibility rested on 'the emphasis on bleak prospects and reduced expectations, on the one hand, and the absolute necessity of defending basic liberal principles, programs, and institutions on the other'.[4] Whereas in a Western context liberals would have been daily confronted with the social and political affirmations of their 'bleak prospects and reduced expectations', in Africa the protagonists encountered in this chapter could use the continent to both inflate the bleak prospects of the West and displace such anxieties in the belief that Africa could serve as a place

---

[3] Randolph Vigne, *Liberals against Apartheid: A History of the Liberal Party of South Africa, 1953–1968* (Basingstoke: MacMillan Press Ltd, 1997), p. 10.
[4] Anderson, *Bleak Liberalism*, p. 25.

where the unique achievements and genius of Whiteness – i.e., the creation and historical dominance of the West – could be resuscitated,
with ever larger numbers of Africans – living and acting according to
universalised White logical and social codes – at the forefront of such
an enterprise.

This all correlated with an effort on the part of inter-racial societies seeking to protect European interests in Africa via the idealisation of a variety of African subjects. That these organisations were so
short-lived, failing in their plan to act as a break-wall against African
nationalism, was a result of the anxiety-ridden contradictions and self-
deceptions that bedevilled their attitudes and practices – and led them
to seek out and believe in wide-spread African support for their programmes and ideals, where there was, in fact, very little.

By many measures, the most significant of these associations was
the Capricorn Africa Society (CAS). In terms of its vision, territorial
scope, metropolitan government contacts and membership it exceeded
the other societies combined (which is not to say that all the societies
considered here were not working collaboratively; I shall return to this
shortly). In important respects CAS was the vanity project of Colonel
Sir David Stirling, founder of the British Special Air Service and latterly
an arms dealer and agent provocateur of the anti-communist right,
both domestically in the United Kingdom and abroad.[5] Following
World War II, Stirling had relocated to Southern Rhodesia from where
he established CAS in 1948. Initially CAS was a conservative, pro-
federation force, which allied itself, rhetorically at least, with the kinds
of self-rule agendas that had characterised Lord Delamere's settlers
in Kenya in the 1920s. In 1950, before CAS had gained any real trac-
tion with other settlers, the British Government and not least Africans,
Stirling wrote in a publication called *Capricorn Africa: The Power
House on the March*, that:

If our people are to have a destiny in Africa then that destiny will be worked
out here in Africa and not in Whitehall ... Africa is now entering upon her
majority ... we must rapidly overhaul our immigration policy and law, so
as to encourage every sort of European to come and make his home here ...
we will need millions if we are to be of any use, if anything is to emerge in

---

[5] See episode one of *The Mayfair Set*, a BBC documentary by Adam Curtis
(1999), available at: www.youtube.com/watch?v=234H8X1-JiA, accessed on
14 June 2016.

the way of civilisation in Africa. We will have to put a stop to crazy political theories and to ideas of African self-determination which can only result in self-destruction. The European will have to control the agricultural develop-ment of Africa if it is not to become another Sahara or Kalahari.[6]

This passage conveys clearly the enduring belief in phenotypical white tutelage of Africans that was apparent among the pre-war protago-nists of Chapters 2 and 3. It is worth, however, briefly pausing here to consider Stirling and what he represented in a bit more detail. As shown by his later involvement with union-busting in the UK and in mobilising the British Government's clandestine war in Yemen fol-lowing an Egyptian-backed coup in 1963,[7] the aristocratic Stirling was not by any means politically liberal or Fabian. Indeed, he shared much in common with an, at that time, small but growing number of Hayekians who were horrified by the advance of the British wel-fare state and Keynesianism in general. The British Hayekian econ-omist John Jewkes wrote in 1948 about the 'melancholy decline of Great Britain', which was 'largely of our own making'. He went on to bemoan:

the fall in our standards of living to a level which excites the pity and evokes the charity of many other countries, the progressive restriction of individual liberties, the ever-widening destruction of respect for law, the steady sap-ping of our instinct for tolerance and compromise, the sharpening of class distinctions, our growing incapacity to play a rightful part in world affairs.

Jewkes blamed these developments on the enlarged and encroach-ing power of the State that had occurred as a result of World War II.[8] These are the anxieties that drove Stirling away from the UK,[9] although as evidenced by his subsequent career, while despondent about the state of British society and broader White vitality at this time, and although he sought in Africa a remedy for this by creating there his vision of 'the good society' based on White racial logics (more

---

[6] David Stirling, *Capricorn Africa: The Power House on the March*, Salisbury, 1950, KNA, MSS/123/104.
[7] Colonel Jim Johnson, Obituaries, available at: www.telegraph.co.uk/news/obituaries/2553726/Colonel-Jim-Johnson.html, accessed on 19 January 2017.
[8] John Jewkes, *Ordeal by Planning* (London: MacMillan, 1948), p. xi.
[9] Richard Hughes, *Capricorn: David Stirling's Second Africa Campaign* (Milton Keynes: Radcliffe Press, 2003), p. 19.

on which shortly) this didn't stop him from simultaneously fighting for his vision of White vitality domestically in the UK as well – i.e., a small state where the fittest survive in a culturally discriminatory, but 'colour-blind', meritocracy.[10]

It is this discriminatory meritocracy (because it displaced race onto culture) that Stirling sought to construct in 'Capricorn' Africa. His strain of colour-blind, conservative, White supremacy remained in tension with some of the more liberal and pluralistic Whiteness that became characteristic of CAS in subsequent years. As such CAS channelled some of both the period-specific liberal and conservative anxieties concerning Whiteness addressed in Chapter 8. In its early years however, and as we can see from Stirling's *Powerhouse on the March* statement, at this stage CAS channelled a sense of entitlement and superiority characteristic of conservative and right-wing settler rhetoric. Indeed, in many ways the early CAS sought to extend British imperial control in Africa, defining 'Capricorn Africa' as 'Bechuanaland, the Belgian Congo, Mozambique, Angola [and] the British East and Central African territories'.[11] To that end CAS initially positioned itself behind the British government attempts to enact Central African Federation between Southern and Northern Rhodesia and Nyasaland, and then to go even further. In 1952 Stirling wrote to the Commonwealth Relations Office that 'The Capricorn Africa Society has from the start supported these proposals [for Federation]'.[12]

In the same letter, Stirling started to flesh out what would make CAS distinct from mainstream conservative settler opinion. Arguing that the Federation proposals required broad-based African support he positioned CAS as central to achieving that aim:

We have been constantly assured that effective steps were being taken by the Governments of the three territories to build up solid African opinion in favour of the proposals, thus providing evidence to convince public opinion in Britain of the unworthiness of the African Nationalist … European

---

[10] For an account of the fightback mounted by the broader Hayekian right in the UK see: Cockett, *Thinking the Unthinkable*. For an account of this struggle in the USA see: Mayer, *Dark Money*; Nancy Maclean, *Democracy in Chains: The Deep History of the Radical Right's Stealth Plan for America* (New York, NY: Viking Press Inc, 2017).

[11] *Capricorn Africa* (Salisbury: 1954), TNA, CO 822/340.

[12] David Stirling to J.G. Foster, Parliamentary Under-Secretary of State for the Commonwealth Relations Office, 30/05/1952, TNA, DO 35/3603.

leadership in Africa cannot endure, and does not deserve to endure, unless it is capable of carrying with it in major decisions affecting their common destiny, genuine and substantial African support.[13]

I will detail the British government's responses to CAS and Stirling in subsequent sections. For now, it is simply worth noting that by positioning CAS in this way, Stirling created the conditions for an implicit meritocratic and social liberalism to take hold within CAS which, in turn, generated idealised claims about (some) Africans, their agency and their contribution to a continental future in which white settler interests would be protected in such a way that would combine with African self-interest. This subsequently became known as 'partnership' and, as we will see, became fantastical – at least by the utopian terms that CAS set out whereby the protection of white settler interests would be welcomed by African populations. The relationship between anxieties concerning the perpetuation of Whiteness in the West and subsequent idealisations of some African subjects as a means by which to safeguard that genius is important here for two main reasons. First, this represented a discontinuity from the largely and solidly socially conservative attitudes explored in Chapter 3, which ranged across eugenicist settler opinion into the ossifying attitudes of humanitarian thinking as well, and which held Africans to be in the 'waiting room' of history. For them, Africa, but not Africans, would be the vehicle by which White vitality would thrive. As subsequent sections will explore, by the 1950s, Africans who met certain cultural standards were deemed very much a part of the forward march of history and were, thus, deemed able to save Whiteness from being a parochial occupation of a West in decline. Secondly, this relationship is important because it lays the groundwork, like much else in this period, for the kinds of idealisations of African culture, politics and economy that we witness in discussions of Africa's post-2007–8 financial crash agency and which will be explored in Chapters 6 and 7.

CAS's growing liberalism manifested in a number of ways, not least that which saw it campaign for the replacement of the 'colour bar' with a 'culture bar', whereby Africans of a certain educational or propertied standard would qualify for voting rights, rights of access to hotels, swimming baths and so on. This is where CAS began to

[13] Ibid.

promote the notion of a 'colour blind' society in Africa that would
nonetheless implicitly protect phenotypically white privilege through
demarcating entry to that society on the grounds of White cultural
norms; norms that phenotypically white people tend to have greater
access to.[14] A typically liberal CAS statement regarding multi-racial
inhabited 'Open Areas' went as follows:

The paramount interest in these areas will be that of civilisation itself, not
the interest of any one race, colour or creed ... the territorial government
will be permitted to lay down conditions in the Open Areas which will
ensure European living standards and proficiency for any trade or calling.
All achieving these standards will have the right to seek employment in
those trades. Political rights in the Open Areas will be enjoyed by Africans
who desire them and have reached the standards of civilisation and culture
held to be requisite for the exercise of such rights.[15]

Affirmations of the kinds of ideal Africans the authors of this document had in mind were not necessarily hard to come across. In the first
book published by an African domiciled in Southern Rhodesia (an
active site for CAS, as well as other inter-racial associations), Bradfield
Mnyanda wrote in 1954 that, 'By all means, let us have a "culture
bar", in place of the present colour bar'. Reverend Esau Nemapare,
a prominent Ethiopianist, wrote, 'The trouble ... is that in Southern
Rhodesia the social bar, which I fully support, is being taken for the
colour bar, which no decent European or African wants'.[16]

As CAS evolved into a broader-based (i.e., beyond Stirling) and
multi-territory organisation, so it began to embrace broader issues.
Again, CAS's liberalism is evident. For instance, in defending the principle of inter-racial marriage, a CAS newsletter based this defence not
on the principle of inter-racial marriage itself, or as an attack on the
conservative defence of the institution of marriage within racially pure
communities, but rather on the principle of individual freedom.[17]

[14] Peggy McIntosh, 'White Privilege and Male Privilege: A personal account of
coming to see correspondences through work in Women's Studies', Wellesley:
Center for Research on Women, 1988, Working paper 189.
[15] The Capricorn Declarations: A Policy for Africa (Salisbury: 1952) ICS, PP.KE.
CAS, File 9.
[16] Michael O. West, *The Rise of an African Middle Class: Colonial Zimbabwe,
1898–1965* (Bloomington, IN, and Indianapolis, IN: Indiana University Press),
p. 196.
[17] Capricorn Chronicle, no.5, 05/06/1956, KNA, MSS/129/18, file G/5.

Another 'partnership' association to begin emerging at this time was the Inter-Racial Association of Southern Rhodesia (IRASR). Established in 1952 to formulate a progressive policy concerning impending Federation,[18] the IRASR consistently concerned itself with more parochial and structural matters than CAS, attempting to make several contributions to Southern Rhodesian government policy throughout the 1950s. For instance, the IRASR lobbied the Native and Labour Board for higher wages for African labourers in the furniture industry[19]; the formation of joint European-African trades unions[20]; and the subsidisation of bus services for African labourers.[21] Nonetheless, in its more reflective moments, the IRASR maintained the centrality of the culture-bar being established by CAS at around the same time. In a draft declaration on African affairs which was never formally published – although it spent many years being circulated among members and being redrafted – and which acted as a kind of quasi-constitution for the IRASR, it was stated that: 'The Africans must welcome the opportunity which European civilisation gives them, to take their place in the modern world and to contribute more efficiently to the needs of mankind'.[22] In other words, Africans would be expected to meet White standards. Unlike the narratives of settlers and humanitarians in the 1920s, here Africans were accorded the ability to reach these standards under their own steam, rather than necessarily requiring phenotypical white tutelage. The result, however, would be the same; a debasement of indigenous cultures and cosmologies.

And yet there were important features that distinguished the IRASR from CAS. The IRASR's engagement with structural factors of wages, transport and labour relations, etc., rendered more clearly the CAS modus operandi that 'personal integrity and courtesy was

---

[18] Minutes of the third annual general meeting of the IRASR (Salisbury branch) held in the Methodist Hall, Third Street, 30/06/1956, ICS, PG.ZW.IRASR 7.

[19] Evidence submitted by the IRASR (Salisbury branch) to the Native Labour Board enquiring into wages and conditions of employment in the furniture industry, 1955, ICS, PG.ZW.IRASR 4.

[20] Evidence submitted by the Salisbury branch of the IRASR to the select committee on the Industrial Conciliation Bill, 1956, ICS, PG.ZW.IRASR 5.

[21] Preliminary evidence submitted by the Salisbury branch of the IRASR to the commission appointed to enquire into transport services of greater Salisbury, 1956, ICS, PG.ZW.IRASR 6.

[22] Draft Declaration on African Affairs, 1953, ICS, PG.ZW.IRASR 2.

more important than structural change'.[23] Furthermore, the IRASR, at an elite level at least,[24] was considerably more reflexive concerning the historical characteristics of Western civilisation than was CAS. A report of comments made by founding member Guy Clutton-Brock at a public meeting recorded him as saying that:

> Man seemed to be inhabited by a false ideology that what had been brought from Europe was Christian civilization – and the African people made the mistake of believing this too ... perhaps the African people might be further along the road of Christian civilisation than Western Europeans [at the advent of initial European contact] ... it was very dangerous to assume that we had got this Christian civilisation here now. This brought the feeling that this ideal state should be defended at all costs and politics became vested with religious authority. It also encouraged paternalism instead of brotherhood.[25]

Of course, in this statement Christian civilisation (and a White social and ethical imagination) is still the apogee of teleological development, although it is rendered as separate from, and superior to, what is at the time taken for phenotypically white Western civilisation. As such, both white Europeans and black Africans are pursuing the same goal, with the result being that both white Europeans and black Africans are equalised, but non-Christian cultures are nonetheless still debased. All the same, such reflexive and less self-important attitudes perhaps explained the IRASR's more vociferous anti-establishment proclamations (when held next to CAS).[26]

---

[23] Allison K. Shutt, *Manners Make a Nation: Racial Etiquette in Southern Rhodesia, 1910–1963* (Rochester, NY: University of Rochester Press, 2016), p. 142.

[24] Subsequent sections will explore attitudes among IRASR's broader membership.

[25] Minutes of the third annual general meeting of the IRASR (Salisbury branch) held in the Methodist Hall, Third Street, on Saturday 30/06/1956, ICS, PG.ZW.IRASR 7.

[26] See, for example, the IRASR's opposition to ever-closer Federation until 'a form of government which is truly representative, i.e. based on a franchise which gives adequate representation to the population as a whole, has been established'– Statement by the National Executive of the IRASR on the subject of the status of the federation of Rhodesia and Nyasaland, Undated, ICS, PG.ZW.IRASR 8. Clutton-Brock himself is an interesting figure here, embodying a journey taken by a number of white 'partnership' protagonists in Southern Rhodesia specifically. Clutton-Brock was one of a number of

Despite the differences between the two societies there were several attempts, at least on the part of CAS, to cooperate with, and even incorporate, the IRASR. In 1957, for instance, CAS made a financial contribution to the IRASR of £200.[27] While incorporation was resisted, however, IRASR minutes show that there was agreement that the two societies should cooperate.[28] Indeed, the journalist Eileen Haddon, one of the IRASR's most prominent activists and sometime chairperson, attended CAS's showpiece 1956 conference on inter-racial cooperation held at Salima, in Nyasaland, attended by settlers, interested observers (including the British security services) and members of the African middle classes from Kenya, Nyasaland, Northern and Southern Rhodesia. Perhaps illustrating the fundamental differences between the two societies, however, a handwritten note by Haddon on the back of the CAS membership card issued to her for the purposes of the conference recorded that 'I did not feel I could, with clear conscience, sign a solemn document concerning a great principle which I wholeheartedly support but includes an ... attempt to solve the franchise question which I am not convinced is the best solution'.[29] This attempt to solve the franchise consisted of a multiple roll along ostensibly cultural/educational lines (in practice however,

---

white liberal settlers who shared in the growing antipathy of Africans to the inter-racial partnership organisations like IRASR. By the end of 1957, Clutton-Brock was becoming an instrumental figure in Joshua Nkomo's Southern Rhodesian African National Congress (the kind of organisation specifically feared and opposed by the inter-racial partnership organisations) and when he died in 1995 became the first white person to be declared a National Hero of Zimbabwe (by President Robert Mugabe). See Ranger, *Writing Revolt*, p. 22; Judith Todd, 'Obituary: Guy Clutton-Brock', *The Independent*, 16 February 1995, available at: www.independent.co.uk/news/people/obituary-guy-clutton-brock-1573319.html, accessed on 28 June 2017.

[27] Letter from the Earl of March, Capricorn Africa Society Treasurer, to the Inter-Racial Society of Southern Rhodesia, 23 February 1957, Eileen Haddon Collection of Southern Rhodesia, CRL, MF2811, Reel 14.

[28] Minutes of the Standing Committee of the Inter-Racial Society of Southern Rhodesia 13 November 1957, ICS, PG.ZW.IRASR 23.

[29] Capricorn African Society Membership Card issued to Eileen Haddon, Eileen Haddon Collection of Southern Rhodesia, CRL, MF2811, Reel 14. As with Guy Clutton-Brock (see note 26), Haddon was another figure who by the final years of the decade had increasingly moved over towards supporting the Southern Rhodesia African National Congress – see Terence Ranger, 'Obituary: Eileen Haddon', *The Guardian*, 22 July 2003, available at: www.theguardian.com/news/2003/jul/22/guardianobituaries.southafrica, accessed on 28 June 2017.

racial). Subsequent sections will return to the Salima conference as it provides a rich resource for exploring 1950s liberal-settler, inter-racial anxieties and idealisations.

For now, however, we will remain with the networks of liberal-settler inter-racialism which were expanding in the 1950s in British Southern and East Africa. Another important figure in this regard is that of the Kenyan politician Michael Blundell. Blundell was part of the liberal wing of the Kenya settler community. Indeed, this was a label he adopted for himself, writing in an edition of his curriculum vitae (in the third person) that 'Blundell has always been strongly liberal. It might have been more apparently so had it not been for the vital need for him to not go too far out of sight of the following on whom he depends for office'.[30] In 1959 Blundell resigned as Minister of Agriculture to lead a new inter-racial political grouping in the Legislative Council (LegCo) called the New Kenya Party (NKP). Although not officially tied to CAS – indeed CAS had prevaricated for a number of years about whether to enter the formal political fray – as with the IRASR there were several areas of overlap and the establishment of a sympathetic correspondence.

Clarence Buxton was the brother of Charles Buxton, who we met as an Imperial Antagonist in Chapter 3. Clarence moved to Kenya in 1912, and after World War I became an Assistant District Commissioner, rising up to the ranks to Acting Provincial Commissioner and retiring in 1940 after a brief stint in Palestine. Far less radical in outlook than his brother (and seventeen years younger), after his retirement he became a Nairobi City Councillor and became active in the CAS Kenya Chapter in the early 1950s, keeping extensive records of the 1956 Salima convention and in general acting as a propagandist for the organisation. When Blundell resigned his ministerial post to lead the NKP grouping, Clarence wrote to him praising his decision to stand down and promising his support for Blundell's future endeavours.[31] Indeed, the NKP

---

[30] Michael Blundell curriculum vitae, Michael Blundell Papers, Weston Library, MSS/66/174, File 3. His Liberalism did not prevent (or perhaps enabled) him from sitting on the 'War Council' established by LegCo during the Mau Mau crisis, on which he was responsible for managing the British military securitisation of Nairobi which was designed to sever Mau Mau supplies, known as 'Operation Anvil'.

[31] C.E.V. Buxton to Michael Blundell, 10 March 1959, Michael Blundell Papers, Weston Library, MSS Afr.s.746, Box 4, File 2, ff 128–135.

cribbed much of their propaganda material from CAS publications, although not without a degree of self-consciousness in the process, with Blundell minuted in a document marked 'Top Secret' as saying, 'This is really a practical document [CAS 'Handbook for Speakers'], undoubtedly prepared by people of considerable ability, but we should keep ours of course for obvious reasons quite separate from it. I have, of course, changed the order of the questions from the Capricorn Handbook'.[32]

Liberal-Settler Inter-Racialism and the Colonial Office

In many ways these associations represented an historical anomaly. The NKP only won 3.2 per cent of the vote in the 1961 common roll general elections, winning four out of 53 seats in the LegCo, being overwhelmed by Jomo Kenyatta's Kenya African National Union (KANU). In the face of growing African nationalism, CAS rapidly withdrew from frontline political agitation and by the early 1960s was focussing most of its energies on providing accommodation and scholarships for African students in London. The IRASR wound itself down in 1959 due to dwindling members and resources and was incorporated into a variety of other liberal-settler campaign groups in Southern Rhodesia, which, due to impending events around Ian Smith's Universal Declaration of Independence in 1965, became somewhat more radical than their inter-racial predecessors.

And yet the designs of these groups were, on their own terms, incredibly ambitious. Of the three groups, it is really only CAS that had designs beyond any particular territory and as a result of this, CAS was often the subject of debate within the Colonial Office, between a range of governors and in other branches of government. The evolution in government thinking concerning CAS is revealing of the society's growing significance in government strategy through the 1950s (from a *very* low base) as well as the anxieties that drove CAS's increasing significance.

To get a sense of just how far CAS travelled in government thinking through the decade, it is telling that at the outset CO policy was to keep Stirling and CAS (and for a long time the two were one and the

---

[32] New Kenya Group, 'Development of the Problems Before Us', 06/1959, Michael Blundell Papers, Weston Library, MSS Afr.s.746, Box 28, File 4.

same thing for the CO) at arm's length. When Stirling approached the CO to back a CAS declaration backing an even broader federation than the three-territory experiment being developed by the British Government between the territorial governments in Nyasaland and the Rhodesias, the response of the CO was almost allergic. In a letter to the Parliamentary Under-Secretary of State for the Commonwealth Relations Office, Stirling had offered a point-by-point explication of the exact benefits that would accrue from the publication of his declaration, which would include attracting support for Federation from trades unions, the Fabian left, and, most importantly, Africans. At the bottom of the letter is a handwritten note added by a CO official that simply reads 'We disagree'.[33] Indeed, the Salima convention held in 1956 had initially been planned by Stirling to take place in 1952, at Mbeya in Tanganyika. The CO managed to delay Stirling for four years, involving a string of correspondence from colonial governors across the three territories of the Federation, plus Kenya and Tanganyika, and which went up as high as the Secretary of State for the Colonies, who requested that Stirling be intervened with, and stopped from rocking the Federation boat.[34]

Indeed, initially many in the CO were rather cutting about Stirling and CAS. One CO official wrote in 1952 that 'we should prefer to see them [CAS] buried'.[35] Over a year later, another official, reflecting on Stirling's CAS declarations which were still circulating around the CO at Stirling's instigation, wrote that 'I have no interest in what I consider a utopian society. The paper was sent to me personally in as much as I have listened (not too diligently!) to some of D.S's [David Stirling's] tirades'.[36]

And yet in the correspondence around Stirling's declarations and proposed convention it is also possible to begin discerning the anxieties that were present within the CO and broader government thinking at the time. These are important, as it is a variant of these very anxieties that began to produce the belief in subsequent years that CAS's ability to bring 'mainstream' African opinion onside might be genuine.

---

[33] David Stirling to J.G. Foster, 30/05/1952, TNA, DO 35/3603.
[34] Note to J.G. Foster, 21/05/1952, TNA, CO 822/340.
[35] Minute by Mr. Jasper of letters and happenings concerning Rev. Michael Scott and Col. David Stirling, 06/06/1952, TNA, DO 35/6731, File 2.
[36] Author unknown, handwritten note, 07/09/1953, TNA, FCO 141/17796, File 31.

Fundamentally, CO and gubernatorial dismissal of CAS was simply related to the latter's unbridled support for a broader federation than that being proposed by the British Government. For instance, Andrew Cohen, Governor in Uganda, a territory not implicated in the tri-territory Central African Federation, wrote that 'nothing but embarrassment is likely to come to Uganda from the activities of the CAS while public opinion here among Africans remains as it is at the present'.[37] Evelyn Baring, Governor in Kenya, wrote in very similar terms.[38] Even CAS's support for Federation within those territories due to be federated was not deemed helpful, in that it 'would [be] likely to wreck prospects of Federation since apparent emergence of a competing scheme would confuse public opinion'.[39] In keeping with the general tone of dismissiveness, the same writer concludes that 'we are not convinced that his claim [to wide African, missionary, press and Labour support] has any substantial basis', and that 'he is notoriously over-optimistic and unreliable in such matters'.

It is notable, then, that as soon as CAS dropped its support for Federation at the very end of 1953, the CO began to view Stirling and the association in a different light. The reversal in CAS policy probably occurred because, despite Stirling's claims to the contrary, CAS was failing to attract African support. A CAS handbook released in 1955 (the same one that inspired the New Kenya Party propaganda) tied this failure to its support for Federation: 'the African who joined the Society was highly suspect by his people. This was explained by the identification of the Society with the campaign for Central African Federation'. The text goes on to admit that 'the Society tended to subordinate human values to the economic and administrative advantages of Federation'.[40]

As a result of this reversal, the CO suddenly became more interested in the role that CAS might play in pursuing British policy and ameliorating Imperial decline, with one official noting at the end of 1953 that 'I should not be surprised if [Stirling's] activities were not on the whole

---

[37] Andrew Cohen to Gorell Barnes, 25/11/53, TNA, CO 822/340.
[38] Evelyn Baring to Gorell Barnes, 16/11/53, TNA, CO 822/340.
[39] Outward telegram from Commonwealth Relations Office to UK High Commissioner in Southern Rhodesia, 24/06/1952, TNA, CO 822/340, File 48.
[40] The Capricorn Africa Society Handbook for Speakers, 1955, ICS, PP.KE.CAS 8/1-17 CAS 6, File 10.

inclined to be helpful to us in the future'.[41] Shortly after this memo
was recorded, William Gorell Barnes, Deputy Under-Secretary of State
at the CO and recipient of many of the sceptical missives concerning
CAS in previous years, circulated a note to the governors of Northern
Rhodesia, Uganda, Kenya, Nyasaland and Tanganyika that seemed to
reinforce this change of attitude. Reporting a meeting with Stirling, he
wrote that he had:

> obtained the impression that he [Stirling] has moved a long way from the
> rather grandiose world of make-believe which surrounded his earlier con-
> ceptions; he now appears to be genuinely trying to make a more realistic
> approach to a limited objective with which I do not think we have any
> reason to quarrel … if these and other liberal ideas such as Blundell has
> recently produced in Kenya can coalesce into a general rallying point which
> will attract moderate opinion of all races, we may yet find that Stirling and
> his society can make a constructive contribution to current problems.[42]

Importantly, we begin to see here the terms against which support
for CAS and related associations were calibrated – i.e., anxieties concerning African nationalism and 'extremist' opinion of both African
and white settler varieties – as well as the emergence of idealisations
concerning 'moderate' African opinion and how widespread this
'moderation' was. Interestingly, while events over subsequent years
showed that British officialdom realised the misconceived nature of
the equivalence between European settlers and African nationalists (by
the very fact that the government ultimately entered into negotiations
with many of the figures that it held, in 1954, to be extremist), this
was an equivalence that, as we will see in the following section, the
liberal inter-racial associations (with the exception of some figures in
the IRASR) never repudiated.

Subsequent to this initial evolution in British government thinking
concerning the liberal-settler inter-racial associations, CAS found a
keen supporter in the Conservative Secretary of State for the Colonies,
Alan Lennox Boyd, who wrote to a British Member of Parliament
that, 'The present policies and philosophy of the Society … seem to
me to be admirable and, so long as it sticks to that line, [I] think the

---

[41] Author unknown, to Mr. Sweany, 09/12/1953, CO 822/340.
[42] Gorell Barnes, to the Colonial Governors of Northern Rhodesia, Uganda,
Kenya, Nyasaland and Tanganyika, 06/01/1954, TNA, CO 822/340.

Society deserves all the support it can get'.[43] Indeed, Lennox Boyd seems to have acted on his own advice, helping to recruit a professional political organiser for the Tanganyika branch at the behest not of CAS, but the Tanganyika Governor, Edward Twining (one of those who, a few years earlier, had sought to keep CAS at arm's length of British imperial policy). In so doing, Lennox Boyd wrote that:

So much depends on whether the sort of ideas for which the Society stands can take a real hold in East Africa, and, although I cannot officially sponsor the movement, I am anxious behind the scenes to do everything I can to help them.[44]

Similarly, while CO internal correspondence over a period of several years reveals that territorial administrators were being advised against joining CAS or other related societies on the grounds of breaking rules concerning political impartiality,[45] other papers illustrate that an offshoot of CAS in Tanganyika, the Tanganyika National Society, had the full support of the governor, who had 'proposed the new society as opposition to TANU [Tanganyika African National Union]', and tellingly that 'Government servants everywhere would be ordered to assist the new society in every possible way'.[46]

As well as the turnaround in Colonial Office sensibilities concerning liberal inter-racialism illustrated by this comment, what we also begin to see is the reason for the centrality of what had only two years earlier been treated as far-fetched, utopian and even a danger to British imperial interests. Fundamentally, with decolonisation in Africa becoming an unavoidable reality, the real question now for British imperial policy was what form newly independent African states would take, which political forces would come to dominate within them and how sympathetic they would be to British commercial interests. This was a set of anxieties (fundamentally wrapped up with the perpetuation of White vitality) that CAS and the other liberal inter-racial associations

---

[43] Lennox Boyd to T.G.D. Galbraith M.P., 22/11/1955, TNA, CO 967/294.
[44] Lennox Boyd to Chief Publicity Officer, Conservative Party Central Office, 21/12/1955, TNA, CO 967/294.
[45] See TNA, FCO 141/17796.
[46] Tanganyika Police Report, Capricorn Africa Society, Tanganyika National Society, a meeting at the house of Robin Johnston, 27/11/1955, TNA, FCO 141/17796, File 95.

were fully plugged into, resulting in a set of idealised fantasies concerning 'moderate' Africans and the likelihood that such moderates would engage in partnership and lend support to liberal inter-racial programmes for the region. Before exploring these idealisations, the following sections address the anxieties that drove them in more depth. As in previous chapters, the evidence will suggest that although material and geopolitical concerns figured importantly, these can only be understood within the broader context of the deeper, racial anxieties in which they were embedded.

The Shadow of Decolonisation and Other Liberal Anxieties

Geopolitical Anxieties

As we have seen, anxieties over decolonisation shaped the evolving attitude of the British Government to the liberal inter-racial societies of British Southern and East Africa. Michael Blundell was welcomed at Downing Street, where briefing notes written for the Prime Minister, Harold MacMillan, indicate the centrality of Blundell's NKP to broader metropolitan government thinking: 'what has happened in the Congo is bound to have its effect on Kenya ... agreement in Kenya between the main races must be a prime aim of policy not just for the Kenya government but for those who care about the future of multi-racial countries'.[47] Blundell himself was fully attuned to this kind of analysis which, of course, also served to further buttress his own political position. NKP documents went to great lengths to present the party as a bulwark against the 'radical racialism' of African nationalism, going so far as to present the advent of common roll democracy as part and parcel of this threat; 'This, in our view, which is illuminated by events elsewhere, would lead rapidly to chaos or to the iron hand of dictatorship'.[48]

[47] Briefing Notes: New Kenya Party meets the Prime Minister, 17 February 1960 and 20 February 1960, TNA, PREM 11/3031. This note no doubt refers to the demands of nationalist Congolese movements for independence from Belgium, which would soon turn into a series of secessionist demands and civil wars driven by a number of domestic and international actors, including Belgium, the United States and the Soviet Union.
[48] New Kenya Party, The Challenge of New Kenya, 1959, Michael Blundell Papers, Weston Library, MSS Afr.s.594, Box 8, File 9.

Indeed, the threat of African nationalism was wrapped up in broader Cold War anxieties. Of course, communists, of the Soviet kind at least, were also white, but they were the wrong kind of white (in that they were not 'White') and if successful would erode all those characteristics historically associated with elite Whiteness – i.e., individual rationalism, property and capital ownership, etc. Into the breach could step non-whites. And if non-whites could be instrumental in the fight against white communism (Blundell's 'agreement ... between the main races') then logically non-whites might be just as able, if not more so, of perpetuating White vitality (understood as a set of civilisational codes) as whites.

Inter-racialism, thus, became a central strategic feature of the anti-communist effort. 'The future of Africa must lie with the West' Blundell wrote, and in that context 'relations between White and Black are of paramount importance'.[49] Similarly, CAS from a very early stage conceived inter-racialism, 'unity and fellowship' as a response to an amelioration for 'the threat – or the reality – of ... communist penetration'.[50] In 1955 a CAS pamphlet put the case even more starkly. Again, the language is suggestive of Stirling's grandiose hand: 'The year 1954, then, will see a struggle between two great Conventions', the pamphlet proclaimed, referring to the Afro-Asian People's Solidarity Conference eventually held in 1957, and CAS's own convention held eventually at Salima in 1956:

I think it is not an exaggeration to say that it may resolve itself into a struggle for good against evil. The Cairo Conference may attempt to appeal for its purpose to the baser emotions which lie in all men, and which we can see expressed in some of the Kikuyu.[51] The Capricorn Convention, on the other hand, will seek to establish an unassailable moral basis of leadership in Africa ... It is vital for Africa's future that it should be Capricorn and not the Cairo Conference which will win their [moderate African] allegiance.[52]

Such geopolitical anxieties might be an expected feature of both metropolitan and settler attitudes towards the oncoming developments of decolonisation. The relationship between these anxieties and the

---

[49] Michael Blundell curriculum vitae, Michael Blundell Papers, Weston Library, MSS/66/174, File 3.
[50] The Capricorn Africa Society (pamphlet), undated, ICS, 8/1–17, CAS1.
[51] This is a reference to the Mau Mau rebellion.
[52] The Capricorn Africa Society Handbook, 1955, ICS 8/1–17 CAS 6, p. 9.

enthusiasm generated by elements of both groups for inter-racial cooperation between 'moderate' elements, however, is an important reminder of both the self-interested nature of such enthusiasm, as well as the anxieties which lay at the heart of the White desire to locate 'moderate' African symbols with which it could affirm itself and protect its interests. In this way, 1950s liberal-settler inter-racialism is an important bridge between pre-war idealisations of Africans and the kinds of anxiety-induced idealisations that characterise post-2007–8 financial crash mainstream analysis of the continent, which will be explored in further detail in Chapters 6 and 7. However, and just like those idealisations displayed in other periods, liberal-settler inter-racialism in the 1950s displayed a broader set of anxieties that transcended the geopolitical and which were equally important.

Economic Anxieties

There was a very large dose of economic self-interest at play in promoting inter-racialism. Most of this was explicit. In a note for fellow delegates at the CAS 1956 convention in Salima, Clarence Buxton asked first 'What ... are the best safeguards for the future security of European enterprise and settlements?' Closely followed by 'the Capricorn doctrines are the best guarantee for racial harmony which is essential as a foundation on which to build'.[53] Stirling himself recounted in 1987 that 'the economic convictions that I had about the potential of Africa were simply not achievable unless we had a decent relationship with the African'.[54]

Indeed, CAS's opposition to African nationalism – although painted by CAS in epochal and dramatic terms (as we saw in the discussion on geopolitics) – was rooted in anxieties about the latter's perceived exclusivism, which would prevent white settlers from allying themselves with the incipient African capitalist class,[55] an anxiety shared by

---

[53] Note for European delegates from Kenya as a result of remarks at Salima Airport on arrival by Roy Buchanan Allen, composed by Clarence Buxton, 15 June 1956, Weston Library, C.E.V. Buxton Papers, MSS Brit.Emp.s.390, Box 2, ff 103.

[54] Archibald David Stirling, IWM Oral History Collection, 18540, Reel 8.

[55] Alistair Ross, 'The Capricorn Africa Society and European Reactions to African Nationalism in Tanganyika, 1949–60', *African Affairs*, 76:305, 1977, pp. 519–35.

some members of the latter group, for a brief period at least.[56] It was these anxieties that drove liberal inter-racialism's desperate search for 'moderate' African partners and which led to CAS in particular (as the most ambitious and trans-territorial of the settler inter-racial associations) attracting the support of international capitalists even when it was struggling to attract the support of the metropolitan political class in London. Such supporters believed that liberal inter-racialism would promote healthy race relations policy, ensure against costly labour shortages and contribute to a calm working environment at a time when organised African labour was growing. This set of beliefs was encapsulated by the motives ascribed to one such financial contributor to CAS's Southern Rhodesian branch, which was described as being made 'presumably on the grounds that the society is doing a good job in promoting good race relations in Africa, and that good race relations are the major interest of the mines'.[57]

Economic anxieties about European and American commercial interests in a series of majority-ruled territories in Africa were expressed in their most full-blown terms by Stirling himself, who toured the finance-houses and corporations of London and New York to trumpet the potential investment payoffs that would exist in Africa subject to the success of CAS's political programme of moderate inter-racial cooperation – and the subsequent protection of Anglo-American commercial interests.[58] The misplaced nature of Stirling's optimism was not so much apparent in the fact that these deals would come off, but more in the fact that they would do so without any form of domestic African opposition, subsequent military oppression and an ultimate breakdown in the conditions amenable to capital accumulation. His central role in facilitating British arms to the Nigerian state during the Biafra war – itself an attempt to protect British oil interests in the region[59] – attests to the fragility of the idealised optimism of his earlier claims.

---

[56] West, *The Rise of an African Middle Class*, p. 177.
[57] Ian McLennan, Office of the High Commissioner for the United Kingdom, Salisbury, to R.W.D. Fowler, Commonwealth Relations Office, 01 February 1955, TNA, DO 35/4705 File 32.
[58] John Russell, British Information Services, New York, to Andrew Campbell, Colonial Attaché, British Embassy in Washington, DC, 18/12/1953, TNA, CO 822/340.
[59] Curtis, *The Mayfair Set*.

Racial Anxieties: Western Civilisation – For One or All?

In spite of all of the above analysis, it would be a mistake to believe that the anxieties that drove liberal settlers in the 1950s into associations like CAS or the IRASR were purely economic and geopolitical. Just as in the 1920s, broader racial and civilisational anxieties were also at play, arguably underpinning the geopolitical and economic factors normally associated with driving the search for comprador elites during this period. It is of course true that different sectors of elite Western societies and classes would have been driven by different mixes of these anxieties, whereby the British Government for instance might have been more concerned by geopolitical challenges than civilisational ones (although the two were, and are, co-constitutive). Nonetheless, as a distillation of White anxieties during this period, the inter-racial associations provide a useful insight into the demarcations of such anxieties. These associations represented, for many, a last chance to get Western civilisation 'right' and thus safeguard White vitality, showing that the former was a universalist creed which could take root and be of generalisable benefit anywhere and everywhere. The inverse of this, being proclaimed to various implicit and explicit degrees by African nationalists and pan-Africanists, conveyed a message that liberal settlers, in their bubbles of privilege, could not bear without recognising the structurally unjust and racialised nature of their situation. In this vein, Susan Wood, an active member of the Kenya CAS chapter, in her address to the 1956 Salima convention, suggested that:

The Capricorn Contract ... gives us the opportunity we have been looking for to live believing in the freedom of the individual and responsibility to one's neighbour and yet to enjoy the great security of knowing that we will not be alone in preserving the standards of civilisation which are so dear to us, but we will have companions equally determined to defend those standards among the other races.[60]

The IRASR, in characteristically blunter terms, nonetheless also channelled anxieties about the vitality of White genius and Western civilisation. In opposing the colour bar in industrial employment, the association argued that:

---

[60] Susan Wood, Address to the Salima Convention, 16/16/1956, Weston Library, C.E.V.Buxton Papers, MSS Brit.Emp.s.390, Box 2.

It is a vitally important problem to solve because it is no advertisement for European civilisation that Europeans should have to secure themselves by preventing employees of another race from doing work which they are capable of doing. It ... plays into the hands of those who contend that economic justice cannot be expected from our system[61]

Such statements channelled the anxious desire to find affirmation for liberal-settler cosmology within those groups who had been historically subjugated and exploited by the system of rule which had perpetuated the former's privileges. If Africans would embrace a White-colonial cosmology, then that cosmology could be said to be functional. What is also interesting here are differences between pre- and post-World War II conceptions concerning the boundaries of Whiteness. In the 1920s we saw that there were very real concerns about the overall vitality and survival of Western civilisation. Africans were largely held to be inadmissible to the club of Western civilisation and were perceived as, at best, docile facilitators and, at worst, threats to its perpetuation. In other words, phenotypical non-whites in that period still represented a threat to the racial purity of Western civilisation; the tie between phenotypical whiteness and Whiteness was secure, even if many whites in the West were not living up to the promise of their supposed racial habitus. By the 1950s such concerns were still apparent, especially with the onset of the Cold War. However, there was also now a more pronounced sense of what Western civilisational decline would look like. The failure to see Western civilisation thrive in Africa, among Africans, was now taken to be a failure of White genius in totality. In other words, White civilisation was nothing if it remained a failing parochial project of phenotypically white people. We can see this position struck by Wood and her concerns about whether Western civilisation could maintain its stronghold in Africa and fulfil its universalist pretensions.[62]

---

[61] Inter-Racial Association of Southern Rhodesia, Draft Declaration on African Affairs, 1953, ICS, PG.ZW.IRASR 2.

[62] Interestingly, this was one point on which British liberals differed from their North American counterparts. Where British liberals were optimistic about finding moderate, 'modern', liberal Africans to carry the legacy of Western civilisation forward, American liberals were far more despondent about the quality of the 'African character' they encountered on their travels in the continent in the 1950s, most likely because unlike British settlers, Americans

Liberal settlers had a very clear idea about what constituted White civilisation. A CAS study group established to discuss the desirability of 'westernisation' in Kenya listed six aspects attached to this label, including the rule of law; 'the high status accorded to women'; Christian tolerance; and science, concluding that 'a degree of Westernisation was both inevitable and desirable in Kenya' albeit with the proviso that 'full use should be made of the contributions of other sources, above all from Africa itself'.[63] The anxiety here, therefore, concerned the question of whether these attributes, all of them thought of as historical achievements of phenotypically white people, and thus together representative of Western and White genius, would survive as anything more than a parochial Western project. For hand-in-hand with this elevated sense of what Western civilisation was – bearing in mind that in the context of discussing westernisation in Africa, this simultaneously implied what the latter *lacked* – came a recognition that these civilisational tendencies were becoming increasingly untethered from phenotypically white people themselves.

Evidence for this can be found in the genesis of CAS, which was based in Stirling's analysis that Europe was in the process of suffering a terminal case of exhaustion, becoming 'sad and socialist'[64] and experiencing an irreversible drain in vitality. 'The fertility of the Western nations', Stirling wrote, 'is falling'; East and Central Africa was the last hope to 'preserve ... the Commonwealth and European civilisation'.[65] It is around such issues that the Imperial Sympathiser from Chapter 3, Joseph Houldsworth Oldham, makes a reappearance. By this stage semi-retired from public life in rural England, Oldham nonetheless maintained regular correspondence with public figures in the political and religious spheres. Stirling had managed to recruit Oldham to the Capricorn cause in 1954 on a visit to the former's home. Despite his biographer's protestations that Oldham's commitment to CAS

---

had little experience of being in Africa. See, Staniland, *American Intellectuals and African Nationalists*, p. 58.

[63] Conference on Education for Nationhood, April 8th–12th 1958, Study Group Chairmen's Reports, Study Group no. 1: To what extent does the achievement of nationhood in Kenya imply westernisation? KNA, MSS/129/18, G5.

[64] Hughes, *Capricorn*, p. 19.

[65] David Stirling to Sir Oliver Lyttleton, Secretary of State for the Colonies, 02/11/1951, TNA, DO 35/3603 – note the similarities of these statements to those of the Hayekian economist John Jewkes, noted earlier in this chapter.

was the aberration of a figure losing touch with his critical faculties,[66] Oldham had always been committed to inter-racialism[67] and CAS was a natural outlet for his beliefs in the centrality of Westernisation and Christianisation to African development. Indeed, for someone supposedly succumbing to decrepitude, Oldham nonetheless managed to publish a well-received book in 1955, *New Hope for Africa*, extolling the virtues of CAS and inter-racialism.

Oldham was in full-step with liberal inter-racialism's analysis of 'racial' African nationalism and what had to be done to preserve Western civilisation and perpetuate White vitality in Africa. Writing to Stirling in 1954, Oldham stated that 'Africans must be given the opportunity of realizing their ineradicable and irrepressible desire for nationhood and self-government within a framework of western civilization or they will seek the fulfilment of these over-mastering passions in an exclusive nationalism and racialism'.[68] *New Hope for Africa* was widely lauded in metropolitan political circles and contributed to the change in attitudes towards CAS.[69] Passages in the book dwell on the question of what was to become of Western civilisation and we, once again, see that the anxieties concerning its perpetuation related to how it could be made to gain a sustainable foothold in Africa; in other words, how Africa might save Western civilisation and, thus, White genius from, and for, the Anglosphere. For instance, Oldham writes that 'western civilisation is itself passing through a crisis. Many of its fundamental beliefs ... are being eaten away by the acids of scepticism',[70] before going on to acknowledge that:

It would ... be a complete misunderstanding of the nature of civilisation to identify the ideals of which we have been speaking with the white community

---

[66] Clements, *Faith on the Frontier*, p. 452.

[67] In 1924 Oldham had written: 'It is a serious question, however, whether even as a stage in evolution it is wise to encourage the growth of political organization on racial lines. Disputes between races are apt to acquire a peculiar bitterness ... a potent cause of misunderstanding and conflict will be removed if associations and loyalties can be based on other interests than the physical bond of race or colour'. Joseph H. Oldham, *Christianity and the Race Problem* (New York, NY: George H. Doran Company, 1924), p. 105.

[68] Clements, *Faith on the Frontier*, pp. 450–1.

[69] See for instance praise for the book in: Alan Lennox Boyd to Chief Publicity Officer, Conservative Party Central Office, 21 December 1955, TNA, CO 967/294.

[70] Oldham, *New Hope*, p. 56.

as such ... It might well happen, and is indeed happening in some instances, that Africans might be the defenders of Christian western ideals against Europeans who are denying them ... the dividing line that really matters in Capricorn Africa today is not that between the races, but that which divides the defenders and promoters of true civilization from those who by their words and actions betray it.[71]

Whereas in the 1920s it was phenotypical whites in Africa who would safeguard Western civilisation from a racially threatened West, by the 1950s even that belief in inherent phenotypical white civility had been eroded. If whites could not be entrusted with the heritage of their historical civilisational genius in Western metropoles and in Africa the job would have to be done by Africans themselves – in partnership[72] of course with the liberal inter-racial associations, themselves the last hope for White vitality in Africa[73]. It was in this process of locating Africans who could fulfil the White civilisational mission in Africa that the geopolitically, economically and civilisationally anxious Whiteness detailed in these past few sections transmuted into a series of idealisations concerning 'moderate' Africans.

The Fantastical Idealisations of Liberal Inter-Racialism

It is important to remember that across British East and Southern Africa during this period the forces of naked settler racism were still on the march. Ian Smith had yet to declare unilateral independence in Southern Rhodesia, the Mau Mau rebellion in Kenya was being met by the brutal response of the Colony's security services (with the assistance of Blundell) and apartheid regimes in South Africa and the Portuguese colonies were far from ready to expire. The liberal interracial associations thus had a twin-pronged set of issues to confront. On the one hand, they sought to convince 'moderate' African opinion that African nationalism was bad for them – although, as we will see, the whole construct of immutable 'moderate' African opinion

---

[71] Ibid., at p. 60.
[72] Note the change in language, from white 'tutelage' in the 1920s to inter-racial 'partnership' in the 1950s.
[73] One example of this belief, among many, can be found in Oldham, *New Hope*, p. 56: 'Africans need the help of Europeans because the latter are the privileged heirs of a high tradition'.

was itself a liberal-settler fantasy. On the other hand, they sought to convince the rest of the white settler opinion that not all Africans were savage brutes who wished to create an 'Africa for the Africans'.[74] They had, however, to achieve the latter without undermining the sense of rightness which attached itself to the entire historical project of white settlement in Africa. Ultimately, they were able to do this in such a way that moderate Africans could be depoliticised and fantasised without denigrating the historical imperial project, while simultaneously offering a critique of the contemporaneous imperial situation, thus meeting the demands foregrounded by both sets of groups they had to win over – i.e., moderate African and settler opinion.

They went about this in the following way; settler racism and domination were no longer appropriate in dealing with groups of Africans who were educated, detribalised and, thus, more civilised and more recognisably White. More importantly however, settler racism and domination were also no longer viable if the white settler communities wished to protect their commercial and property interests in the face of rising African nationalism. This did not mean, however, that white settler racism and domination were *never* appropriate or viable. In her speech to the CAS Salima convention in 1956, Wood proclaimed that: 'Our domination in the past was derived largely from circumstances. When the European came to Africa it was inevitable that he took the land as he had experience of the wide issues of life that was needed in a country that was as yet untouched by the growth of modern civilisation.'[75] Similarly, Stirling wrote to CAS members that, 'I am not suggesting that our attitude in Southern Rhodesia has been wrong in the past, but only that it is becoming wrong in the present and will be disastrously wrong in the future',[76] while the IRASR stated that 'in the sixty years since the Occupation ... Africans have advanced and there are now a large number of Africans who are already more or less adapted to European civilisation',[77] implying again that the original occupation and the means by which it was conducted were justified.

---

[74] A term first popularised by pan-Africanist Marcus Garvey and used repeatedly in CAS propaganda against the aims of African nationalists.
[75] Susan Wood, Address to the Salima Convention, 16/16/1956, Weston Library, C.E.V. Buxton Papers, MSS Brit.Emp.s.390, Box 2.
[76] David Stirling, Address to Members, 1954, TNA, CO 822/340.
[77] Draft Declaration on African Affairs, 1953, ICS, PG.ZW.IRASR 2.

So, to recap, racism and domination were justified historically because Africans weren't civilised enough 'back then' (an assertion designed to placate settlers) but now growing numbers of Africans were civilised and had to be admitted into the higher echelons of the political and economic domain – an assertion designed to appeal to so-called moderate Africans. It is in this sense that the transition from race to culture discussed in Chapter 4 does not seem to have been driven so much by what John Hobson has called 'colonial-racist guilt syndrome'[78] as by anxiety about White vitality, both in the West and in Africa.

Liberal inter-racial idealisations about moderate Africans, their civilised characteristics (their Whiteness) and tendency towards political and economic cooperation, therefore, had to be at a high pitch; otherwise both lines of argument would fall down. However, the criteria by which Africans could be admitted to Western civilisation had to remain incredibly severe in order to ensure that only 'moderate' African opinion flourished – as against the 'racialism' of radical African nationalism. As a result, the liberal inter-racial associations went to great lengths to admit only certain forms of African behaviour as 'civilised'. This entailed a double movement of idealisation: first, idealising the role of liberal-settler inter-racial associations in shepherding forth inter-racial African polities; and second, idealising the equanimity of those few Africans who actually qualified to become members of these polities.

The first and entirely self-referential aspect of liberal-settler inter-racial idealisation is evident across the rhetoric, propaganda and the key protagonists of the three societies. CAS was 'the last real chance for Africa' in the face of those enemies of Africa whose aim was 'to discount any movement which leads directly towards a lessening in racial tension'.[79] As we have seen, this theme of the liberal inter-racial associations as providing an alternative to the 'racialism' of radical African nationalism was recurrent and it served to bolster the self-regard within which these societies held their own potential as makers and changers of history. The main contribution these associations thought they could make was to create a common patriotism for white settler

[78] John H. Hobson, 'Re-embedding the Global Colour Line', p. 83.
[79] G.R.A.M. Johnston to Secretary of State for the Colonies Alan Lennox Boyd, 07 June 1955, TNA, CO 967/294.

and African alike in Africa, thus, overcoming both white settler and African racialism. This, of course, necessitated the claim that there had hitherto been no such indigenous common civilisational communities. Stirling wrote that, 'The Black ... has never produced a civilization of its own; nor, when it has adopted the civilization of a conqueror has it been able to sustain it when the support of the conqueror was withdrawn',[80] while Clarence Buxton proclaimed that 'a common African patriotism has no basis in history. Capricorn aims at creating it'.[81] An Africa constructed along CAS's inter-racial policies would produce 'a galaxy of African philosophers, scientists, writers and artists',[82] where none had existed before.

The liberal inter-racial associations positioned themselves as the transcendental agents of post-War Africa. One of the IRASR's founders, the liberal Southern Rhodesian politician and lawyer Hardwicke Holderness, attended CAS's Salima convention and commented that 'here were people who were determined to reject the barren doctrine of racial nationalism and establish one patriotism and one allegiance'.[83] Oldham pushed the message in his influential 1955 book, when he opined that he could 'see nowhere on the horizon any other force that gives promise of doing what the Capricorn Africa Society might be the instrument of doing' in ushering in 'a radical change of direction'.[84]

According to the liberal-settler inter-racial associations, therefore, everything was thus dependent on liberal inter-racialism. In some ways this kind of self-justification is not necessarily very surprising, but the pitch of the assertions being made, their manic quality, that not simply Africa but Western civilisation itself would crumble if liberal inter-racial warnings were not heeded and programmes followed, speaks to the anxieties driving these societies and their supporters (including in Whitehall and Westminster) at this time. Indeed, a small insight into the fragility of this idealised self-regard is provided by the responses of ordinary (white settler) association members to the proposals being

---

[80] Stirling to Sir Oliver Lyttleton, Secretary of State for the Colonies, 02 November 1951, TNA, DO 35/3603.
[81] Clarence Buxton, Note for European delegates from Kenya as a result of remarks at Salima Airport on arrival by Roy Buchanan Allen, 15 June 1956, Weston Library, C.E.V. Buxton Papers, MSS Brit.Emp.s.390, Box 2, ff 103.
[82] Oldham, *New Hope*, p. 55.
[83] Minutes of the third Annual General Meeting, 30/6/1956, CRL, Eileen Haddon Collection of Southern Rhodesia, MF2811, Reel 2.
[84] Oldham, *New Hope*, p. 7.

discussed at the elite levels of these organisations. A questionnaire circulated in May 1953 by the IRASR, the most left-liberal of the groups discussed here, to gauge member attitudes to its Draft Declaration on African Affairs (which, after several years, never evolved out of its draft stages) elicited the following kinds of responses:

I am one of those who feel that such a happy state of affairs [as partnership] will only come with the extension of Christ's Kingdom on Earth. Dr. H.J. Knight

To bring about the honourable cooperation of all races for the benefit of the whole community, in accordance *with the spirit of the federal white paper*. A.L. Macmillan, *emphasis added*

There should be no bar based on colour or race alone ... [but] we cannot do away with a 'culture or civilisation' bar. At whatever cost we must maintain the highest European standards. J.R. Martin

Whilst [the African] cannot be held back, I believe it to be to his detriment to push him forward at the speed you propose.' C.R. Miskin[85]

These responses are by no means unrepresentative and show that liberal-settler inter-racialism was some way adrift of even those corners of white settler opinion it counted as its own, let alone the 'moderate' African opinion it sought to court (more of which shortly).

If this self-regard was overly idealised, then the optimism with which liberal inter-racialism constructed narrow terms on which Africans could be admitted to Western civilisation was no less so in its attempts to establish boundaries and celebrate those who could overcome them. Remember that the IRASR and CAS, while sympathetic to each other, were unable to bridge the divide between the latter's support for a multiple electoral roll and the former's adherence to a common roll. For CAS the multiple roll was a means by which to ensure that only Africans who could meet certain property or educational standards could ascend to the same voting rights as white settlers. This was an extension of the broader civilisational benchmarks that CAS had established for African admittance to CAS, European areas, businesses and so on and which took on a cultural, rather than racial, nature – although which, of course, in practice were implicitly racial. These included 'a behaviour and manners bar' and a 'health and hygiene bar'.[86]

[85] CRL, Eileen Haddon Collection of Southern Rhodesia, MF2811, Reel One.
[86] The Capricorn Africa Society Handbook, F1d, 1955, ICS, PP.KE.CAS, File 8/1–17.

And yet the IRASR were not particularly different in their appraisal and promotion of civilisational standards. Alert to the dangers posed to the polity by a common roll populated by uneducated and, thus, potentially 'racialist' voters 'the proper solution is not to abolish the common roll ... but to arrange the franchise so that only reasonably responsible people, irrespective of race, qualify'.[87] Africans who had transcended their supposed racial habitus were to be welcomed into Western civilisational practices, for, like 'members of a family do when they grow up' these were Africans who could be relied upon to conduct themselves politically responsibly[88] – i.e., not threaten white commercial and property interests through adopting excessively nationalist positions.

The NKP, meanwhile, recognised the racialised nature of the culture bars being proposed by liberal inter-racial opinion; 'In our country, racial and economic differences lie together. The usual historical economic conflict is thus, in our case, exacerbated by race'. But their response was to police this cultural division no less ferociously. 'The only solution', they argued, 'is vigorously to tackle the basic problem of low living standards, so that there may rapidly emerge from the poorer majority people having similar interests, and similar ideals, to those economically more advanced'.[89] In other words, Africans as they existed in rural and many urban slum areas were not qualified to avail themselves of equal rights with white settlers, or to share the same political or cosmological space. Oldham, too, argued in this vein, writing that 'tribal loyalties ... [are] too restricted in their range to be compatible with the twentieth century world into which Africa is inevitably being drawn'.[90] This all, of course, coheres with the tropes of Modernisation Theory explored in Chapter 4, which relegated 'tribe' to the pre-modern. In Oldham's case his position is magnified because as we saw in Chapter 3, in the 1920s he had been a passionate advocate of keeping Africans in tribal areas under tribal authority, to begin with. Furthermore, as with the more general tropes of Modernisation Theory, there were biopolitical and affective emphases contained within such analyses whereby Africans had to develop the

---

[87] Draft Declaration on African Affairs, 1953, ICS, PG.ZW.IRASR 2, p. 9.
[88] Ibid., at p. 16.
[89] The Challenge of New Kenya: A policy statement for the New Kenya Party, ICS, GB 0101 PP.KE.NKP, p. 3.
[90] Oldham, *New Hope*, p. 26.

'many moral qualities that can ennoble life'[91] and where 'the question for the original Africans is no longer of our clearing the path for them, but rather of their taking up the burdens of adult responsibility [and] self-discipline'.[92]

The racial and civilisational anxiety that drove liberal inter-racialism produced this relegation of the non-modern to the realms of the *pre-modern* and simultaneously produced optimistic idealisations about those who could affirm White standards (including related geopolitical and economic agendas) and confirm that even if White vitality was declining in the West and among some groups of phenotypical whites, it was emerging and solidifying itself in Africa, among Africans. And so, Michael Blundell praised 'those African peasant farmers who are emerging, through a planned and consolidated programme, as *a modern* agricultural community', counter-posing them to 'the suspicious attitude and conservatism of those around them'.[93] Similarly, Stirling was fulsome in his praise for those 'many intelligent Africans' who saw that their 'best chance of personal advancement lies in backing our case rather than that of the African Nationalist' and who, once inspired by CAS, 'will explain our joint purposes to other Africans',[94] a notion which, as we will discover shortly, was a largely fanciful one again driven by the idealised and necessary self-regard concerning the centrality of CAS's mission in Africa.

One of the outcomes of these optimistic idealisations was a denial of affective politics to those deemed unfit for membership of the kind of civilisation envisaged by liberal-settler inter-racialism. This is because the contours of what constituted acceptable African behaviour were so narrow. As such, a marker of admittance to Western civilisation (as defined by liberal inter-racialism) was that Africans had to 'forget the racial differences of the past'[95] if they wanted to attain full voting rights: 'the reservation of seats for minority interests must be retained,

[91] Ibid., at p. 54.
[92] William M. MacMillan, 'African Growing Pains', *African Affairs*, 52:208, 1953, p. 197.
[93] Speech by Michael Blundell to the Conference on Education for Nationhood, Nairobi, April 1958, KNA, MSS/129/18, File G/5, *emphasis added*.
[94] David Stirling to J.G. Foster, Parliamentary Under-Secretary of State for the Commonwealth Relations Office, 30 May 1952, TNA, DO 35/3603.
[95] The Challenge of New Kenya: a policy statement for the New Kenya Party, ICS, GB 0101 PP.KE.NKP, p. 3.

until such time as racial prejudice disappears'.[96] Indeed, the whole CAS critique of African nationalism was, in part, based on its affective content, that it was based on an 'emotional appeal' to 'black racialist extrem[ism]',[97] while the NKP extolled that 'our enrolled members are sensible men of all races', simultaneously warning that '[foreign] money will only come if there is no threat of strikes, boycotts and disturbances'.[98] This did not mean that all forms of emotion were deemed unwelcome. Stirling wrote approvingly that 'any day hundreds of Italians, Negroes, Scandinavians, and coloureds can be seen filing past the Lincoln Memorial [in Washington, DC] with much the same look on their face. They all file past as Americans, and the look in their faces is similar because they are sharing the same emotion derived from an ideology accepted by them all'.[99] This was a form of ordained emotional politics that, rather than the mix of anger, frustration, joy and emboldenment expressed in anti-colonial politics was predicated on respect for authority and solemnity, emotions that cohered to a set of White social codes born out of a deferential European feudal and class system. This approach sought to incorporate Africans into Western civilisation so long as they did not threaten white settler commercial and property interests and offend, or seek to usurp, privileged classes more broadly. This is a major area of distinction between the 1920s and 1950s anxious Afro-idealisations. Whereas in the former it was inconceivable that any African might partake of the same rights as white people (and become 'White') within any definable timeframe, by the 1950s the timeframe had – often by dint of the agency of Africans and other colonised peoples demanding change themselves – become much more defined and immediate. Implicit rules, thus, had to be created by which only some Africans – deemed respectful of white settler and Anglospheric commercial and property interests – might be admitted to partake in the kinds of rights enjoyed by phenotypical whites as full members of Western civilisation. It was these kinds of Africans who could be celebrated, while the others would be, as we have seen, admonished for being 'racialist extremists'. Chapter 7 will illustrate

---

[96] Plan for Success, The New Kenya Party, ICS, GB 0101 PP.KE.NKP, p. 4.
[97] Capricorn Africa, 1954, CO 822/340, p. 6.
[98] The New Kenya Group Newsletter, No. 2 August 1959, Weston Library, Michael Blundell Papers, MSS.Afr.s.594, Box 8, File 9.
[99] David Stirling to Edward Twining, Governor of Tanganyika, 06 May 1953, CO 822/340.

how this form of anxious idealisation has continued to be an important feature of contemporary 'Africa Rising' narratives. For now, this discussion functions as a means by which to begin exploring how the responses of those subjected as both 'good' and 'bad' Africans served to puncture these kinds of idealisations, even if this was often beyond the comprehension of the white liberal-settler activists themselves.

African Responses to Liberal Inter-Racialism

As one might expect, there were members of the nascent African capitalist classes attracted to the settler inter-racial associations. The IRASR branches in Salisbury and Bulawayo were at various points chaired by African members, such as the labour activist Charles Mzingeli and the founder of the Southern Rhodesia Bantu Congress Thompson Samkange, who was also active in CAS. Boaz Omori, subsequently editor of the *Nation* newspaper in Kenya, was also an active CAS participant, while six of the 46 LegCo members who signed the founding NKP statement were Africans.[100]

Even among this small group of settler inter-racial sympathisers, however, there were divisions that served to highlight the anxieties of liberal inter-racialism in the 1950s concerning White vitality. In particular, the place of Africans within the liberal-settler inter-racial associations immediately served notice of just how idealised settler members of the societies had been in their construction of 'moderate' African opinion.

Two Speeches at Salima ... and the Return of Harry Thuku

Far from fulfilling the optimism of the settler inter-racial associations, many of the African members simply served to illustrate in even starker detail the anxiety-driven idealisations of the former's White imaginations. Omori, future editor of the *Nation* newspaper in Kenya, might be the most interesting case of this, primarily because his excoriating criticisms of other Africans set him quite apart from the far more carefully racially coded language of his white settler association

---

[100] See Kenya a Nation: A statement of policy presented by a number of members of Kenya Legislative Council of all Races, 25 March 1959, ICS, GB 0101 PP.KE.NKP, p. 4.

compatriots. In a speech at the CAS Salima convention in 1956, Omori talked about the ignorance of most Africans and warned that they would have a propensity to vote for tyranny if given the right to do so. He continued:

You cannot trust a child to handle a sharp knife. And wise parents always keep the knife in safe custody until the child is old enough to realise the danger of misusing it. Similarly the vote ... can bring disastrous results to a society that misuses it. It is important therefore, that it should not fall into the wrong hands ... the responsibility of returning members of the Legislature should be left to those people of all races who are best qualified and equipped for it ... the vote is not a natural right since a citizen has to work hard to earn it[101]

Similarly, a figure familiar from Chapter 3 chose this period to make his return to the political fray. Having retired from politics to take up farming in the 1930s following his unsuccessful attempts to convert the nationalist Kikuyu Central Association into a collaborationist vehicle, Harry Thuku began reappearing on platforms in the 1950s to denounce the Mau Mau rebellion and was indeed an invited member of a special government committee to report on 'the sociological causes underlying Mau Mau' and to make proposals 'on the means for ending it'.[102] It seems that in settler inter-racialism Thuku found a way to marry his collaborationist leanings with a pseudo-nationalist politics. As a result, Thuku released a statement of support for the NKP shortly after the group formed. Although not as scathing as Omori, Thuku's statement repeatedly reinforces the idea that equality is only achievable through meritocracy, finally arguing that NKP policy would lead to 'progress for all races ... on the basis of ability only'.[103] His support for the NKP is, therefore, couched in terms which would automatically result in the denial of rights for the majority of Africans who did not meet the narrow standards of civilised behaviour and education laid down by white settler inter-racialism.

[101] Speech by Boaz Omori at the Capricorn Convention, Salima, Nyasaland, 16/06/1956, Weston Library, C.E.V. Buxton Papers, MSS Brit.Emp.s.390, Box 2.
[102] Rosberg and Nottingham, *The Myth of Mau Mau*, pp. 335–6.
[103] Harry Thuku Statement of Support for the New Kenya Party, 21 April 1959, Weston Library, Michael Blundell Papers, MSS.Afr.s.746, Box 20, File 7, Ff. 27–28.

Of course, statements such as those of Omori's and Thuku's are
unsurprising given that African societies are as more and less penetrated by gender, generational, ethnic and economic divisions as any
other. Indeed, by dint of having access to a European secondary education and, in some cases, higher education as lawyers and journalists,
African members of settler inter-racial associations in the 1950s were
invariably members of a highly selective and tiny elite, more empow-
ered than most to be visibly seen to meet the standards of Western
civilisation. But this is also the fundamental point; white settler inter-
racialism had erected a romanticised notion of African societies,
attributing various positive and negative characteristics to different elements of them, but only in very narrow terms, posing both 'emotional'
and pre-modern masses and nationalists against educated, 'modern/
moderate' elites. The latter, however, were assumed to be keen on and
able to engage and placate the former. Statements like Omori's and
Thuku's disabuse such optimistic notions and illustrate the ways in
which sections of educated African opinion were as (unsurprisingly)
jealous of protecting their own privileges as white settlers were.

The Southern Rhodesian activist Thompson Samkange gave a different and contrasting speech to the Salima convention, although it
too, in its own way, would have served to puncture settler inter-racial
idealism had the latter not been so hubristic. Samkange's speech was
a warning and one that sought to place the responsibility for African
nationalism's appeal not on 'emotional' and immature Africans, nor the
machinations of the 'Indian and Egyptian Imperialists' often blamed
for African anti-colonial agitation,[104] but on the white settler – and as
we have seen in some cases African – denial of rights to the majority
of Africans. The emergence of African nationalism, including where
it took more exclusivist characteristics, was 'the natural reaction to
the continued refusal of the Europeans to accord to us that dignity,
freedom, and security which is the right of every human being'. He
concluded: 'If we are unable to assert ourselves and gain full status
and dignity as individuals, then we will be forced to assert ourselves
as a race.'[105] It is a testament to settler inter-racial hubris, certainly in

[104] David Stirling, Memorandum to all Members, 20 July 1953, TNA, FCO
141/17796, File 28a.
[105] Speech by Thompson Samkange at the Capricorn Convention, Salima,
Nyasaland, 16 June 1956, Weston Library, C.E.V. Buxton Papers, MSS Brit.
Emp.s.390, Box 2.

the case of CAS (which never adopted the common electoral roll) if not so much the IRASR, that such a statement caused no discernible reflection on the position that white settler inter-racialism occupied in denying rights to the majority of Africans in the territories in which it was concerned.

In Conclusion: Puncturing White Settler Idealism

In general, and as one might expect, African nationalists were scathing about settler inter-racialism and the associated societies. On a visit to Salisbury in December 1958 the leader of the Nyasaland African Congress, and in years to come President of Malawi, Hastings Banda, denounced '"moderates" and "Capricorns"'.[106] In the months follow-ing the announcement of Blundell's new LegCo NKP grouping, KANU members of the Kenyan Legislative Council took turns in mounting withering personal attacks against Blundell personally and the NKP in general, accusing Blundell of using inter-racialism as a cover for the protection of settler privilege.[107] Another Nyasaland nationalist, Kanyama Chiume, thundered against CAS years earlier in 1954, get-ting straight to the products of the anxieties that were driving settler inter-racialism – i.e., fears of imperial decline and White civilisational vitality and historical ingenuity:

[W]e at this end have [not] swallowed the Capricorn emotional pill ... [been] buried in the Capricorn political grave ... the Capricorn version of Imperialism ... The Capricorn Society should not try to shed crocodile tears in being sorry for having taken an active part in helping to bring six and a quarter million people in Central Africa under the rule of 160,000 Europeans, for its aim now, as it has always been, is to bring about an even larger dominion in which only those who shall respond to the Capricorn jazz flute shall be entitled to a vote.[108]

Meanwhile, and moving beyond the core of elite African national-ists, Special Branch reports out of Tanganyika in 1954 declared that

---

[106] John McCracken, *A History of Malawi, 1859–1959* (Suffolk: James Currey, 2012), p. 351.
[107] African Nationalists on Blundell, Weston Library, Michael Blundell Papers, MSS Afr.s.746, Box 5, File 4, ff 58–60.
[108] M.W. Kanyama Chiume, The Capricorn Society: A Rejoinder, *The African and Colonial World*, 1(18), TNA, FCO 141/17796, Files 56 and 56a.

Africans there 'generally regard [CAS] as yet another means whereby the European hopes to maintain his hold on the African territories',[109] while at a public meeting in Bulawayo in 1952 an African representative of CAS was told to leave shortly after he had started speaking. The meeting later passed resolutions to 'issue warnings to rural Africans to beware of the agents of the Society ... and to refuse to join the Society'.[110]

Despite being chronically under-evaluated in the scholarship on British late-imperial history in Africa, the associations considered in this chapter were significant enough to have been given audiences at the very heart of the British governmental apparatus, which gave increasing and eventually full consideration to the prospect that white settler-liberal inter-racialism held out for continuing neo-imperial relations of power between Britain and its soon-to-be former colonies.[111] For many Africans however, liberal-settler inter-racialism was a threat and menace. This is an obvious point, perhaps, but the main implication is not so much to do with what it tells us about African opinion, but rather the nature of anxieties about Whiteness and Western civilisation amongst elite white opinion in the 1950s. Being a threat and a menace to Africans was the exact opposite of what CAS, the IRASR, NKP and other fellow travellers understood themselves to be. Whereas the British governmental machinery well understood, at least initially, the implications of liberal-settler inter-racialism vis-à-vis African opinion, it is notable that there is little evidence that CAS, the IRASR or NKP understood themselves in these terms; their documents, personal as well as public, never explicitly reveal ulterior motives of the kind assigned to them by their African opponents. And yet nonetheless, driven by the geopolitical, economic and civilisational anxieties noted in prior sections, the liberal-settler inter-racial associations explored here channelled idealised notions about themselves and Africans that, under sustained analysis, could barely mask the pernicious outcomes such idealisations represented – i.e., the exclusion of the majority of

[109] Special Branch Intelligence Survey 1954, TNA, FCO 141/17796, File 76a.
[110] 'Capricorn Members asked to Resign', *Bantu Mirror*, 25 October 1952, TNA, DO 35/6731, File 13.
[111] It is also worth noting that the CAS Salima convention in June 1956 attracted media coverage from tens of widely read news publications and agencies. A total of 29 clippings, some of them very lengthy and mostly very sympathetic, are on file at TNA, DO 35/4705.

Africans from being authors of their own national and pan-continental histories.

And so, much more so than in the 1920s, when anxiety-induced idealisations in their various iterations could not far escape the eugenicist bent of the period – and thus saw Africa as a territory, rather than a peopled continent, where White vitality could be salvaged – the anxiety-induced idealisations displayed by the settler inter-racial associations of the 1950s relates in important ways to the kinds of 'Africa Rising' narratives that became more prevalent in the years after the 2007–8 financial crash. This includes the manner by which both sought to identify Africans who conformed to White norms in order to salvage Whiteness from a crisis-ridden West in decline. The next two chapters will explore the broader socio-cultural interest in Africa that has emerged since the crash, alongside the kinds of political and economic analysis characteristic of the 'Africa Rising' narrative. It will be shown that in both cases, whether it is cultural expressions of African beauty, film and culture (Chapter 6), or celebrations of African democracy and economy (Chapter 7), such optimism and positivity about the African presence in Western society and international order has been predicated on a series of anxieties about Whiteness and related financial, political and military insecurity.

6 | Afropolitanism and the White-Western Incorporation of Africa

This chapter occupies a slightly more ambiguous ground than the previous contextual chapters. This is for two reasons. Firstly, with the advent of ever-faster communication technologies, the spatial dimension of how Whiteness is constructed and where it locates itself has become ever more blurred. As we will see, Whiteness can no longer be easily accommodated in a frame that is geographically limited to an Anglo-American or European context, settler or otherwise. Of course this has been an explicit theme running through some of the preceding chapters; firstly, that Whiteness is a project that requires an affirmation of itself in Others as a means by which to affirm its own vitality, and secondly, that by operating as a set of codes and rationalities, Whiteness has never been the pure preserve of people with a particular phenotypical presentation, something that has worked historically to exclude groups of people with *and* without light-skinned phenotypical presentations –and something that has come to characterise the fluid boundaries of Whiteness more observably through the course of the past hundred years. The second reason for the more ambiguous nature of this chapter is that in many contemporary socio-cultural and political narratives about Africa, people identifying as being of African heritage are more to the fore than in any previous period. This presents a number of challenges for trying to locate a White narrative of Africa in the contemporary Western gaze, as it is those defined as and who define themselves in some way as Black and/or African who are doing much to shape the contours of debate in Western arenas previously dominated and demarcated by phenotypically white privilege.

It is, however, important to recognise that, as we have witnessed in earlier chapters, certain versions of Africa and Africans have always been admitted into the porous circles of White privilege; that admittance cohering with the function of assuaging anxieties about White vitality. With that history in mind, this chapter takes a sceptical view of the ways in which pluriform, critical, reflexive and agentic African narratives are projected to audiences constructed as White and Western by the agents of popular mediation – i.e., news and culture websites, film, music and so on. The extent to which such agents of popular mediation unconsciously or consciously construct its audiences as White is hard to measure, but is most certainly persistent, albeit uneven. Take, for example, mainstream Hollywood cinema where race has both always been present, but also naturalised to the extent that it has been absent.[1] Phenotypical whiteness and the logics of Whiteness in particular have become taken-for-granted components of Hollywood productions, with an ongoing stream of controversies and campaigns only acting to shed further light on this. The #OscarsSoWhite campaign, launched after the 2016 Oscars ceremony (when no non-white actors were nominated for the second year running) shined a light on a perhaps more obvious lack of phenotypical diversity within mainstream Hollywood and Anglospheric film. That this campaign seemed to be addressed by the victory of a film that explicitly mined particular African-American experiences, *Moonlight*, the following year, did not of course mean that on-screen phenotypical diversity had been solved, much less the racialised logics that underpin film production. Instructive perhaps in terms of illustrating how spaces, in this case film, are made White regardless of who is on screen, is a controversy concerning the actor Matt Damon. Damon was one of three judges on a show called *Project Greenlight*.[2] During a discussion about diversifying the production crew of the film that was being put together on the show, Damon's co-judge, African-American producer Effie Brown, suggested that diversifying the production crew would be an important step in addressing certain problems with racial stereotyping in the characterisation and scripting of the film. Damon's response was first of all to suggest that, 'When we're talking about diversity, you do it in the casting of the film, not in the casting of the crew', and furthermore

---

[1] James Snead, *White Screens/Black Images: Hollywood from the Dark Side*, Colin MacCabe and Cornell West (eds.) (Abingdon, New York, NY, Routledge: 1994/2016).

[2] The premise of the show is as follows: 'Project Greenlight is a documentary series about filmmaking from executive producers Matt Damon and Ben Affleck. Starting with a digital competition on July 24, the series will be a revealing and uncensored look at the challenges facing a first-time director as cameras roll from pre-production and casting through principal photography and post-production', available at: www.hbo.com/project-greenlight accessed on 3 May 2017

that 'if you suddenly change the rules of this competition at the 11th hour, it just seems like you would undermine what the competition was supposed to be about, which is about giving somebody this job based entirely on merit, and leaving all other factors out of it. It's just strictly a film-making competition. I think the whole point of this thing is that you go for the best director, period'.[3] Damon's comments were instructive for two reasons. Firstly, the suggestion that diversity is only important in the casting, and not 'crewing' of a production illustrates the invisibility with which Whiteness operates within debates about diversity. Indeed, the comment makes that invisibility visible, because it speaks to the assumption that race is only something we see, largely phenotypically, and not something that operates socially and culturally, 'behind the camera', so to speak. Secondly and relatedly, Damon went on to suggest that meritocracy is something that functions more or less frictionlessly; the person who gets the job will do so 'based entirely on merit', he claimed. However, just as privilege is socially constructed by intergenerational transfers of wealth, luck, skin colour, gender and so on, so is disadvantage. As such, meritocracy merely acts to mask how some people have privileged access to certain spaces at the expense of others.[4]

Damon subsequently apologised for these comments, but this discussion is important because it shows how, in the cotemporary context, so much popular Anglospheric culture is raced.[5] As such, when people who have been traditionally silenced are suddenly afforded cultural spaces to present themselves and their narratives, it is pertinent to ask why and how this is happening. How have these people and their narratives come to occupy legitimate ground within a White cultural space? Answering this question is not, then, about trying to undermine the professed agency of people who have been collectively and historically denied audiences to hear them express themselves as such. Nor is it to suggest that such opportunities themselves escape

---

[3] All quotes taken from Ben Child, 'Matt Damon apologises for diversity in film gaffe as #damonsplaining trends', *The Guardian*, available at: www.theguardian.com/film/2015/sep/17/matt-damon-damonsplaining-apology-diversity-race, accessed on 3 May 2017.

[4] For a critique of the assumptions that underpin the supposed functionality of meritocracy see: Little, *Against Meritocracy*.

[5] For an older, but still relevant analysis, see Stuart Hall, *The Whites of their Eyes: Racist Ideologies and the Media* (New York, NY: Lawrence and Wishart, 1981).

the racialisation of non-whites, with such individuals more likely to be asked to write about, or speak to, issues concerning 'Black' or 'Asian' issues, racism, etc.[6] Rather, the aim of this chapter is to explore why it is that, in the various political and economic conjunctures of the early twenty-first century, certain forms of African subjectivity have been given increasingly mainstream platforms and audiences in ways that have rarely, if ever, occurred before.

Of course, in part this is a story about technology, diaspora and culture, whereby it has never been easier than now to communicate to a global audience and to find niche and sub-population groups who collectively identify with the protagonist of the communication and who then act to develop a foothold for such communicated narratives among a broader social group. Nonetheless, there remains a politics of both supply and demand here. While it may never have been easier to communicate over distance, through tweets or blogs or Instagram, this remains a technology limited to those privileged with the access and the time to reflect and nurture a series of thoughts and impressions into analysis, prose or poetry. Similarly, such messaging for a global audience must be recorded/translated into a European language, mostly although not always English or French. On the demand side, those footholds in a broader social conversation must navigate through a whole series of majoritarian prejudices and stereotypes concerning Africa and Blackness, as well as majoritarian anxieties concerning White vitality. Such anxieties revolve around the current state of European democracies[7] and social and national unity in the face of disintegrating – and arguably mythical – political, social and cultural consensus.[8]

---

[6] When *The Guardian* newspaper ran an all-black comment and opinion edition as part of Black History Month in 2014, this was presented as an otherwise exceptional opportunity for black writers to publish pieces that went beyond race. See, Chris Elliot, 'The readers' editor on ... showing that black writers can write about far more than race', 2 November 2014, available at: www .theguardian.com/commentisfree/2014/nov/02/guardian-readers-editor-black-writers-write-about-anything, accessed on 11 July 2017.

[7] European Social Survey, 'Europeans' Understandings and Evaluations of Democracy: Topline Results from Round 6 of the European Social Survey', 2012, pp. 12–13, available at: www.europeansocialsurvey.org/permalink/800ea36f-3a8d-11e4-95d4-005056b8065f.pdf, accessed on 24 July 2017.

[8] For instance: British Social Attitudes Survey, 'Key findings: A kind-hearted but not soft-hearted country', No. 34, 2017, available at:

This chapter will argue that a key product of this 'supply and demand' politics is the figure of the Afropolitan, often, but not always, related to the fashion, literary or style icon. This is a figure that has emerged in the early part of the twenty-first century to dominate certain quarters of more progressive and cosmopolitan cultural and social debate, particularly with reference to African culture, film, literature and fashion, and that has been driven by a generation of younger, diasporic, self-defined African authors, bloggers, designers and other social, cultural and economic entrepreneurs. The following pages will offer a working definition of 'the Afropolitan', including an engagement with debates concerning the political and social claims of those who adopt this label, which have not been without controversy. Very briefly, these debates have centred around the degree to which those who adopt this term and make claims from an Afropolitan position are embedded in elitist privilege divorced from the lives of the majority of people of African descent, whether living on the continent or in the diaspora. I will explore these debates more fully in what follows. For now, it is relevant to note that being an author that passes for and is privileged as white,[9] and is structurally privileged in lots

---

www.bsa.natcen.ac.uk/latest-report/british-social-attitudes-34/key-findings/context.aspx?_ga=2.139194163.1267568276.1500897376-1033311816.1500897376, accessed on 24 July 2017.

[9] In keeping with other phenotypically white authors who have written about Whiteness, this seems an appropriate time to briefly reflect on my own positionality (see Dyer, *White*, p. 4; David Roediger, *The Wages of Whiteness: Race and the Making of the American Working Class* [London: Verso, 1992/2007], pp. 4–5). I am light skinned, and of a mixed Sephardic (Jews from Arab countries of Spanish heritage), Mizrachi (Jews historically indigenous to Persia, Babylon and Palestine) and Ashkenazic (Jews from Eastern Europe and Russia) heritage. In my day-to-day life, where I choose not to wear a *kippa* (Jewish skullcap), the colour of my skin means that I am less likely to be stopped and searched by the police, less likely to feel out of place within the largely white academy and largely able to conduct my life with the 'invisible weightless knapsack of assurances, tools, maps, guides, codebooks, passports, visas, clothes, compass, emergency gear, and blank checks' that defines white privilege (McIntosh, 'White Privilege'). Nonetheless, I have always been aware of my Otherness and the degree to which in many contexts I 'pass'. Exceptions to this make my self-consciousness more pronounced. This mostly happens when I am stopped at supermarket checkouts and asked if I am Spanish or Portuguese (My answer: 'No'; their response 'So where are you from then?' My internal monologue: 'Here we go ...') or when I have to make my excuses from professional or social commitments because of religious restrictions that admittedly I choose to opt into (and out of!) but that nonetheless mark my

of other ways too, potentially lends extra degrees of fraughtness to this debate. In light of this, what is of interest to me is not whether Afropolitans are channelling a similar form of elitism often characteristic of broader normative cosmopolitan political theory,[10] but rather how and why this Afropolitan moment has been packaged and mediated for Western societies understood to conform to historical logics of White rationality and vitality, now in decline. In other words, after centuries of largely negative, belittling and more or less overtly racist coverage, why are people of African descent finding such a broad range of artistic and cultural platforms open to them, largely through the subjected figure of the Afropolitan? Does this represent a softening of the Western gaze, or is there a more symbiotic relationship at play that unites anxieties concerning the perpetuation of Whiteness with a certain type of African and/or Black self-expression at this particular point in time? It is to these questions that the rest of this chapter now turns.

Afropolitanism and Its Discontents

In this section I will briefly lay out some definitional terrain concerning the emergence of Afropolitanism as a field of significance in contemporary debates around African agency and subjectivity. The emergence of the Afropolitan subject has not been free of internal contestation. It is, therefore, important to appreciate the contours of these contestations in order to then bear witness to how these have been sanded down and commodified for majoritarian consumption. As this terrain

---

difference. As discussed earlier there has been a close historical relationship between Christianity and Whiteness (Pasha, 'Religion and the Fabrication of Race'). For the structural positioning of Jews as a 'buffer class' in order to make 'ruling classes invisible', see April Rosenblum, 'The past didn't go anywhere: making resistance to antisemitism part of all of our movements', 2007, available at: www.buildingequality.us/prejudice/antisemitism/rosenblum/the-past.pdf, accessed on 11 January 2018.

[10] Examples of contemporary cosmopolitan canonical texts include Daniele Archibugi, *The Global Commonwealth of Citizens: Toward Cosmopolitan Democracy* (Trenton, NJ: Princeton University Press, 2015); David Held, *Cosmopolitanism: Ideals and Realities* (Cambridge: Polity Press, 2010). For criticisms of the ideas contained within these texts as elitist and anti-democratic, see Chantal Mouffe, *On the Political* (London, Routledge, 2005), pp. 90–108; Clive Gabay, *Civil Society and Global Poverty: Hegemony, Inclusivity, Legitimacy* (London: Routledge, 2012), pp. 66–103.

unfolds in the following paragraphs, it will become clear that the vast majority of these debates have taken place beyond the traditional zone of scholarly and academic interrogation – i.e., universities, scholarly publishing houses, etc. Rather, and reflecting the kind of Africa being summoned up through the deployment of the term 'Afropolitan', we find most of these debates occurring in cultural magazines, online blogs and fanzines, literature festivals, cultural reviews, and so on. As such, the 'Afropolitan archive', for want of a better term – i.e., the places where a language and form attached to the Afropolitan moment can make itself known – does not correlate to the traditional (i.e., colonial[11]) conception of an archive. For that, it is no less telling.

In many respects debates around Afropolitanism, whether supportive or otherwise, have been 'audience-generated' in the sense of blurring the line between cultural producers and consumers. As I suggested earlier, this means that making a judgement on Afropolitanism in the context of debates concerning race and racialisation can potentially become extremely problematic. This reinforces the sense, then, in which it is perhaps more important to interrogate the space that has opened for this 'Afropolitan moment' and that has allowed this moment to transcend itself in certain important respects.

This transcendence can be related back to a viral essay written by the cultural commentator Taiye Selasi in 2005 and published online in *The Lip* magazine. Selasi has since commented that 'I'm always loath to say that I coined the term [Afropolitanism], because I know that I heard it somewhere, and then I applied it, like all good writers. But that was powerful enough'.[12] In the original essay, Selasi defined Afropolitans in the following terms:

Like so many African young people working and living in cities around the globe, they belong to no single geography, but feel at home in many. The newest generation of African emigrants, coming soon or collected already at a law firm/chem lab/jazz lounge near you. You'll know us by our funny blend of London fashion, New York jargon, African ethics, and academic

[11] See Mudimbe, *Idea of Africa*; Ann L. Stoler, *Along the Archival Grain: Epistemic Anxieties and Colonial Common Sense* (Princeton, NJ: Princeton University Press, 2010).
[12] Taiye Selasi and Stephanie Sy, 'Taiye Selasi talks to Stephanie Sy', *Al Jazeera*, 19 February 2015, available at: http://america.aljazeera.com/watch/shows/talk-to-al-jazeera/articles/2015/2/19/taiye-selasi-talks-to-stephanie-sy.html, accessed on 11 July 2017.

successes. Some of us are ethnic mixes, e.g. Ghanaian and Canadian, Nigerian and Swiss; others merely cultural mutts: American accent, European affect, African ethos. Most of us are multilingual: in addition to English and a Romantic or two, we understand some indigenous tongue and speak a few urban vernaculars. There is at least one place on The African Continent to which we tie our sense of self: be it a nation-state (Ethiopia), a city (Ibadan), or an auntie's kitchen. Then there's the G8 city or two (or three) that we know like the backs of our hands, and the various institutions that know us for our famed focus. We are Afropolitans: not citizens, but Africans of the world ... What distinguishes this lot and its like (in the West and at home) is a willingness to complicate Africa – namely, to engage with, critique, and celebrate the parts of Africa that mean most to them. Perhaps what most typifies the Afropolitan consciousness is the refusal to oversimplify; the effort to understand what is ailing in Africa alongside the desire to honor what is wonderful, unique. Rather than essentialising the geographical entity, we seek to comprehend the cultural complexity; to honor the intellectual and spiritual legacy; and to sustain our parents' cultures.[13]

Much ink (or its online equivalent) has been spilt over just this excerpt from the essay. For Selasi, and those who admire her positioning, these words represent an opening up of identity, particularly an African as multiple and future-oriented identity that has for so long been refused by a colonial epistemology of state, nation and individualism, an epistemology that by necessity ossifies and nativises all but the privileged White (white and non-white) elite; only they may be cosmopolitan, rootless and cultured, while the non-modern Others remain static, backward and outside of historical time.[14] In this vein the *MsAfropolitan* blogger Minna Salami contends that Afropolitanism can be deployed in order to extract a new sense of being in the world and present alternative images of Africa and Africans that 'speak from the present moment into the future'. In this sense, Salami argues that Afropolitanism is explicitly not an identity, but a 'space exploring what it means to be a person of African heritage in a glocal world ... [It is a space where] ideas of identity are both contested and explored, as well as communicated and expressed'.[15] What distinguishes the Afropolitan

---

[13] Taiye Selasi, 'Bye-Bye Babar', *The Lip*, 3 March 2005, available at: www .thelip.robertsharp.co.uk/?p=76, accessed on 11 July 2017.

[14] Shilliam, *Black Pacific*, p. 4.

[15] Eva Rask Knudsen, Ulla Rahbek, Kwame Anthony Appiah, Emma Dabiri, Minna Salami and Asta Busingye Lyderson, 'The Authors in Conversation with

space from a diasporic space is that it, in theory at least, exists within Africa as well as beyond it. In this sense, Achille Mbembe attempts to foreground histories of migration to, from and within Africa that have long defined the African continent. Where Selasi and Salami focus on 'glocal' Africans, or 'Africans of the World' with their multiple identities, accents, languages and wardrobes, Mbembe seeks to foreground the 'world in Africa' and how this has defined Africa's 'way of belonging to the world' over time.[16] In similar terms, Simon Gikandi has argued for a recognition of two types of Afropolitan; those who, due to their material exclusion, are rendered inadmissible to the clubs and 'chem labs' and, indeed, the territories of the West, but who through their smartphones know about events happening in Europe or the USA sometimes before people living in those places do. These are people who live in and between worlds, but do not physically travel in the same way that the second, more elitist group do, represented by those like Selasi and Salami. For Gikandi, it is the former who are potentially more interesting, while it is the latter who write and are written about.[17]

It has, thus, predominantly been the Selasi-inflected Afropolitanism that has emerged as both a subject of critique and a subject of broader majoritarian consumption. Indeed, Selasi, raised in the USA and the UK by her Ghanaian father and Nigerian mother, herself summed up what Afropolitanism meant to her when she stated: 'Enough with people telling me what I'm not. Enough with people saying, "You're not really American. You're not really black. You're not really British. You're not really Nigerian. You're not really Ghanaian." Enough with the nots. I am this'.[18] Such a conception of Afropolitanism has led some to criticise it for being elitist and out-of-touch with the lived

---

Kwame Anthony Appiah, Emma Dabiri, Minna Salami, and Asta Busingye Lyderson', in Eva Rask Knudsen and Ulla Rahbek (eds.), *In Search of the Afropolitan: Encounters, Conversations and Contemporary Diasporic African Literature* (London, New York, NY: Rowman and Littlefield, 2016), p. 156.

[16] Achille Mbembe, 'Afropolitanism', in Njami Simon and Lucy Durán (eds.), *Africa Remix: Contemporary Art of a Continent* (Johannesburg: Johannesburg Art Gallery, 2007), p. 27.

[17] Eva Rask Knudsen, Ulla Rahbek, and Simon Gikandi, 'The Authors in Conversation with Simon Gikandi', in Eva Rask Knudsen and Ulla Rahbek (eds.), *In Search of the Afropolitan*: Encounters, Conversations and Contemporary Diasporic African Literature (London, New York, NY: Rowman and Littlefield, 2016), pp. 48–9.

[18] Selasi and Sy, 'Taiye Selasi talks to Stephanie Sy'.

daily experiences of many people living in Africa and beyond. For instance, by far the most common form of African migration/African diasporic living concerns those who lack the social and financial capital commonly associated with the Afropolitan subject. These are the office and road cleaners, or hospital orderlies, people who take on low-paid work as an alternative to the joblessness or other forms of privation they may have faced had they stayed in their countries of birth. Are these people Afropolitan? As per Selasi's definition they certainly 'belong to no single geography' and will be multilingual, speaking in 'indigenous tongue and ... a few urban vernaculars'.[19] However, according to some Afropolitan advocates, such low-paid 'Africans of the world' do not qualify as Afropolitans,[20] presumably because they do not engage in the kinds of cultural circuits (the 'law firm[s]/chem lab[s]/jazz lounge[s]') that give the Afropolitan subject its African/post-African identity.

It would be a mistake to treat this debate without any shades of grey. All of the prominent figures in the propagation of the Afropolitan subject/space are fully engaged in the history and present of racial discrimination faced by people of African and other non-white heritages within Africa and beyond. Indeed, this history and present is what self-consciously drives their embrace of Afropolitanism as a means by which to both recognise the African contribution to world-making as well as transcend the racial and territorial categories of Blackness and African-ness, both of which have been historically used to deny people of African descent their humanity and record of/contribution to world-making. There is also a consciousness of the elitist nature of these debates, with Salami writing that 'Afropolitanism is largely shaped by people who have time for ideological ruminations and cultural expression. People who are struggling for food, or fleeing wars, or struggling with other disabling structures, sadly rarely have the luxury to debate ideology, be it feminism, Marxism, socialism'.[21]

---

[19] Selasi, 'Bye Bye Barbar'.
[20] Knudsen, Rahbek, Appiah, Dabiri, Salami, and Lyderson, 'The authors in conversation with Kwame Anthony Appiah, Emma Dabiri, Minna Salami, and Asta Busingye Lyderson', p. 165.
[21] Minna Salami, '32 views on Afropolitanism', *MsAfropolitan*, 7 October 2015, available at: www.msafropolitan.com/2015/10/my-views-on-afropolitanism .html, accessed on 1 December 2016.

Nevertheless, it is notable that the popular aesthetic of the Afropolitan subject to have emerged in majoritarian discourse has been one that conforms to, and confirms, the vitality of White logics of consumerist rationality. This is not the same as arguing that people of African descent should not be expected to be as materialist or consumerist as anyone else. This risks creating the kind of romanticised Africa that pervaded idealisations of the continent in the 1920s. This kind of romanticisation is indeed still apparent in popular depictions of the continent.[22] Addressing this issue of exactly how 'Modern' Africans are allowed to be, Olufemi Taiwo writes, 'It is almost as if an African like me who deliberately embraces Modernity ... must be a dope; someone who is suffering from a pathological dependence on white people as well as a severe case of self-hatred'.[23] It is the argument of this book that Modernity is indeed rooted in colonial history and that the financial capital necessary to be the successful rational self-maximiser of the liberal imagination has been, and continues to be, reliant on oppression and slavery.[24] In other words, the choice to choose this T-shirt or that T-shirt, this kind of tea or that kind of tea, this phone or that phone, continues to rely on the kind of indentured slavery[25] that has underpinned the growth of the consumer market since the sixteenth century when what were then considered luxury goods first appeared in Northern Europe, imported from Caribbean slave plantations.[26] But to argue that this means one particular group of people should reject the material outputs of this historical colonial-Modern process because they have been victimised by it, is to circle around and engage

[22] See for instance Oxfam's 2012 campaign that sought to 'show Africa's potential' and 'make Africa famous' through a series of images that foregrounded images of African natural environment, rather than, for instance, urban landscapes, or even just people. See Oxfam, 'Show Africa's potential not just its problems, says Oxfam', 28 December 2012, available at: www.oxfam .org.uk/media-centre/press-releases/2012/12/show-africas-potential-not-just-its-problems-says-oxfam, accessed on 23 August 2016.
[23] Olufemi Taiwo, *Africa Must be Modern: A Manifesto* (Bloomington, IN: Indiana University Press, 2014), p. xv.
[24] Walter D. Mignolo, 'Delinking', *Cultural Studies*, 21:2, 2007, pp. 449–514; Bhambra, 'Historical Sociology'.
[25] For a comprehensive overview of the prevalence of slavery in contemporary global supply-chains see: www.antislavery.org/includes/documents/cm_docs/2016/p/products_of_slavery_and_child_labour_2016.pdf.
[26] Maria Mies, 'Colonization and Housewifization,' in Rosemary Hennessey and Chris Ingraham (eds.), *Materialist Feminism: A Reader in Class, Difference, and Women's Lives* (Abingdon: Routledge, 1997), pp. 175–85.

in the same kind of 'waiting room'/not-ready-yet racism characteristic of attitudes towards African development in important arenas of
intellectual, public and policy debate over the course of centuries. One
can hold all of this to be true and yet still recognise the colonial and
slave-based dimension of the kind of Modernity Taiwo is seeking to
embrace.

So, the issue that this part of the book takes up, then, is not whether
it is 'okay' for people of African descent to subject themselves as
Afropolitan/colonial-Modern or not. Rather, it is how a particular
aesthetic of Africa has been generated through the emergence of the
Afropolitan subject, which largely does away with the critiques of
racism, discrimination and enforced identitarian politics discussed by
commentators such as Selasi or Salami and, instead, sands this away
and conforms to/confirms the vitality of White logics of consumerist
rationality at a conjuncture when anxiety about such vitality is prevalent (something Chapter 7 explores in greater detail).

This means that, despite the efforts of the Afropolitan commentariat
to 'complicate Africa',[27] what we end up with is just another simplified Africa, packaged up for consumption, rationalised according to
logics of Whiteness. This maps on very closely to similar historical
efforts to negate Africa's plurality, which has been discussed in previous chapters. The major difference between these instances and the
first decades of the twenty-first century is that this is now much more
widespread and Africa being commodified is one in which Whiteness
can be reflected far more clearly than in previous periods. The late Ali
Mazrui saw hope in this, arguing that this century would see the final
phase of 'the historical conceptualization of Africa ... the realization
that the continent is the ancestry of the human species ... and a major
stream in world civilization. A transition occurs ... to the paradigm of
Afrocentricity – and from the Dark Continent to the Garden of Eden.
This final paradigm globalizes Africa itself'.[28] Projecting Africa as a
'Garden of Eden', however, is precisely one of the major ways in which
Africa gets simplified, rather than complicated. Whether it is through
campaigns such as the 'Make Africa Famous' Oxfam initiative (see
note 22) or through volunteerism or 'safari tourism', 'a "traditional

[27] Selasi, 'Bye Bye Barbar'.
[28] Ali Al'Amin Mazrui, 'The Re-invention of Africa: Edward Said, V.Y. Mudimbe
and Beyond', *Research in African Literatures*, 36:3, 2005, p. 71.

Garden of Eden" Africa' speaks to 'the way outsiders would like to see the continent'.[29] And so, as much as Mazrui saw in twenty-first century fascination with the continent a recognition of Africa as a 'major stream in civilization', and as much as this might be the case among the Afropolitan and cosmopolitan elites of the blogosphere and academy, unfortunately this development has an underside – one dominated by anxieties concerning Whiteness whereby Africa and its 'emergence' in global historical time is projected as an affirmation of the mythologised historical genius of Whiteness.

Consuming Afropolitanism

Having argued that it is in the manner of how it is consumed that we must analyse this Afropolitan moment, it is of merit to look towards Afropolitan scholarship as one site where this consuming takes place. This may seem counter-intuitive, but only if we hold that academic scholarship is in some way value-neutral and 'objective', presenting facts rather than constructing narratives of its own. One major title (one of very few at the time of writing) to have been released on Afropolitanism is Eva Rusk Knudsen and Ulla Rahbek's *In Search of the Afropolitan Subject*. Primarily a literary study, the book is also structured around a series of interviews with prominent commentators on the emergence of Afropolitanism as a site of debate, including Kwame Anthony Appiah, Simon Gikandi, as well as online proponents and critics of the concept such as Minna Salami and Emma Dabiri.[30] It is in the book's introduction, however, that the authors' normativity concerning Afropolitanism as a concept and vehicle is most prominent. The two authors are phenotypically white and work in Europe. This is not to say that authors of this appearance and location cannot work on these issues, but with such a heritage it is more than ever incumbent to be reflexive about the privileges brought to bear through sitting with this appearance and location. Put another way, people with lighter skin pigmentation are not 'White' until they uncritically occupy, inhabit and project logics that have been used in order to develop the privilege of people with such phenotypical

---

[29] Bücsher, 'The political economy of Africa's natural resources', p. 143.
[30] For the latter's critique see Emma Dabiri, 'Why I'm not an Afropolitan', *Africa is a Country*, 21 January 2014, available at: www.africasacountry .com/2014/01/why-im-not-an-afropolitan/, accessed on 02 December 2016.

presentations (understood as White) over the past 500 years.[31] And it is these logics that feature in Knudsen and Rahbek's text, in keeping with a post-colonial theoretical intellectual canon that can sometimes stand accused of indulging liberal fantasies of privileged individual rationality/agency.[32]

Several examples of this can be drawn from Knudsen and Rahbek's introduction. For instance, while recognising that transnational mobility is not confined to an inter-continental diaspora, the authors, cognisant that their approach is 'potentially skewed and tipping a balance that ought to be observed' nonetheless foreground 'passages between Africa and the West, and [view] Afropolitan stories from that angle as part of an intercontinental global phenomenon'.[33] As a literary analysis, this move's violence is twofold: first, it self-consciously foregrounds and projects African mobility to the inter-continental. But as a literary analysis – and this next point is borne out by the novels chosen by Knudsen and Rahbek for their analysis – they also reduce this mobility to an elitist, liberal homage of international jet-setting, reminiscent of the figure of the Afropolitan in Selasi's 2005 'Bye Bye Barbar' essay. There are no drowning refugees here, nor low-paid domestic workers, but purely individuals privileged enough to be able to reflect on their identity, lives and relationships and act accordingly. This does not have to be an either-or debate. Refugees and domestic workers might also reflect on their identities, embark on relationships and are, of course, internationally mobile, even if the conditions they exist in dictate that these reflections and relationships are more likely to become truncated and precarious. Nonetheless, what this means is that Knudsen and Rahbek's choice is a false dichotomy, which effectively reduces African mobility to something that looks a lot like the lives and associated problems thought to pervade people living according to White logics and rationalities in Western societies – i.e., identitarian insecurity, crises of faith, and so on. To be fair to Knudsen and Rahbek, despite setting out as they do in their introduction, they do devote a chapter of their

---

[31] Mills, *Racial Contract*, p. 106.
[32] Epifanio San Juan Jr., 'Postcolonialism and the Problematic of Uneven Development', in Crystal Bartolovich and Neil Lazarus (eds.), *Marxism, Modernity, and Postcolonial Studies* (Cambridge: Cambridge University Press, 2002), pp. 221–40.
[33] Eva Rask Knudsen and Ulla Rahbek, 'Opening: In Search of the Afropolitan', in Knudsen and Rahbek, *In Search of the Afropolitan*, p. 5.

book to 'less-fortunate Afropolitans'[34]; but it is the final chapter of the book (bar a brief post-script) and is full of hedges and caveats. So, the 'African ... legal and illegal migrants behind counters of chicken and chip shops ... can be construed as less-fortunate, *possibly vernacular* Afropolitans'.[35] Continuing in this hedged vein, Knudsen and Rahbek argue that such subjects are 'in a manner of speaking' part of the ongoing dialogue that constitutes the Afropolitan moment.[36]

Apart from this late-appearing and highly caveated chapter (one of ten substantive chapters in the book) many of the protagonists in the novels Knudsen and Rahbek discuss are of the privileged cosmopolitan type. They face lack of personal fulfilment in jobs and relationships and crucially possess the financial and/or social capital to do something about this.[37] Reinforcing this sense of elitism is the notable fact that not a single one of Knudsen and Rahbek's interview subjects are based in the African continent. This is not to say that living on the continent of Africa is indicative of where one might sit on the question of Afropolitanism and what it represents, or vice versa.[38] But it nonetheless seems significant and representative of the way Knudsen and Rahbek frame their study that this is the case. Ultimately, Knudsen and Rahbek's framing of, or to adopt their term, 'search for' the Afropolitan subject reinforces the kind of subjectivity only too familiar to a White cosmopolitan gaze that is becoming increasingly anxious about, and disrupted by, the rise of authoritarian right-wing populism and the collapse of economic orthodoxies.

In many ways Knudsen and Rahbek's writing on Afropolitanism is reminiscent of the idealisations of African subjects that have featured in previous chapters. This is not because they conform to racialised tropes of Blackness (they don't) but rather because what they want

---

[34] Eva Rask Knudsen and Ulla Rahbek, 'Less Fortunate Afropolitans, "Lapsed Africans", and Class Conundrums', in Knudsen and Rahbek, *In Search of the Afropolitan*, pp. 265–87.

[35] Ibid., at pp. 286–7, *emphasis added*.

[36] Ibid., at p. 287.

[37] See for instance, Sefi Atta, *A Bit of Difference* (Boston, MA: Interlink Books, 2012).

[38] A report for the news network CNN bears this out, featuring as it does a number of Nigerians, Ghanaians and South Africans talking about Afropolitanism in the terms discussed earlier on in this chapter. See Mark Tutton, 'Young, urban and culturally savvy: Meet the Afropolitans', *CNN*, 17 February 2016, available at: http://edition.cnn.com/2012/02/17/world/africa/who-are-afropolitans/index.html, accessed on 5 December 2016.

to see – 'Afropolitanism ... as a space of inquiry ... a contingent and dialogically constituted way of being African in the world ... through encounters and conversations across difference'[39] – leads them to statements and claims that simply contradict themselves. For instance, when trying to rebut the accusation that Afropolitan literature conforms to White ways of living and being, ignoring the more deprived conditions of some of those who live on and leave the African continent (becoming internationally mobile as a result), Knudsen and Rahbek write that 'this is an overhasty generalisation ... suggest[ing] that Afropolitanism has already petrified into "classic responses" and assigned the thematics of individual identity and travel exclusively to the African "outsider" who does not live on the continent'.[40] The example they deploy to substantiate this claim is Sefi Atta's 2012 novel *A Bit of Difference*, which they argue is a 'realist Afropolitan novel'[41] because much of it is set in Lagos, Nigeria. While this is a novel in which the major protagonist moves back to Lagos from London – thus inverting many other Afropolitan literary tropes of leaving the continent – it begins in an airport arrivals lounge in the United States and remains a story of being liminal and of traversing different spaces and identities from a position of social and economic privilege. Relatedly, in tackling the experience of someone moving *back* to Africa (specifically Nigeria) the novel foregrounds a feature of international mobility much more rarely experienced by many in the African diaspora whose lack of material resources makes their mobility a generally more one-way affair. In that sense, the novel conforms to notions of international mobility that occupy a relatively smooth and unfettered space – as opposed to the life-threatening nature of mobility for economic and conflict refugees – as well as individualism and identitarian anxieties – which the novel is rooted in. Of course, such notions normally define a set of White experiences, generally accorded to people who are phenotypically white. Particularly when it comes to international mobility, people who are not phenotypically white may still expect to face more barriers to travel than their phenotypically white co-travellers. However, this does not make these Afropolitan literary

---

[39] Eva Rask Knudsen and Ulla Rahbek, 'Afropolitanism: A Contested Field and its Trajectories', in Knudsen and Rahbek, *In Search of the Afropolitan*, p. 42.
[40] Knudsen and Rahbek, 'Less Fortunate Afropolitans', p. 8.
[41] Ibid., at p. 9.

tropes less White, given the arguments already presented in various chapters concerning the increasing disconnect between whiteness (skin colour) and Whiteness (access to and reproduction of various social codes and privileges historically understood to belong to phenotypically white people). Again, the point here is not to criticise Atta for writing about these issues, whether they reflect her own personal experiences or not.[42] Rather, the issue is of how such renditions of African agency become popular and popularised in the first place.

Knudsen and Rahbek's book represents one kind of audience ripe for the Afropolitan moment; the liberal-scholarly elite. Here, Afropolitanism is consumed as a means by which to affirm that while right-wing populism grows in the West and illiberal fanaticism and/ or authoritarianism in other parts of the world, the kind of liberal cosmopolitan, 'citizen of the world' project beloved of certain parts of the academy since the end of the Cold War[43] is alive and well among Africans. That this sensibility concerning the onward march of liberal values traverses disciplines and political commitments, from the neo-liberal/neo-realism of Francis Fukuyama's *End of History*[44] to the post-colonial theoretical tradition of Knudsen and Rahbek, where they argue that the messages within Afropolitan literature 'relate directly to the world *we all live in*,'[45] indicates that anxieties about White vitality and the desire to locate self-affirming subjects that can be described as 'African' is not the preserve of one particular political philosophy, be they regressive or progressive.[46] Indeed, in keeping with the other chapters of this book, it is clear here that the Afropolitan moment resonates most with progressive liberal audiences (as we saw in Chapter 4 for example, regressive authors and their audiences might

---

[42] As already discussed, another way of racialising non-white authors is to assume that they can only write about their own raced experiences.

[43] For instance, Archibugi, The Global Commonwealth of Citizens; Held, Cosmopolitanism.

[44] Francis Fukuyama, *The End of History and the Last Man* (New York, NY: Free Press, 1992).

[45] Knudsen and Rahbek, 'Afropolitanism: A Contested Field', p. 42, *emphasis added.*

[46] It is worth reiterating a point made earlier here. Scholars from the post-colonial tradition are unlikely to be enamoured of ideas concerning White supremacy, but this does not mean that, if socialised by the privilege of their skin colour and other structural advantages, they might not nonetheless reproduce logics that privilege modes of being historically attainable largely only to groups of people with lighter skin pigmentation.

share the anxieties of liberal elites, but not their hope that White historical genius might be safeguarded and revitalised by African socialisation into White racial codes).

It is these liberal audiences that have consumed Afropolitanism more broadly beyond the academy and circles of literary critique. The growing prevalence and prominence of African culture, art, food and other commodities within the spheres of White privilege speak to Africa's 'being in the world' that percolates through the Afropolitan literature surveyed by Knudsen and Rahbek. Again, the point here is not to necessarily question the content of the growing numbers of African fashion, food or film festivals, but to put into question the reasons for their growing popularity. For every 'Africa on the Square'[47] (what might a 'Europe on the Square' look like? Or even an 'Asia on the Square'?) there is an 'Africa Utopia', an annual series of talks, workshops, music and performances held at the South Bank centre in London that 'celebrate the arts and culture of one of the world's most dynamic and fast-changing continents'.[48] Clearly one of these events delves deeper and more critically into what is signified when we talk about 'Africa' than the other. The point is, however, that both are manifestations of the post-financial crash era, growing in popularity and centred in a post-imperial metropolitan centre.

Examples of how Africa's 'being in the world' is selectively packaged for majoritarian audiences abound. Fundamentally what we find within many of these instances is a commodification of Africa, all of which represents the ways in which civilisational anxieties and material drivers intertwine and are co-constitutive. African art for instance, has prompted, we are told by an auction-house press release, 'a new scramble for Africa'. It goes on to say that 'Africa is the new China when it comes to art ... The Romans had a phrase for this: "There is always something new out of Africa" ... Today that new thing is art, and the scramble is to acquire it, as the educated view in the capitals of the world is that South African and African Art is a bull market, with one's investment liable to return a handsome profit in the years

---

[47] A one-day annual festival of African food and culture in Trafalgar Square, London. See www.london.gov.uk/events/2016-10-15/africa-square, accessed on 8 December 2016.

[48] Africa Utopia, available at: www.southbankcentre.co.uk/whats-on/festivals-series/africa-utopia, accessed on 23 May 2017.

ahead'.[49] Where this kind of idealisation of Africa – here through its art – maps onto some of the arguments in previous chapters relates to the African subject's precise role in this. Whereas previously Africans had been objectified as romanticised brutes in the 1920s and as perhaps not always-ready individual/de-tribalised 'Moderns' in the 1950s, today Africans are able to take the place of their phenotypically white forebears in making money out of a commodified Africa. This is made apparent when the press release continues, in a moment of reflection on the imperial objectification of the continent, that:

Picasso and many of his contemporary artists saw in Africa the wellsprings of their own creative drive. They acknowledged Africa's creative genius and their work pays homage and tribute to it. Now the African artists are claiming for themselves some of that acclaim and some of the kinds of sums earned by those master artists whose names are household words.[50]

As we saw in Chapter 2, Picasso (along with many of his contemporaries) during his 'primitive' stage, produced art that objectified Africa, with this objectification emerging as a key demarcation of African 'difference'.[51] In the post-crash years, Africa has emerged, instead, as a site where similarities may be found, but only those that conform to, and confirm, the universality and vitality of White social codes concerning individuality and the commodification of creativity. We see these kinds of codes reinforced repeatedly. In a much-shared piece from 2012, 'Young, urban and culturally savvy: Meet the Afropolitans', journalist Mark Tutton proclaims that 'Afropolitanism implies a certain type of cool', where 'coolness' becomes a recurring motif in how this Afropolitan moment is commodified for majoritarian Western audiences.[52] 'Chic Afropolitan shopper[s]' according to *Vogue* magazine, 'are never too far from their must-have handbags',[53] whereas fashion

[49] Barnebys UK Press Release, 'Spotlight is on African Art – Growth Greater than Gold: Barnebys, the World's Largest Art and Auction Search Engine, Notes Tenfold Growth in Value of African Contemporary Art', 21 September 2016.
[50] Ibid.
[51] Mudimbe, *The Idea of Africa*, pp. 56–60.
[52] Tutton, 'Young, urban and culturally savvy'.
[53] Marjon Carlos, 'Inside Nigeria's It-Bag Obsession', *Vogue*, 2 November 2016, available at: www.vogue.com/13498878/nigeria-lagos-fashion-and-design-week-prada-gucci-hermes-chanel-accessories-alara/ accessed on 5 December 2016.

shows deploy Afropolitanism (which, according to *Elle* magazine's write-up of Cape Town Fashion Week, is 'a local buzz word') in order to 'boost upscale African fashion round the world'.[54] These are, of course, incredibly superficial representations of 'African culture' (itself an incredibly problematic term). And yet, for all the protestations that Afropolitanism is 'a conceptual space in which African heritage realities are both interrogated and understood with the tools and nuances of modern-day globalisation',[55] it is these kinds of representations, channelled through a variety of fashion features, food, film and literature festivals and not the reflexive, self-interrogating narratives of authors and popular culture bloggers, that are entering the mainstream of majoritarian and metropolitan White discourse in the West.

From Afropolitanism to 'Africa Rising'

In this chapter I have sought to lay out the contextual backdrop through which Africa has been refracted in Western societies since the financial crash of 2007–8. This refraction has taken place not via the medium of skin colour, but rather through certain logics that conform to, and confirm, the vitality of Whiteness. As logics of Whiteness spread across the globe, they are increasingly being reflected back to and through societies and discourses constructed as phenotypically white as a means by which to confirm the perpetuation of mythologised historical achievements commonly associated with White originary genius. This is, of course, nothing new, but the regularity and volume with which a White-refracted Africa appears in Western cultural and political discourse speaks to the ways in which those dynamics are noted in earlier chapters, whereby slowly but surely Whiteness and what it means has been disentangled from skin colour, have become increasingly dominant in the ways in which Africa gets packaged for majoritarian consumption in some quarters. This does not mean that other versions of Africa do not persist in majoritarian public discourse; versions that conform more closely to conventional

---

[54] Alice Pfeiffer, 'A Closer Look at South Africa's "Afropolitan" Chic', *Elle*, 1 August 2014, available at: www.elle.com/fashion/news/a25076/a-closer-look-at-south-africas-afropolitan-chic/, accessed on 5 December 2016.

[55] Salami, '32 views on Afropolitanism'.

racist stereotypes of the continent.[56] Rather, it is simply that the more positive and cosmopolitan narratives to have emerged in the years since the financial crash are similarly embedded in problematic tropes that ahistoricise and depoliticise the continent, mainly because in both negative and positive accounts of Africa there is a fundamental inability to see beyond Whiteness as the bar against which peoples and cultures should be set. Tzvetan Todorov argued of Christopher Columbus that his inability to appreciate diversity among the Indian peoples of North America was a result of 'the failure to recognise the Indians, and the refusal to admit them as a subject having the same rights as oneself, but different. Columbus has discovered America, but not the Americans'.[57] The very same might be said of the manner by which Whiteness sees and needs Africa in the post-crash period. And as much as this has been a cultural phenomenon, it has also, and perhaps more coherently, been a political and economic one too, something that, in partnership with an analysis of the anxieties driving such idealisations of the continent, is explored in Chapter 7.

---

[56] See for instance the following by the *The Guardian's* Africa correspondent Jason Burke: 'Has Africa had its fill of Strongmen?', *The Guardian*, 11 December 2016, available at: www.theguardian.com/world/2016/dec/11/africa-strongmen-angola-dos-santos-zimbabwe-mugabe-uganda-sudan, accessed on 20 December 2016. Despite finishing with a map that reveals that only seven of Africa's 54 sovereign territories conform to whatever definition of 'strongman rule' is being deployed by the newspaper's relevant editorial team, the article nonetheless rests on a set of generalisations concerning liberal democracy and its function in Africa. For a critique of such tropes see: Alison Ayers, 'Beyond the imperial narrative: African political historiography revisited' in Branwen Gruffydd-Jones (ed.), *Decolonizing International Relations* (Lanham, MD: Rowman and Littlefield, 2006).

[57] Todorov, *The Conquest of America*, p. 49.

7 | *Africa Rising, Whiteness Falling*

Just over a decade separated the two visions of Africa in Figure 7.1. In some ways they were starkly different and yet in others they channelled distinct continuities. On the one hand, it is impossible to escape the staggeringly different prognoses for this place, Africa, summoned up by the two front covers of *The Economist* magazine. The image from 2000, with its black backdrop and conjoining of the map of the continent with an image of a young man resting a rocket launcher on his shoulder, was a clear message to the magazine's audience that Africa was a place beset by violence and death. As its headline stated, the situation was 'hopeless'. For those with an interest in how Africa has been imagined in Western imaginaries since the European enlightenment, here was an obvious rendition of Georg Hegel's infamous assertions that Africa was 'still involved in the conditions of mere nature,[1] "existing" ... beyond the day of history'.[2] With its dark backdrop and violent foreground, in this image the entirety of the continent – with all of its regional and sub-national differences – was nothing but a nihilistic swamp of pre-modernity.

The image to the right of *The Economist's* 2011 front cover is seemingly very different. It is colourful, joyful and optimistic. A child runs with a kite across an empty vista. The sun is rising, its rays poking up into the early morning sky. Like the sun, Africa too is 'rising'. Just a little more than a decade after the 'Hopeless Continent' front cover, it was the publication of this edition of *The Economist* that stimulated the project presented in this book and drew me into exploring the broader literature and set of sensibilities that had emerged and cohered around the conclusion that this was 'Africa's Moment'.[3] And yet, although aesthetically different, this second image also channelled

[1] Georg Hegel, *The Philosophy of History* (New York, NY: Dover Publications, 1837/1956), p. 99.
[2] Ibid., at p. 91.
[3] Severino and Ray, *Africa's Moment*.

(a)

Figures 7.1a and 7.1b Two visions of Africa, 2000 versus 2011 (images used with permission from *The Economist* Newspaper Limited, 13 May 2000 and *The Economist* Newspaper Limited, 3 December 2011)
Notes: The Economist Newspaper Limited, 'The Hopeless Continent', London, 13 May 2000; The Economist Newspaper Limited, 'Africa Rising', London, 03 December 2011.

Figures 7.1a and 7.1b (Continued)

some problematic ideas about a place called 'Africa' – in this case represented by the rainbow-coloured flag which is probably a reference to South Africa. Indeed, this is where one could begin picking the image apart. If Africa is not simply one country, then South Africa is certainly not a whole continent, and what happens there is not necessarily representative of anywhere else. More symbolically, the image of the child, running across an empty territory, is just as evocative of historical renditions of Africa as the 2000 front cover was, in this sense speaking to Africa's supposed 'emptiness' and the childlike nature of its peoples. And if this seemingly more hopeful, optimistic and positive image of Africa was also rooted in old and racialised ideas about the continent, then how far was it actually possible for similarly positive coverage to escape such stereotypes when embedded in anxieties concerning Western politics, economies and societies, and, concomitantly, White vitality?

This is the question that this chapter will explore, building off the arguments of the previous chapters that sought to explore the manner by which Whiteness as a set of social codes has become dislocated from skin colour in important (although not all) respects. In particular, this chapter follows in Chapter 6's footsteps with its insistence that contemporary fascination with African culture, literature and – in this chapter – politics and economy, affects a sanding down of events in the continent in order to hold a positive mirror image up to a White historical genius that those holding the mirror fear would otherwise be in terminal decline.

This chapter firstly and briefly introduces the broader 'Africa Rising' narrative that has emerged since the 2007–8 financial crash and then establishes the highly anxious and idealised–stereotyped renditions of Africa and Africans that have emerged in these debates. Next, the chapter will explore the anxieties concerning Whiteness that underpins much of the 'Africa Rising' rhetoric. In keeping with the rest of the book, this is an argument that suggests that material explanations alone cannot provide a full explanation of why such a narrative has emerged when it has,[4] nor how this narrative discursively relates to previous iterations of Afro idealisation. The chapter will end with a consideration of some of the affective and biopolitical elements of

---

[4] Briefly, such explanations would suggest that Africa is here serving as a 'spatial fix' for a crisis of capitalism in the West – David Harvey, 'Globalization and the "Spatial Fix"', *geographische revue* 2, 2001, pp. 23–30. Given that the Africa Rising narratives we are dealing with here have emerged since the 2007–8 financial crash, this is a convincing argument. However, the chapter will suggest this can only provide a partial picture of what has been driving these narratives.

'Africa Rising' narratives as well as the ways in which such agendas are countered by those subjected as 'African'.

Exploring Post-Crash 'African Rising' Debates

Although in 2000 the World Bank published a report entitled *Can Africa Claim the 21st Century?*,[5] this stands out as a highly unusual publication for its time (see *The Economist* front cover that opens this chapter for a much more indicative representation) with the question mark ending the title serving as an important limitation on the degree to which Africa was thought to be transcending the West politically and economically. It is really only after the 2007–8 financial crash that we begin to see a sustained and broad narrative about Africa's rise. Multi-lateral organisations, major investment consultancies, government departments, government advisors, policy informers – representatives of all of these groups came out in the wake of the crash with positive proclamations of Africa's rise. No such broad narrative existed prior to this.

While at the turn of the century we saw celebrations of Africa's 'Renaissance', most famously by Thabo Mbeki,[6] then South Africa's vice-President, these were mainly confined to members of various African governing elites, seeking to attract foreign investment and to fulfil their hegemonic aspirations on the continent.[7] Importantly, the African renaissance narrative was largely missed by the main-stream Western news and opinion-forming organisations, such as *The Economist* with its contemporaneous 'Hopeless Continent' front cover in 2000.

Post-crash 'Africa Rising' narratives then were of an entirely different qualitative nature to these earlier proclamations of an African renaissance. Where the former were almost entirely ignored by main-stream political and economic commentators outside of Africa, the post-crash narrative has been of a far more diffuse nature and less driven by key African governments. It, of course, remains the case that African governments buy into this narrative, however, which provides

---

[5] No author, *Can Africa Claim the 21st Century?* (Washington, DC: World Bank, 2000) available at: www.siteresources.worldbank.org/INTAFRICA/Resources/complete.pdf, accessed on 22 August 2017.
[6] Mbeki, 'The African Renaissance Statement'.
[7] Ajulu, 'Thabo Mbeki's African Renaissance'.

extraversionary opportunities for investment and personal prestige/ national development. Just one example of this would be the obvious prestige which accrued to the government of Mozambique for hosting the 2014 International Monetary Fund 'Africa Rising' conference,[8] a country which, if 'rising', nonetheless displays a national poverty rate which remained almost static (at over 54 per cent) between 2002 and 2009[9] and where life-expectancy in 2014 remained hovering at just over 50 years of age.[10]

This post-crash narrative differs very much from the coverage of the continent that was prominent even as recently as the early 2000s and 1990s, when very few in mainstream Anglospheric academia and the media were talking in terms of Africa's 'agency',[11] 'moment',[12] or that it was 'emergent'.[13] Most *fin de siècle*, popular, politico-economic analysis of Africa was distinctly pessimistic. Much more common at that time was the talk of Africa's 'new barbarism' and 'coming anarchy',[14] of the continent being, as we have seen, 'hopeless'. The next section will explore these more recent narratives in greater depth.

For now, as I alluded to in the previous chapter, it is important to note that post-crash 'Africa Rising' narratives are far from being dominant in how the continent is narrated and represented in Western societies.[15] Furthermore, the optimistic scholarly-policy texts referenced

---

[8] See www.africa-rising.org/index.htm, accessed on 25 February 2015.

[9] See www.data.worldbank.org/country/mozambique, accessed on 9 March 2014.

[10] United Nations, Human Development Report 2014, 'Sustaining Human Progress: Reducing Vulnerabilities and Building Resilience. Explanatory note on the 2014 Human Development Report composite indices for Mozambique', available at: www.hdr.undp.org/sites/all/themes/hdr_theme/country-notes/ MOZ.pdf, accessed on 22 June 2015.

[11] Harman and Brown, *African Agency*.

[12] Severino and Ray, *Africa's Moment*.

[13] Rotberg, *Africa Emergent*.

[14] Robert Kaplan, 'The Coming Anarchy: How Scarcity, Crime, Overpopulation, Tribalism, and Disease are Rapidly Destroying the Social Fabric of Our Planet', *The Atlantic*, 1994, available at: www.theatlantic.com/magazine/ archive/1994/02/the-coming-anarchy/304670/, accessed on 3 July 2017.

[15] Coverage of the West African Ebola crisis is one example, which included the widely-read US news publication Newsweek releasing an edition fronted simply by a picture of a monkey (see: Gerard Flynn, and Susan Scutti, 'Smuggled Bushmeat Is Ebola's Back Door to America', 29 August 2014, available at: www.newsweek.com/2014/08/29/smuggled-bushmeat-ebolas-back-door-america-265668.html, accessed on 05 September 2015). This was not unexceptional; disease and race, specifically Blackness, have a long history

above number in the tens rather than hundreds of titles; the literature is not particularly theoretically or historically informed, cherry
picking convenient statistics and events to build a narrative of Africa's
growing political and economic significance. The claims found in this
literature have garnered significant backlashes[16] and given the bursting
of Africa's commodities bubble already appear, at the time of writing,
out of date. And yet, the very fact of the faddishness of these forms
of representation begs two questions: firstly, why did this narrative
of Africa's 'rise' emerge when it did, and secondly and relatedly, why
did it become – and in some senses still continues to be – so pervasive, across political, economic, policy and popular culture sites?
The International Monetary Fund held its 'Africa Rising' conference
in 2014; Jean-Michel Severino and Oliver Ray's 'Africa's Moment'
appeared being read by one of the main protagonists in the popular
Netflix drama *House of Cards*, while mainstream popular journals
have continued to produce coverage that popularises the notion and
the narrative of Africa's rise.[17]

We can witness the contingent and paternalistic nature of post-crash
Africa Rising narratives through a reflection on what happens when
those subjectified as 'Africans'[18] act in ways contrary to ethnocentric

---

of being intertwined in the Western imagination (see, for instance, Susan
Sontag, *AIDS and its Metaphors* (New York, NY: Farrar, Straus, Giroux,
1999); T. Adeyanju Charles, *Deadly Fever: Racism, Disease and a Media Panic*
(Blackpoint, NS: Fernwood Publishing, 2010).

[16] Dulani, Mattes, and Logan, 'After a Decade of Growth in Africa'; Taylor,
Africa Rising?

[17] *The Economist* for instance has continued to publish positive coverage of the
continent.

[18] As at other points throughout this book, it is interesting to reflect on the
blurred lines of distinction between constructs of race and class that apply to
the category 'African'. It would be hard to argue that figures such as former
UN Secretary General Kofi Annan, or billionaire entrepreneur Mo Ibrahim,
are subjected to the same demands and interventions as those rendered
'African' (and everything that it signifies i.e., proclivities for violence and
sexual irresponsibility, uncivility, etc. [see for instance, Penny Griffin, 'The
World Bank, HIV/AIDS and Sex in Sub-Saharan Africa: A Gendered Analysis
of Neoliberal Governance', *Globalizations*, 8:2, 2011, pp. 229–48]) by the
historical ethnocentric and Eurocentric mythologisation of the continent.
Indeed, this further reinforces the ways in which race has become something
that is coded into certain forms of behaviour and being, rather than one
simply resting on skin colour, although as the journalist Gary Younge has
eloquently argued, the latter remains crucial; it is hard for instance to imagine
a Black man being elected president of the United States with the same

standards of peaceful conduct which derive from a mythologised Western past where violence is viewed as an aberration[19] and where explanations of 'unacceptable' African behaviour quickly resort to intrinsic tribalist or brutalist tropes. For instance, the initial reticence of international and bilateral donors to criticise Paul Kagame's regime in Rwanda, for fear of re-opening the 'tribal' box, could be understood as an evident case of the resort to brutalism in understanding conflicts in Africa rather than looking to legacies of inequality derived from the colonial period or regional geopolitics.[20] Indeed, this is another good example of how the subjects of Afro-idealisation can extravert such attitudes to their own ends. Although the situation is now beginning to shift, Paul Kagame's ability to evade international opprobrium for so long[21] has, in part, been predicated on his ability to sell Rwanda as an African 'success story'[22] that fits neatly with celebrations of the continent's rise among the policy-informers and analysts featured in this chapter and that coheres to standards of politico-economic performance, including high economic growth and regular elections, reflective of a mythologised White historical genius.

Thus, it is that Africa 'rises' when subjected Africans act according to White norms and is 'hopeless' when they do not. It is, though, perhaps unsurprising that donor governments and international organisations idealise Africans when they appear to be cohering to preferred political and economic norms, and denigrate them when they are not. The point, however, is how ephemeral these idealisations have been and how related they have been to conventional historical Western intellectual

---

record of adultery, misogyny and children fathered with different partners as Donald Trump (see Gary Younge, 'Being a Black Man in White America: A Burden Even Obama Couldn't Escape', available at: www.theguardian.com/us-news/2017/jan/17/obama-legacy-black-masculinity-white-america, accessed on 26 January 2017).

[19] Richard Reid, *Warfare in African History* (Cambridge: Cambridge University Press, 2012), p. 147.

[20] Mahmood Mamdani, *When Victims Become Killers: Colonialism, Nativism, and the Genocide in Rwanda* (Princeton, NJ: Princeton University Press, 2002).

[21] In a remarkable passage in 2013 Robert Rotberg records that, despite the kidnappings, murder and repression of political opponents 'which *have* happened' (*emphasis added*), Kagame 'remains a visionary with a high order of analytical intelligence' who has brought 'real material and spiritual gains to Rwandans' – *Africa Emerges*, p. 214.

[22] Danielle Beswick, 'Genocide and the Politics of Exclusion: The Case of the Batwa in Rwanda', *Democratisation*, 18:2, 2010, pp. 490–511.

and popular tropes about African brutality. Therefore, far from being an antithesis to the more familiarly racist tropes about the continent, the subsequent sections will illustrate that contemporary idealisations of Africa, in fact, correspond to such tropes, drawing on a pattern (hopefully now familiar) of myths and standards generated in contexts of systemically White supremacy that have produced knowledge about Africa in the past. As I suggested in Chapter 1, while an effort to resite Western capitalism to provide a 'spatial fix' for Western over-accumulation[23] plays a role in all of this, the tone of much of the texts and proclamations that feature in this chapter are suggestive of a deeper set of anxieties that transcend purely material concerns and are, in fact, racial. It is these broader anxieties that the next section considers.

The Anxieties of Post-Crash 'Africa Rising' Narratives: It's (not all) the Economy, Stupid!

Despite differences in imagined audience and disciplinary and professional background, post-crash idealisations of Africa projected a set of political and economic ideas about, and constructions of, 'Africa' that cohered to the anxiety/idealisation nexus that began to emerge through Modernisation Theory, which the book began to discuss in Chapter 4. It is, for instance, noteworthy to consider the role of 2007–8 financial crash in contributing to the production of these idealisations – and not purely in a material and economic sense.

The idealisations of Africa contained within the pages of current affairs magazines and the books written by business and policy experts in the shadow of the 2007–8 financial crash appeared to be based, at least in part, on anxieties about the sustenance of Western economic, political and social models – all of which, as was explored in Chapter 1, cohere around practices historically associated with socio-economically privileged people who have been phenotypically white. *The Economist* magazine, for example, reported that 'Investors in Africa are buying a big-picture story of progress ... given the troubles in large parts of the rich world, many will feel there is a lot more to gain than to lose'.[24] The slew of investment guides to Africa that

---

[23] Harvey, 'Globalization and the "Spatial Fix"'.
[24] The Economist, 'The Hottest Frontier: Strategies for Putting Money to Work in a Fast-Growing Continent', 6 April 2013, available at: www.economist.com/printedition/2013-04-06, accessed on 30 July 2013.

proliferated in this period[25] might also be seen in this light. These breathless celebrations of Africa's politico-economic emergence can be read as a desire to seek vindication of 'the Western Way' which detaches White genius from phenotypical whiteness and the West, understood in territorial terms as occupying a place experiencing the very opposite of what is being claimed to be happening in Africa – i.e., low growth rates, social upheaval and geopolitical uncertainty. In short, post-crash idealisations of Africa saw in the continent's supposed rise, a validation and hope for the perpetuation of a mythologised White past, specifically in the emergence of an African homo economicus. This illustrates the ways in which post-crash idealisations of Africa's 'rise' had both material, but also socio-psychological, underpinnings.

It is arguably in this light that Severino and Ray spoke to the underlying anxieties concerning White vitality driving a fascination with African numbers and bodies, when they contrasted Africa's 'demographic dynamism' with 'our sluggish European societies'.[26] Similarly, Robert I. Rotberg writes of Africa's 'demographic surge' and what this could mean for African productivity,[27] while Vijay Mahajan contrasted Africa's booming population with Europe's, which 'in contrast, is ageing rapidly'.[28] One might argue that this simply betrays a materialist impulse to re-site capitalist accumulation away from the West. African demographic youth, their labour and consumerism, will provide the vigour required to reboot the global economy. And yet there is a distinctly racial undertone to these anxieties. For instance, anxieties about ageing European societies and Africa's 'demographic dynamism' do not map onto the realities of European and Western demography in a territorial sense. Racially, however, these anxieties make more sense, for it is largely those demographic groups that fit a White stereotype (to the exclusion of, for instance, phenotypically white Eastern European immigrant groups in Europe, as well as other more obviously non-white immigrant communities) that are ageing and producing less children.[29] In other words, it isn't that Europe and the West

---

[25] Mahajan, *Africa Rising*; Mataen, *Africa*; Robertson, '*The Fastest Billion*'.
[26] Severino and Ray, *Africa's Moment*, p. 1.
[27] Rotberg, *Africa Emerges*, p. 12.
[28] Mahajan, *Africa Rising*, p. 128.
[29] For overall statistical data see: 'Population Structure and Aging', EuroStat, available at: www.ec.europa.eu/eurostat/statistics-explained/index.php/Population_structure_and_ageing, accessed on 1 March 2017; for predictions

are experiencing demographic decline, but some phenotypically white groups therein are. In addition, these anxieties are incredibly ephemeral. Not even twenty years before these claims were being made, Robert Kaplan was infamously using very similar figures of African demographic growth and European demographic decline to argue that Africa represented a barbaric threat to world order – a 'coming anarchy'.[30] Arguably, this fascinated idealisation of African demography is related not simply to the demographic decline of some phenotypically white groups, but economic and political decline in the West more broadly, just as Kaplan's more self-evidently racialised tropes concerning Africa in the 1990s was underpinned by post-Cold War triumphalism concerning the liberal political and economic project.[31]

These kinds of anxieties drove broader geopolitical and economic concerns that patterned proclamations of Africa's rise. High profile speeches by then-President Francois Hollande of France and former Prime Minister of the United Kingdom Tony Blair concerning Africa's place in the international order, underline this point. These speeches were primarily Afro-centric. They did not contain long reflections on the state of Western economies and societies and yet, nevertheless, anxieties about the vitality of these economies and societies slipped through. Of course, Hollande exemplifies a Francospheric, rather than Anglospheric, set of attitudes, histories, prejudices and so on. However, the greater convergence between 'spheres' of history and culture characteristic of the post-Cold War era is perhaps most prominent among governing and capitalist elites[32] and, as such, Hollande's pronouncements in a highly billed 2012 speech at the Senegalese Parliament

---

of aging among ethnic minority communities in the UK that shows how many of these groups continue to illustrate larger, younger demographic characteristics, see Nat Lievesley, 'The Future Ageing of the Ethnic Minority Population of England and Wales', Runnymede Trust, 2010, available at: www .runnymedetrust.org/uploads/publications/pdfs/TheFutureAgeingOfTheEthnic MinorityPopulation-ForWebJuly2010.pdf, accessed on 1 March 2017.

[30] Kaplan, 'The Coming Anarchy'. This in itself can be seen as drawing on an older interwar genealogy of anxieties (discussed in Chapter 2) concerning the demographic threat of the 'darker races' to be found in the scientifically racist work of those such as Lothrup Stoddard.

[31] Hobson, *The Eurocentric Conception of World Politics*, p. 286; See also Cox, 'Is the United States in Decline Again?'

[32] Leslie Sklair, *The Transnational Capitalist Class* (Oxford: Wiley-Blackwell, 2001).

in Dakar can provide insights similar to those gleaned from more
squarely Anglospheric figures.

It is interesting to compare this speech to that of his immediate predecessor, Nicolas Sarkozy's, who gave a similarly billed speech (one
that would supposedly reset France-Africa relations), also in Dakar,
at the city's university in July 2007. That speech, just months before
the breaking news of the global financial crisis, was criticised for its
colonial paternalism,[33] containing passages that rendered the continent as out-of-time and stuck in its own repetitive self-referentialism.[34]
Hollande's speech was notable for its change of tone, no doubt driven
by the vociferous criticism of his predecessor's 2007 speech[35] – and
perhaps explaining the decision to revisit the country for the former's
speech. In Hollande's speech, delivered to the Senegalese parliament in
2012, he proclaimed that Africa's role was 'to give this world a more
human purpose, to take your place, to shoulder your responsibility'
before going on to say that 'no global challenge can be tackled without Africa. All the essential responses already involve your continent:
the economy, raw materials, the environment, energy, global governance'. Africa was 'excellently placed to be, tomorrow, the continent of
growth, development and progress'.[36]

Former UK Prime Minister Tony Blair deployed Africa as one of his
'legacy' projects, via his Africa Governance Initiative. During a speech
on a 'New Approach to Africa' in 2012, Blair hinted at the geopolitical
concerns motivating some elements of contemporaneous idealisations

[33] Mbembe, 'Nicolas Sarkozy's Africa'.
[34] The following passages are indicative: 'The tragedy of Africa is that the
African has not fully entered into history ... Africa's challenge is to enter to
a greater extent into history ... Africa's problem is to stop always repeating,
always mulling over, to liberate itself from the myth of the eternal return ...
Africa's problem is that it lives the present too much in nostalgia for a lost
childhood paradise'. See: No author, 'The Unofficial English Translation of
Sarkozy's Speech', available at: www.africaresource.com/essays-a-reviews/
essays-a-discussions/437-the-unofficial-english-translation-of-sarkozys-
speech?showall=&limitstart=, accessed on 3 July 2017.
[35] See for instance: No author, 'Africans Still Seething over Sarkozy Speech',
Reuters, 5 September 2007, available at: www.uk.reuters.com/article/uk-africa-
sarkozy-idUKL0513034620070905, accessed on 3 July 2017; Mbembe,
'Nicolas Sarkozy's Africa'.
[36] Francois Hollande, 'Speech by M. François Hollande, President of the
Republic, to the National Assembly of Senegal', 12 October 2012, available
at: www.uk.ambafrance.org/President-Hollande-s-keynote, accessed on 3 July
2012.

of African demography, politics and economy when he drew attention to the fact that Chinese investment was outstripping Western investment and that 'the stellar rise of China on the continent of Africa' represented 'real issues ... for concern'.[37] Two years earlier, Blair had, similarly to Hollande, spoken of Africa as 'a strategic interest for us ... Security, resources, food, water: you name it and we have an interest in how Africa develops'.[38] China's post-millennial interest in Africa, alongside that of India, Emirati States and Brazil has in many ways matched that of the West's, and, as we can see from Blair's statement, has been a feature of the geopolitical anxieties that have patterned Western analysis of Africa. What is striking about these states' engagements with Africa is the extent to which they have recreated the kind of resource and land-grabbing characteristic of the European imperial phase,[39] but are absent of the kinds of racial anxieties that characterise contemporary Western proclamations of Africa's rise.[40] And so, while the actions of these states might be recreating important historical (imperialistic) and ideological (neo-liberal) features of Western engagements with Africa, they differ in, and thus render more clearly, the racial anxieties that have driven important components of post-crash Western idealisations of the continent.

Western geopolitical concerns overlap with economic ones. A Goldman Sachs' report argues that 'failure to invest now will see others rush in',[41] and that, again, 'Africa has a major role to play in resolving the world's commodity, food and labour constraints in the near, medium and long term'.[42] Taken together, these geopolitical and economic anxieties point to the pendulum-like way with which places called 'the West' and 'Africa' get imagined, underpinned by anxieties

---

[37] Tony Blair, 'A New Approach to a New Africa' Tony Blair Africa Governance Initiative, 19 March 2012, available at: www.africagovernance.org/africa/news-entry/a-new-approach-to-a-new-africa/, accessed on 17 March 2014.

[38] Tony Blair, 'Speech Text: Tony Blair: Making Government Work Will Transform Africa', Speech at Center for Global Development, 17 December 2010, available at: www.cgdev.org/article/speech-text-tony-blair-making-government-work-will-transform-africa, accessed on 3 July 2017.

[39] Padraig Carmody, *The New Scramble for Africa* (Cambridge: Polity Press, 2011), Chapters 3, 4 and 8.

[40] See for instance, in the case of China, Deborah Brautingam, *The Dragon's Gift: The Real Story of China in Africa* (Oxford: Oxford University Press, 2009), pp. 1–12; Chapter 11.

[41] Goldman Sachs, 'Africa's Turn'.

[42] Ibid., at p. 3.

concerning White vitality, as refracted through economy and politics. As we have seen in previous chapters, this radical shifting occurs simply because of the hard work required to maintain enough evidence to sustain the various idealisations that we have seen are inherent to Western imaginaries of Africa.

And yet, as has been argued with reference to post-crash idealisations about Africa in this section, it is not simply that anxiety undermines optimism concerning the perpetuation of White historical genius, for anxiety also drives this optimism in a self-reinforcing loop. In other words, an idealised fantasy of Africa is constructed to address anxieties concerning Whiteness as much as these anxieties themselves constantly act to undermine White self-confidence – thus necessitating the construction of further idealised 'Africas'.

Africa Rising (Self-Mythologisation)

Of course, being anxious about the supposed decline of White vitality presupposes that there was some sort of political and economic golden age when a White Europe was in flush, autonomously generating wealth and universal political ideals devoid of the material and ideational influence of other regions, colonised or not. 'Africa Rising' texts betray this self-mythologisation through perpetuating a discourse of White historical genius. Just one example of how contemporary praise for Africans can quickly bleed into instructions for how they should govern themselves – and which betrays a sense of historical White institutional genius – can be found in the launch of Tony Blair's Africa Governance Initiative, where he proclaimed that:

> [T]here is a new generation of leaders in politics, business, and civic society who don't simply have a new competence about how they approach their tasks; but a new attitude, a new frame of thinking, a new way of looking at their own situation ... The biggest obstacle to Africa's development is governance ... This is not only about transparency ... It is also about effective government ... the new Africa needs a new approach from African leaders.[43]

The ability to make such pronouncements undoubtedly rests on the certainty that White historical genius offers a model of politics and

---

[43] Blair, 'A New Approach to a New Africa'.

governance that has 'been there and done that'. Contemporary ideal-isations about Africa thus rest on a powerful feature of White ethno-centrism, namely, that as much as it creates myths about the objects of its attention, it simultaneously creates myths about the provenance of White political and economic excellence (incubated in the West) even if, in line with the previous section on anxiety, these are increasingly becoming understood to be historical and failing.

This celebration of a mythologised Western history is held up, as Alison Ayers argues, as a universal standard whereby those who trumpet the importance and growth of liberal democracy in Africa[44] have sought to turn particular Western histories, sanitised of their own often-violent constitutive elements, into 'turnkey institutional import[s]'.[45] A particular idea of Africa is thus summoned, based on a selective reading of elections and multi-partyism,[46] to reflect and affirm this mythologised democratic Western past cleansed of the very colonial violence that made limited forms of democracy and economic redistribution in the West, for a brief period, possible.[47]

So, a myopically viewed African present is constructed and an image of a mythologised and racialised Western past is sustained. We see this at play within the at times celebratory, at times cautious, idealisations expressed about the state of African democracies where Steven Radelet, for instance, talks approvingly about how more African countries are meeting the indicators that represent 'basic standards of democracy', which include 'basic standards of political rights and civil liberties, more freedom of the press, a much more vibrant civil society, greater transparency, and stronger checks and balances ... less conflict and

---

[44] For instance, Radelet, *Emerging Africa.*
[45] Ayers, 'Beyond the Imperial Narrative', p. 158.
[46] This acclaimed provenance of democracy in Africa is repeatedly undermined by many studies (i.e. Mkandawire, 'Rethinking Pan-Africanism'; Graham Harrison, *The World Bank and Africa: The Construction of Governance States* [Abingdon: Routledge, 2004]; James Ferguson, *Global Shadows: Africa in the Neoliberal World Order* [Durham, NC: Duke University Press, 2006]), most notably the biannual Afrobarometer survey of respondents across 35 African states, which repeatedly reveals extremely low levels of public belief in the quality of democracy in these countries, and indeed, not insignificant numbers of people who would prefer a return to one-party rule (www.afrobarometer .org – see for example Briefing Papers 140, 152 and 159).
[47] For an analysis of the relationship between the material and financial proceeds of the British Empire and the construction of the British welfare state, see Gupta *Imperialism and the British Labour Movement*, Chapters 8 and 9.

political violence, stronger adherence to the rule of law, and lower levels of corruption'.[48] Similarly, Rotberg asks how it might be possible to 'assist these badly governed, mostly authoritarian, places to learn how to govern themselves more adequately'.[49] Of course, in reality very few countries in the world, not least those countries considered to be 'Western', would perform very well when held to these standards, particularly when viewed from the experience of minorities or refugees where, even though one would argue that in some cases the latter groups are safer and better provided for than in their countries of origin, this is a *relative* rather than absolute comparison. It does not suddenly mean that refugee countries of destination have become, or have ever been, centres of welcome and virtue for the deprived, destitute and suffering. The universal standards Radelet, Rotberg and others refer to when they are talking about 'adequate standards' of governance, or 'sensible economic policies',[50] therefore, are, of course, not universal at all, derive from a sense of White ethnocentric exceptionality and in doing so, paint a picture of 'The West' as having historically embodied the height of pluralism, peace and democracy in absolute terms – even if all of this is unravelling in the current conjuncture. That there is a dissonance between this and the various anxieties that also drive contemporary idealisations of Africa, is not a contradiction given that the past can be glorified even while the present is bemoaned.

Anxiety-driven idealisations of Others have always reified and valorised the present of the colonised. This has been evident, from the idealisation of 'noble savages' ripe for conversion in the missionary era, through to the figure of the 'childlike ... negroid Bantu',[51] which underpinned the architecture of South African Apartheid. Contemporary Africa Rising narratives repeat this pattern with one important difference: today, idealisations of Africa are constructed in terms that mirror and/or replace the mythologised and racialised Western, phenotypically white enlightened subject, something the next section turns to in greater detail.

[48] Radelet, *Emerging Africa*, p. 14.
[49] Rotberg, *Africa Emerges*, p. 84.
[50] Radelet, *Emerging Africa*, p. 16.
[51] Smuts, *Africa and Some World problems*, p. 74.

Africa Rising (Recognition)

One implication of the claims posited above is that idealisations of Africa become an implied celebration of White historical institutional genius as much as it is a celebration of perceived African achievement. This is necessary in order to maintain the fantasy that, although in decline, the vitality of ideas construed as emanating from the genius of phenotypically white people and Western institutional arrangements persist. This is because the explicit anxieties about the trajectory of Western modernisation and White historical genius are assuaged in part by the belief, or hope, that Africa, and in particular the extracted African homo economicus of contemporary international economic and development policy,[52] represents the salvation of mythologised White achievements, especially the golden age of the high consumerist society of Rostowian Modernisation Theory. Western imaginaries and idealisations of Africa are, thus, always projecting something familiar in their Others; some material that can be fashioned into a recognisably White image. So while, for example, the growing numbers of African film, fashion, music or food festivals that are occurring in Western metropoles may in part represent the 'civilising mission in reverse',[53] they also represent this tendency to extract an Africa which is consumerist, Modern and entrepreneurial,[54] a denial of difference that leaves other forms of dynamic African cultures ossified in museum ethnology and art exhibitions.[55]

Confirming this project of idealised self-affirmation, post-crash accounts of an emerging and vibrant African middle-class abounded.[56] 'The demand story is clear – 3bn consumers by 2050' proclaimed Goldman Sachs[57] while Vijay Mahajan beseeched us to take notice

---

[52] Williams, 'Constructing the Economic Space'.
[53] Ellis, *Season of Rains*, p. 2.
[54] Dabiri, 'Why I'm not an Afropolitan'.
[55] Mudimbe, *The Idea of Africa*, pp. 56–60.
[56] One might want to compare the following analysis with the growing predilection among politicians and scholars across the political spectrum in many Western societies to refer to 'the squeezed middle' class. For the persistence and prevalence of this debate across Western and OECD countries, see: The Squeezed Middle Class in OECD and Emerging Countries: Myth and Reality, OECD/World Bank Issues paper, 1 December 2016, available at: www.oecd.org/inclusive-growth/about/centre-for-opportunity-and-equality/Issues-note-Middle-Class-squeeze.pdf, accessed on 23 August 2017.
[57] Goldman Sachs, 'Africa's Turn', p. 8.

of Africa's 900 million current consumers.[58] The accounts of who make up this new class of African consumer highlights this tendency to seek self-affirmation. Central to post-crash politico-economic idealisations of Africa, these 'Africans' are understood to be acting like acquisitive and entrepreneurial 'Westerners', thus assuaging anxieties about White vitality and concomitant social and economic models beyond the West – for this is where such models will have to thrive, if the anxieties detailed earlier are borne out. For instance, the management consultancy Deloitte provides a helpful list of markers by which we might identify a 'middle-class African' (titled: 'The African Middle Class: Who are They?'). There is just one characteristic that defines 'what they are generally not', and that is simply that they are not rural – 'They do not derive income from farming and rural economic activities'. There, then, follows a long list of characteristics that tell us what 'they generally are'. These include being urban, educated, salaried, young, acquisitive and aspirational.[59]

The easy dismissal of what constitutes a 'non-acquisitive' African – i.e., that they are simply rural (or old, informally educated, communitarian, etc.) – finds a parallel in political analysis of the African middle class. The following celebratory passage draws on an episode of postelectoral violence in Kenya in 2007–8, which led to up to 3,000 people losing their lives. It similarly conveys the division between recognisably White, norm-affirming Africans and 'chaotic', unrecognisable Other Africans:

The riots hit the Kenyan middle class in their ideals ... but they did not accept this passively; they put pressure on the two main political parties to end the violence and begin talks ... made sure that the commitments made were kept, and that the country did not fall back into chaos ... They present themselves freely to their compatriots, with a certain pride, as models to be followed, *the incarnation of a resolutely African modernity.*[60]

Again, everything that an acceptable form of contemporary African subjectivity is not can be reduced to one signifier – chaos. In addition, although the evidence is scant, such that exists suggests that the degree to which the growing numbers of middle-class Africans will, in fact,

[58] Mahajan, *Africa Rising*, Front cover.
[59] Deloitte 'The Rise and Rise of the African Middle Class', p. 2.
[60] Severino and Ray, *Africa's Moment*, p. 92. *Emphasis added.*

act beyond their own class and ethnic interest is questionable.[61] This reinforces the sense in which this belief in the African middle class seems at least partially based in the kind of fantastical and detached self-referentialism characteristic of historical imperial encounters with native peoples.[62]

At a surface level, of course, being optimistic about one's ability to sustain imperial or neo-imperial relations and being optimistic about the capacity of Africans to achieve modernisation and economic development involves a different set of practices and attitudes. However, given that the outputs of both colonialism and an ethnocentrically framed process of modernisation have implied material gains for agents of imperial, neo-imperial and 'post-imperial' power, both the overt Othering racism of colonial attitudes characteristic of many of the protagonists encountered in Chapters 2 and 3, and the recognition-seeking attitudes of post-crash Afro-idealists lead to the same results. These include a search for Africans who fulfil the relevant criteria of affirming White understandings of politics and economics and who, as a result exist, as a promise of the perpetuation of White political and economic vitality, even if as Africans they are mostly not phenotypically white.

The subjects of post-crash Afro-idealism are, thus, validated through a process of self-referential Whiteness. In this vein, many of the works cited in this chapter contain stories of personal encounters between the authors and surprising self-referentially norm-affirming African subjects. Severino and Ray admire the gym membership and Blackberry of their protagonist[63]; for Dowden, what is surprising is his protagonist's honesty[64]; and for Rotberg it is their commitment to party-based rather than kin-based politics.[65] Similarly, Dowden talks about the downtown Lagos businessman he meets who wants to make money but 'doesn't want to fawn on the Big Men business-politicians'[66] as if there has ever been, or is still in many places, much

---

[61] Cheeseman, 'Does the African Middle Class Defend Democracy?'
[62] Todorov, *The Conquest of America*, p. 36.
[63] Severino and Ray, *Africa's Moment*, p. 91.
[64] Dowden, *Africa*, p. 523.
[65] Rotberg, *Africa Emerges*, p. 6.
[66] Dowden, *Africa*, p. 521.

choice in the matter.[67] Rotberg, too, notes that 'there is a coterie of entrepreneurs and executives that is much less dependent than before on governments for favours'.[68]

Pluralism, consumerism and liberal politics, then, are the keys to the future for an Africa that can be conceived and recognised through a White ethnocentric lens and practitioners of such a politics are to be praised, while those dissenting, who are so angry and disillusioned with their situation that they engage in violent or other divisive behaviour, are to be blamed for Africa's problems and deemed external to Africa's imagined future – just as they have been made central to the violence and related problems of Africa's imagined past. For now, it is the individualistic, entrepreneurial and consumerist African who is praiseworthy, precisely because such behaviours are seen to be under threat within many stagnating Western societies.[69] As we have seen in previous chapters, in the past it has been other African figures that have been central to such forms of idealisation. This tendency for phenotypically white elites to want to see an image of themselves is part of a process of constructing African subjects who conform to idealised White renditions of economy and society, predicated on anxieties about the perpetuation of White supremacy – even if rarely expressed in such blunt terms. In the post-crash conjuncture, these anxieties were framed as threats to Western influence in Africa and the sustainability of historically mythologised forms of governance and liberal society in the West itself.

In seeking to displace supposedly White achievements onto Africa as a means of 'saving' these achievements from Western decline, Africa

[67] Janet Roitman, 'A Successful Life in the Illegal Realm: Smugglers and Road Bandits in the Chad Basin', in Peter Geschiere, Birgit Meyer, and Peter Pels (eds.), *Readings on Modernity in Africa* (Bloomington, IN: Indiana University Press, 2008), pp. 214–20.
[68] Rotberg, *Africa Emerges*, p. 2.
[69] In the UK context, Brexit has only served to make this stagnation more evident in a certain kind of elite liberal policy context. Writing after the referendum in a piece ostensibly about Africa, Richard Dowden wrote that 'The tribes of Britain will now be at war with each other. The Scots will demand another referendum and will vote to leave. Northern Ireland will be vulnerable to civil war again. Are they really going to build a fence along the border? Sinn Fein will go back to war if they do. And the Welsh will not be slow to realise they do not want to be tied to an impoverished England'. See Richard Dowden, 'What will Brexit mean for Africa?' available at: www.royalafricansociety.org/blog/what-will-brexit-mean-africa, accessed on 23 August 2017.

becomes a place in which Whiteness and the institutions and ideas that have historically privileged phenotypically white elites (as well as other groups of phenotypical whites at various points in time) can be affirmed, not simply by defining White sustenance in relation to Black savagery – the conventional argument deployed by critical and post-colonial scholarship – but also by reassuring itself of the validity of White genius in light of anxiety about the sustainability of this vitality in the West itself. This is a dual idealisation, on the one hand, of an eth-nocentric Western history and, on the other hand, of the African pres-ent. Holding up the picture of Dorian Gray into which the West has been able to empty its own flaws[70] is, thus, not the only function Africa has served within historical Western mythologisations of the conti-nent. Indeed, one might argue that post-crash idealisations of Africa reversed the situation, placing the West and its phenotypically white-majority populations in the picture rather than posing in front of it. This is because Africa became a site for White norms and the mytholo-gised genius that underpins them, to be affirmed and perpetuated, even and especially when they are held to be faltering in Western societies, or as a place to reclaim supposed past glories. This shares a number of striking similarities with the kinds of rhetoric deployed by the inter-racial society activists considered in Chapter 5. As was illustrated, they too saw in Africa the potential to save the historical achievements of White genius, even if they were more circumspect about the ability of Africans alone to forge ahead and safeguard such achievements, in keeping with the geopolitical anxieties of the period. It is in this spirit that we might understand a passage of Francois Hollande's speech to the Senegalese parliament: 'If Africa, the cradle of humanity, can manage to live democracy and make it a reality ... then Africa will be the continent where the very future of the planet will be played out'.[71]

---

[70] Achebe, *An Image of Africa*, p. 19.
[71] Hollande, 'Speech by M. François Hollande'. It is worth noting that none of Hollande's contemporaneous speeches in other parts of the Global South engaged in this kind of lofty rhetoric. During his presidency Hollande made state visits to both India and China and across a series of speeches spoke of far more instrumental matters such as economic partnership and climate change. For India see: Speech by President François Hollande at CEOs forum, Chandigarh, 24 January 2016, available at: www.in.ambafrance .org/Speech-by-President-Francois-Hollande-at-CEOs-forum, accessed on 22 August 2017. For China see: Reuters Staff, 'France's Hollande says EU, China must resolve trade disputes', available at: www.uk.reuters.com/article/

The Self-Conducting Politics of Contemporary Africa Rising Narratives

While all of the above continues to tell us something about both the ways in which Africa gets idealised and about the developments of Whiteness more broadly – namely that the delineations and boundaries of Whiteness are driven by existential anxieties, none more so than in the present – there are further material implications to the forms of knowledge that are produced about Africa in Western imaginaries. Just as ideas about Africa that, in the past, centred on African brutality and childishness served as a justification for the various European imperial projects from the seventeenth century onwards, more idealised and positive ideas about the continent also get deployed in ways that materialise and personify. Historically such positive idealisations have formed the backbone for endeavours designed to 'raise up' or 'protect' an ossified form of African culture. Indeed, this was the logic underpinning many of the humanitarian interventions detailed in Chapter 3, which constructed Africans as in need of protection from the vagaries of modern life.

In the contemporary period, however, these material implications are more subtle and almost incidental-seeming. And this isn't simply because it is no longer really possible to directly advocate for the imperial control of other countries – even if some do think Africa would be better off if the Europeans had never left[72] – but also because that is not why positive idealisations of Africa have material and governing implications. These implications actually arise because of the purpose that positive idealisations of Africa serve – i.e., to reassure anxieties about Whiteness. If claims are going to be made regarding the 'maturity' of African democracies, or the peaceable and consumerist habits of the 'African middle-class', then something or somebody needs to make sure that African subjects are indeed acting according to these

---

uk-france-china-hollande-idUKBRE95705H20130608, accessed on 22 August 2017. Even if Hollande's Dakar speech was designed to repair relations with African governments and public opinion, why not engage in the kind of rhetoric characteristic of his other state visits to parts of the Global South? I have argued in this section that, at least in part, the Dakar rhetoric reflected the unique place Africa holds in Western imaginaries as a place to salvage White vitality at times of excessive racial anxiety.

72 See for instance Niall Ferguson, *Colossus: The Rise and Fall of the American Empire* (London: Penguin, 2009).

norms. This is not intentional, but a necessary by-product of Afro-idealisation, because, if it turns out that in fact African subjects are not conforming to these norms, then the idea that Africa might be in the process of saving White institutional and ideational genius becomes undermined. At this point such idealisations would have to come face-to-face with the anxieties driving them and the historical failures of that supposed genius, a scenario fragile White narratives of internal genius are unequipped to deal with.[73]

And so it is that we find a whole range of anxieties about Africa's ability to 'carry the flame'. Will its demographic boom *really* pay-off by providing a mobile and educated workforce for the continent, or will it result in conflicts over resources and violent resentments over unfulfilled promises[74]? Can Africa's democratic march be broadened and deepened, or are 'old tribal loyalties' ready to spill over at any moment[75]? It is as a response to anxieties like these that those generating positive idealisations of Africa seek to find Africans who can provide self-affirming norms. But it is also as a response to these anxieties that these positive idealisations of Africa deploy technology and the internet as tools by which to keep Africa on the 'straight and narrow' of liberal market democracy.

So, for example, Rotberg discusses how Africa's political future is dependent on essentially turning Africans into individual mobile panopticons of surveillance,[76] armed with smartphone technology to report on incidents of government misspending, graft, violence, public sector performance and so on.[77] Richard Dowden's often more-sensitive account of his time on the continent also engages in breathless praise for the role of mobile technology in facilitating political transparency – although he does, too, note its potential drawbacks, namely the ability of governments or other forces to spread messages of hatred

---

[73] DiAngelo, 'White Fragility'.
[74] For these concerns, see: Rotberg, *Africa Emerges*, p. 12; Radelet, *Emerging Africa*, pp. 145–6.
[75] For these concerns, see; Radelet, *Emerging Africa*, pp. 142–3; Dowden, *Africa*, p. 530.
[76] My interpretation of Rotberg's argument. For more on mobile panopticons, and self-surveillance, see Jennie Germann Molz, '"Watch us Wander": Mobile Surveillance and the Surveillance of Mobility', *Environment and Planning A*, 38, 2006, pp. 377–93.
[77] Rotberg, *Africa Emerges*, pp. 142–3, 149, 176.

quickly and widely.[78] It is, of course, difficult to argue with putting the means of holding powerful forces to account into peoples' hands. That is not the point being made here, however. Quite apart from the individualised (as opposed to structural) sense of power transmitted via these idealisations of technology in Africa, the African subject to emerge in these accounts is preconceived and already known. As Engin F. Isin and Evelyn S. Ruppert have argued, approaches that celebrate the power of technology to bring 'power to the people' tend to reify a subject 'whose conduct already pertains to good civic behaviour ... [and who] inhabits forms of conduct that are already deemed to be appropriate to being a citizen'. The embodiment of different lived experiences, which may produce different kinds of non-liberal claims, is thus lost.[79]

And yet it is the very messiness produced by Africa's most recent form of insertion into the global economy that these accounts of techno-savvy, entrepreneurial democrats reduce to footnotes. The next section foregrounds these footnotes. Their importance is that by representing alternative possible subjects produced by the way the global economy manifests in Africa, they explicitly challenge positive idealisations of the continent and reveal the project of liberal market democracy which these idealisations seek to mythologise and, implicitly, facilitate to be riddled with unsustainable contradictions. It is the impossibility of foregrounding these alternative forms of subjectification under the conditions of contemporary capitalism in Africa that makes 'Africa Rising' narratives so idealised in the first place.

De-idealising Africa

At a general level, contemporary commentators all idealise Africa's most recent iteration of its integration into the global economy. They do this in two ways. First, Africa, we are told, is rising. What does this mean? It means that 'Africa is no longer cut off from the rest of the world'[80] and that 'though we often think of it as old, Africa is a new place in almost every way'.[81] More substantively, Radelet asserts

---

[78] Dowden, *Africa*, pp. 524–5.
[79] Engin F. Isin and Evelyn S. Ruppert, *Being Digital Citizens* (London: Rowman & Littlefield International, 2015), p. 8.
[80] Dowden, *Africa*, p. 252.
[81] Berman, *Success in Africa*, cover notes.

that 'the number of countries meeting basic standards of democracy in Africa has grown from just 3 in 1989 to more than 20 today ... there has been marked improvement in the quality of governance'.[82] But, as Alison Ayers has noted, this kind of position is a problematic one to sustain, as it presumes 'a non-history of democracy in Africa ... There is an African history (or histories) of political community and democracy autonomous of the orthodox Western neoliberal notion that dominates the so-called democratisation project'.[83] Africa 'Emerges',[84] 'Emerging',[85] 'Rising'[86] – such renditions as these, and those that opened this chapter, position an Africa existing 'out of time'[87] and even when portrayed in a positive light, only exerting an agency that coheres with White logics of temporality and modernity (i.e., that all societies everywhere have or will follow a path to prosperity derivative of the West). Thus, Africa is rising now because it is perceived to be embracing patterns of consumption and liberal political and economic institutions that cohere with imaginaries concerning the mythologised historical genius of Whiteness. All alternative forms of living and being in the world are absent and, thus, implicitly relegated in significance.

The second sense in which Africa's most recent integration into the global economy is idealised concerns the effects of this process. 'In the cycle now underway', Africa 'will be the biggest winner'[88] suggests investment consultant Charles Robertson. His analysis is based on the idea that while global growth in the rest of the world, including the BRICs, stalls, sub-Saharan Africa is so under-exposed to this slowdown that it 'will barely feel that gravitational pull'.[89] Severino and Ray suggest that it is now 'impossible for Africa to do anything but hurl itself full-pelt into the adventure of growth',[90] while a Goldman Sachs report notes that while 'previous scrambles for Africa didn't produce lasting economic benefits ... there are contributing factors creating a happy confluence that has produced some startling

---

[82] Radelet, *Emerging Africa*, p. 14.
[83] Ayers, 'Beyond the Imperial Narrative', pp. 157–8.
[84] Rotberg, *Africa Emerges*.
[85] Radelet, *Emerging Africa*.
[86] Mahajan, *Africa Rising*.
[87] Ellis, *Season of Rains*, p. 9.
[88] Robertson, *The Fastest Billion*, p. 244.
[89] Ibid., at p. 248.
[90] Severino and Ray, *Africa's Moment'*, p. 79.

economic growth'.[91] Others have rebutted these arguments, suggesting both that Africa's 'rise' is simply a new version of dependency[92] and that as Africa's growth has been largely commodity driven, it is not sustainable.[93]

The purpose of the argument here is not to interrogate whether Africa is 'rising' or not. Rather, the aim is to consider how fallible the idealised image of Africa found within contemporary commentary and consultancy analysis is. For it is the very macro-economic processes that such analyses portray as central to Africa's rise – i.e., deregulation of trade barriers, flexible labour markets, floating currencies, etc.,[94] which drive a political economy far removed from the idealisations of the 'Africa Rising' analysis. Indeed, this is a political economy that speaks directly to the anxieties of these idealisations which in its criminality can be perceived as a mirror for the self-destructive tendencies of Western capitalist economies and societies (although, as we will see, there are other ways of interpreting this) understood as constituting the apogee of White genius (or now White genius in decline).

Where we have seen 'Africa Rising' commentators idealise the African middle-class and assign its emergence to the confluence between more orthodox macro-economic policy and globalisation, it is these very processes, and particularly the latter, which have driven the emergence of a different form of upwardly mobile, entrepreneurial and consumerist economic subjects, the Nigerian 419 con-artists or Cameroonian feymen responsible for a wide range of internet and email scams and who, according to Basile Ndjio, 'herald a Second Coming of capitalism, not in its millennial, neo-liberal and global manifestations ... but rather in its criminal, felonious, venal expressions'.[95] When Steven Radelet, author of *Emerging Africa*, writes that,

[91] Goldman Sachs, 'Africa's Turn', p. 2.
[92] Taylor, *Africa Rising?*
[93] No author, 'After the 'rising' – Now Reform and Realism', *Africa Confidential*, 57:2, 2016, available at: www.africa-confidential.com/article/id/11448/After_the_'rising'_%E2%80%93_now_reform_and_realism, accessed on 28 January 2016.
[94] See, for example: Berman, *Success in Africa*, pp. 71–95; Mataen, *Africa*, pp. 81–105; Robertson, *The Fastest Billion*, pp. 19–38.
[95] Basile Ndjio, 'Overcoming Socio-Economic Marginalisation: Young West African Hustlers and the Reinvention of Global Capitalism' in Emmanuel Obadare and Wendy Willems (eds.), *Civic Agency in Africa: Arts of Resistance in the 21st Century* (Suffolk: James Currey, 2014), p. 95.

'They are savvy, sharp, and entrepreneurial, capable of combining the best of both worlds ... They are fed up with the unaccountable governments and economic stagnations of the past and bringing new ideas and new vision'[96], he could just as well be writing about Ndjio's 'young West African hustlers'.[97] Of course, Radelet is not talking about them and yet they are produced by, and re-appropriate, the very same system that also produces Radelet's entrepreneurs, yet this relationship is silenced by the celebration of one and criminalisation of the other. Once again, to address this relationship would be to undermine and, thus, make less secure the project on which the historical project of Western economic development and Modernity (all associated with White genius) has stood and, thus, the denial of this relationship is simultaneously an assertion of the pacific nature of the capitalist economic model.

This argument is reinforced by the claims of the anthropologist Janet Roitman, whose work problematises some of the implicit logics that underpin the idealisations of the 'Africa Rising' narratives and, importantly, does so through the foregrounding of the agency of those very people who are, via their criminalisation or absence in such narratives, denied a place in Africa's uneven journey through the global economy. Roitman illustrates the manner by which not only are hustlers and other workers in African informal and/or illicit economies produced by Africa's current terms of integration in the global economy, they also form a fundamental plank of the modern African state that commentators, like Radelet and Rotberg in particular, are so praiseworthy of. Roitman asserts that 'the state is dependent on these [illicit] economies for rents and the means of redistribution ... they make important, or even essential, contributions to the national political economy'.[98] As such, these illicit operators see themselves (and indeed are) very much part of the modern African economy. When they establish formal associations (for operators of 'informal' economic activity) 'they are ... not necessarily resisting capitalism, integration into the world economy or

---

[96] Radelet, *Emerging Africa*, p. 20.
[97] Ndjio, 'Overcoming Socio-Economic Marginalisation'.
[98] Janet Roitman, 'New Sovereigns? Regulatory Authority in the Chad Basin', in T. Callaghy, R. Kassimir, and R. Latham (eds.), *Intervention and Transnationalism in Africa: Global-Local Networks of Power* (Cambridge: Cambridge University Press, 2001), p. 241.

the state',[99] and the trans-nationalisation of their economic activities suggests, in an arguably un-coincidental echo of Steven Radelet, 'the possibility of an emergent African middle class developing across the bounds of national states and outside the bounds of national regulatory authority'.[100]

And so, even though some of those operating in this realm partake in activities deemed to be criminal (and that do inflict degrees of suffering on those who fall prey to the various scams operated from within some sectors of African informal and illicit economies) these activities are produced by the same conditions of integration into the global economy that produce Radelet's and other's office-dwelling, norm-affirming African middle-classes. These are also activities that are practised by subjects who, through fusing religious identification with gangsta rap, Hollywood and the accumulation made possible through their economic activities, are irredeemably Modern and capitalist.[101]

Ultimately then, the very processes and subjects idealised within the 'Africa Rising' narratives are fallible when held alongside the agency of those excluded from these narratives' frame of analysis. It is important to recall here that when commentators talk about Africa's rise, this is understood in terms of Africa 'catching up' with the West, and its phenotypically white populations. Africa 'will rapidly impose itself in the globalization game'[102] as if Africa's insertion into the global economy is a new phenomenon. With globalisation understood as a racialised Western innovation bequeathed upon the world through a lineage of neo-classical political economy, Africa's rise signifies an affirmation of the vitality of ideas and institutions that have historically privileged phenotypically white people (thus making these ideas and institutions 'White'). However, as we have seen, the conditions of Africa's contemporary place in the global economy also produces pathologies that undermine those same ideas and institutions (or at least relate to them in highly ambivalent ways). Ignoring the relationship between the ideas, institutions and practices they praise, and the pathologies these produce, is the only way to maintain the notion that while White vitality might be in decline among phenotypically white people in the West, all will ultimately be well with the economic, political and social

---

[99] Roitman, 'A Successful Life in the Illegal Realm', p. 217.
[100] Ibid., at p. 218.
[101] Ibid., at p. 216.
[102] Severino and Ray, *Africa's Moment*, p. 3.

achievements that have flowed from this historical vitality as they materialise in Africa.

Conclusions

It is perhaps especially the case in this chapter, that you, the reader, might get the impression that the argument being presented here coheres to a kind of 'damned if they do, damned if they don't' form of analysis. If Africans are criticised, this draws on historically racist and colonial tropes, and if Africans are praised, the same thing is happening. And yet there is a fairly straightforward solution to this. For what is distinctive about the contemporary accounts of Africa addressed in this chapter is their generalised pan-continentalism. Very few talk in terms of specifics, be that countries, regions, ethnic groups or so on, or at least when they do talk in specifics, it is only to reinforce White norms. There are far too many examples of this pan-continentalism to recount here and this should already be clear from preceding sections,[103] but a couple more examples would include Severino and Ray asking us to meet 'Africa's billion at a particular moment on its journey, that of its awakening',[104] or Tony Blair telling us that, 'This could be Africa's century. It should be'.[105] In these and other cases, Africa is conceived of as emerging to pick up the mission of White genius and the Western civilisational project.

A resolution, in part, then would be to stop talking in such universalistic terms, a form of thinking about Africa that has itself a distinctly late-nineteenth-century European imperial provenance.[106] Of course, the anxieties that drive much of this positive idealisation makes recognising the diverse and contradictory nature of the African continent more complex, for to recognise all of this would be to abandon the fantastical idealisations (of self, as well as Other) of contemporary Western imaginaries. The following and concluding chapter will pick

---

[103] Think, for example, of management consultant Jonathan Berman telling us that, 'Though we often think of it as old, Africa is a new place in almost every way'.

[104] Severino and Ray, *Africa's Moment*, p. xiv.

[105] Tony Blair, 'Speech Text'.

[106] Helen Tilly, *Africa as a Living Laboratory: Empire, Development, and the Problem of Scientific Knowledge* (Chicago, IL: University of Chicago Press, 2011), p. 1.

up on this argument, that it is not homogenising imaginaries of Africa as such, but Whiteness, which requires disassembling. Before that, Chapter 8 will pay attention to the genealogy of the kinds of idealisation that have been explored throughout the book and how the messiness obscured by this idealism has always exceeded the limitation of the Western gaze behind it.

8 | *Making Whiteness Strange*

This triumphant discourse seems relatively homogeneous, most often dogmatic, sometimes politically equivocal, and like dogmatisms, like all conjurations, secretly worried and manifestly worrisome.[1]

Three Vignettes

Vignette #1:

A few weeks before pro-Harry Thuku demonstrators were gunned down in Nairobi, a tour of missions in Nyeri, some 100 kilometres from Nairobi, was conducted by mission-trained members of the Kikuyu Association – the ostensibly representative body formally recognised by the colonial administration – the same association that had ejected Thuku from its membership months earlier. The report of the tour suggests that it was designed to gauge local opinion concerning Thuku and to propagandise against him. However, the author of the report exhibits a mixture of disgust, surprise and despair at what he encounters.[2]

At their first stop, the Gospel Mission Society in Kihumbuini, the author records that a member of his group 'explained to them that he had come to greet them and to compel them to deny master Harry Thuku as they know how Harry Thuku is doing ... one way is for them to follow Harry Thuku and the other way was to follow the Kikuyu Association'. The report continues by detailing the arguments put forward against Thuku: that it was the government and missions that built schools and workshops, not Indians, and so how could the Indians be the best friends of the natives as Thuku had claimed? And yet despite

---

[1] Jacques Derrida, *Spectres of Marx* (London: Routledge, 1994), p. 56.
[2] The subsequent details of this tour are all drawn from: James, P.K. n.d., The Kikuyu Association, The Five Delegation of the Kikuyu Association to Nyeri, Canon Harry Leakey and Charles Richards Papers, Weston Library, MSS. Afr.s.633, Box 17/2.

this concerted attempt to sway local opinion in favour of the mission
and government-sanctioned Kikuyu Association 'the meeting separated
unagreed ... their decision was [for] Harry Thuku to be their leader'.

At their next stop, the Kikuyu Association delegation barely got
their arguments heard at all. At a meeting called for 4 pm they were
told that "they [the mission members] are recognising Harry Thuku as
their leader, as they [are] quite convinced that Harry Thuku is mainly
contending for them'. On reporting back to the mission head, a Dr.
Reverend Philip, they were told that he did not believe that many of
his 'boys' would be East Africa Association (EAA) members. However,
'we told him that some of them are the member (sic) of the EAA'. The
author concludes the report by writing that Thuku 'is a leader of all
the unruly boys, who are separated with the churches and who have
been put away from the Government's work'. This leaves the impression that EAA support in the missions was in the minority and, yet,
the mission trip was an absolute failure. The Kikuyu Association delegation did not report managing to convince any of the missions they
visited to desist from following Thuku.

Vignette #2:
David Stirling, the destiny-making colonel, the man who single-
handedly created the mythical UK Special Air Service, certain that
through his individual will he could shape the future prosperity of
Africa, and through Africa the anti-Communist West, stands up to
address an audience in Bulawayo to regale them of the opportunities available to them if they sign onto the Capricorn vision of an
inter-racial Africa. Stirling runs through his well-rehearsed lines,
among them that 'African leaders who understood the European view
were turning from bitter destructive racialism to constructive African
nationalism'. Members of the audience rise to their feet, shouting him
down with cries of 'Europeans must be driven in the sea!'[3]

Vignette #3: An email I recently received
The moment, it seems, may already be passing. By this I am not referring to anxieties about the Western decline and the end of a recognisable international order and thus the ebbing of White vitality. As I write
this, with the normalisation of the right in French electoral politics,
the shambles of Brexit, ethno-nationalists governing Hungary, Poland

---

[3] *Manchester Guardian*, 30 May 1957, TNA, DO35/4706 File 105a.

and the United States, the public re-emergence of organised ethno-nationalists in Germany – all of this has left both liberals and conservatives[4] wringing their hands in Spenglerist fashion about the plausible decline of the West.[5]

---

[4] For exemplars of liberal anxiety, see Thomas Friedman, 'Where did "We the People" Go?', *New York Times*, 21 June 2017, available at: www.nytimes .com/2017/06/21/opinion/where-did-we-the-people-go.html, accessed on 23 August 2017; Jonathan Freedland, 'If Donald Trump Wins, It'll Be a New Age of Darkness', *The Guardian*, 4 November 2016, available at: www.theguardian .com/commentisfree/2016/nov/04/if-donald-trump-wins-new-age-endarkenment, accessed on 23 August 2017; Jonathan Freedland, 'The 1930s Were Humanity's Darkest, Bloodiest Hour. Are You Paying Attention?', *The Guardian*, 11 March 2017, available at: www.theguardian.com/society/2017/ mar/11/1930s-humanity-darkest-bloodiest-hour-paying-attention-second-world-war, accessed on 23 August 2017. Meanwhile, conservative commentator Bill Kristol, in a perhaps or perhaps not tongue-in-cheek moment, compared the United States' current predicament to the decline of the Roman Empire: See Julia Manchester, 'Bill Kristol: US Reliving Decline and Fall of Rome under Trump', *The Hill*, 2 July 2017, available at: www.thehill.com/blogs/ blog-briefing-room/news/340443-bill-kristol-us-reliving-decline-and-fall-of-rome-under-trump, accessed on 23 August 2017.

[5] Although Spengler was rather more sanguine about it. See Oswald Spengler, *The Decline of the West* (Oxford: Oxford University Press, 1918/1991).

What has passed, rather, is the high-point of post-crash celebrations of Africa's rise. While some of those who initially trumpeted it continue to do so,[6] others, such as Robert Rotberg, have rapidly changed their position, worrying now, with reference to Africa's 'demographic dividend' about where 'the food to feed these new millions will come from? How will they be governed? Are current methods of political management adequate? … Where will the clean water come from to slake the thirst of these new, mostly urban, and mostly unemployed masses?'[7] As African states have largely failed to fully escape their dependency on foreign demand for commodities, particularly in China where demand has dropped off, so the lustre has gone off some of the more idealised predictions and predilections detailed in Chapter 7.

However brief though, what this book has illustrated is a longer tendency by which 'Africa' has never solely been a place of negation that has enabled the phenotypically white West to walk tall. In addition, it has also been a place where the project of Whiteness, that sense of universalisable institutional, social, political and economic genius associated historically purely with phenotypically white people in the West, might be perfected, away from the deteriorating character of phenotypically white social groups in the West. As such, the logics upon which international order is held to have been based since Westphalia might be perpetuated. In this we find what it is that connects Joseph Oldham, Lothrup Stoddard, David Stirling, Daybreak in Udi, African Fashion Week and *The Economist* magazine. More and less overtly racist, more and less overtly paternalistic – or not at all paternalistic in the avowedly racist work of Lothrup Stoddard – more and less authored by African voices, it is not these characteristics that necessarily conjoin these figures, films, publications and events. Rather, it is the mirror they all hold up to various elitist conceptions of Whiteness and the relationship between phenotypical whiteness and the practice of something called 'Western civilisation'. This book has argued that, over the past century, we have seen the arrogance of elite phenotypical

---

[6] See, for instance, Richard Dowden, 'Britain Must Seize the Chance for More Trade with Africa', *The Times*, 25 January 2017, available at: www .royalafricansociety.org/blog/britain-must-seize-chance-more-trade-africa, accessed on 23 August 2017.

[7] Robert Rotberg, 'Will Africa Keep Rising?', 19 September 2016, available at: www.robertrotberg.wordpress.com/2016/09/19/will-africa-keep-rising/, accessed on 23 August 2017.

white supremacy slip, all the while that the centrality of Whiteness to the imagination and mechanics of international order has been maintained. As I have argued at various points, the relationship between whiteness (phenotype) and Whiteness (a system of privilege that rests on a set of supposedly universal and ahistorical codes that represent a civilised status) has started to break apart, without the latter being displaced as a social, political and economic set of ordering logics. This has been the result of a series of crises that have rocked the foundations of the relationship between phenotypical presentation and civilised behaviour, all the while maintaining Whiteness as the true civilised ideal and, thus, fundamentally denying the legitimacy of difference within social and international hierarchies.

Of course, I write this all in the context of rising ethno-nationalism in many parts of the world, including in the Anglosphere. Surely then, the presence in the White House of a White supremacist, one who seems to at the very least ally himself with people who believe in racial hierarchy, race and the superiority of the phenotypically white race, and who allegedly talks about non-white places as 'shithole countries', must challenge any argument about the deteriorating relationship between phenotypical presentation and civilised behaviour? Whether this period itself turns out to be short-lived remains to be seen. However, whether it is PayPal founder billionaire (and member of Donald Trump's transition team) Peter Thiel taking New Zealand citizenship and purchasing a sheep farm in the countryside as a bunker against impending civilisational collapse (Nippert, 2017)[8] or Donald Trump's crude analysis that America needs to be made 'great again' and rescued from 'American carnage', there are plenty of indicators that those who imagine themselves as the inheritors of a great

[8] In Thiel's own words: 'The great task for libertarians is to find an escape from politics in all its forms – from the totalitarian and fundamentalist catastrophes to the unthinking demos that guides so-called social democracy. The critical question then becomes one of means, of how to escape not via politics but beyond it. Because there are no truly free places left in our world, I suspect that the mode for escape must involve some sort of new and hitherto untried process that leads us to some undiscovered country' (Peter Thiel, 'The Education of a Libertarian', 13 February 2009, available at: www .cato-unbound.org/2009/04/13/peter-thiel/education-libertarian, accessed on 20 February 2018). There is a much longer tradition of economic libertarians seeking to detach themselves from politics – See Nancy Maclean, Democracy in Chains: The Deep History of the Radical Right's Stealth Plan for America (New York, NY: Viking Press Inc, 2017).

White tradition remain pervaded by anxieties as to the vitality of that tradition.

Returning to the central arguments I have made in this book, however, what I have tried to show is that anxieties about White vitality are not the sole preserve of the right – or those who would self-identify as white supremacists – and that those who identify as liberals and progressives have been even more likely than those on the right to seek affirmation of their values in places where they feel such values can be transplanted, namely a *terra incognita* such as Africa. I have made these more general claims based on the implications of some specific cases, although Chapters 2, 4 and 6 sought to provide a broader socio-cultural context for claims like these. It is worth briefly reflecting back on the specific cases and broader contextual arguments in order to qualify the above claims. After doing this I will return to the vignettes that opened this chapter. Their function is to foreground what goes on while people invested in the perpetuation of Whiteness aren't looking; another core argument of this book has been that the various anxieties concerning White vitality that have pervaded Western imaginaries of Africa over the last century have resulted in the idealisation of certain African subjects, subjects that can affirm the perpetuation of Whiteness. The vignettes that open this chapter all open up a vista on how the idealised subjects of White anxieties – the tribal African, the bureaucratic African, the entrepreneurial middle-class African – all operate in ways that confound the idealisations of White anxiety.

A key implication of the arguments presented over the preceding chapters is that for at least the past century, socially constructed versions of Africa have been integral to maintaining faith in the vitality of Whiteness – the latter understood as a form of legacy project. By this I mean that increasingly over the past century, Africa has become a place where the achievements of White genius might be rescued from a failing phenotypically white West, and perpetuated. At first, the place of eugenicism in mainstream social, political and intellectual thought dovetailed with, or even produced, an Africa that required phenotypically white people to tutor a largely savage, tribal, African population in, at least, some basic forms of civilised behaviour. Race was here understood to exist ontologically and hierarchically and rural Africans were idealised as a means by which to offer evidence of this hierarchy, its necessity and the centrality of phenotypically white people to the perpetuation of Whiteness beyond the West. What we saw in Chapters 2 and 3, however, is that in the aftermath of the World War I, a range of political, economic and social ruptures created increasing levels of elite anxiety concerning the vitality of Whiteness in the (Anglospheric) West. As such, the colour line became more significant than a simple means by which to divide the territories and peoples of the world. It also became important in justifying white settlement in Africa as a means by which to perpetuate a vulnerable domestic Whiteness somewhere other than in the West, where it was under threat from communism, militarism, feminism and more. If Africans were admitted to be able to organise politically and economically on their own terms, then Africa, the last habitable *tabula rasa* on the planet, would not be able to serve as a place where Whiteness might be saved from the growing deteriorations of the white West. This was the threat posed by Harry Thuku. It was not simply that Thuku posed as a challenge to the supremacy of European settlers and British hegemony in Kenya Colony – and the economic concerns of both. Nor was Thuku simply an insult to the paternalism of missionaries and assorted humanitarians. More than this, Thuku also served as a terrifying harbinger of what would happen to all the treasured and supposed historical achievements of Whiteness if he was allowed to succeed in whipping up a majority of indigenous public opinion against colonial rule. Being so completely Othered, Africans would be incapable of safeguarding these historical achievements and so individuals like Thuku and the movements that followed him, simply had to be crushed – just as unthreatening rural Africans had to be idealised – if Whiteness was to be perpetuated. However, as the opening vignette of this chapter reveals, in at least some cases, rural Africans confounded settler, government and humanitarian idealisations and were just as political as their urban 'semi-educated' counterparts.

Moving forward thirty years, Chapters 3 and 4 marked a key transition in the ways in which anxieties about White vitality mobilised a different set of attitudes to Africa and Africans. The end of World War II made eugenicism largely persona non-grata among policy-making/informing elites in the West. Strains of conservative eugenicism remained – no less so in artistic and cultural quarters as political ones – but broadly speaking, culture replaced colour as the bar against which civilisation was to be set. As such, the post-war period witnessed major efforts to socialise and incorporate significant enough sections of non-white societies into White social, political and economic codes so as to head off the major anxieties pervading –still largely phenotypically – white Western elites in this period; namely, rapid unmanaged decolonisation resulting in a race war. The trajectory of the inter-racial associations considered in Chapter 5, and particularly the Capricorn Africa Society (CAS), perfectly encapsulated this transition from conservative eugenicism to liberal socialisation. The very transition itself, however, was affected precisely by anxieties concerning how the supposed historical achievements of White genius would survive the new emerging post-war international order. As much as these anxieties transcended any particular territorial region of the world, applied to Africa the move was most marked. Unlike in the Indian subcontinent, where political organising and indirect rule had long punctured, at least in part, the imperial gaze, or those parts of South and Central America that had gained their independence in the previous century, in many cases under phenotypically white leadership, the move from idealising non-threatening rural Africans to idealising urban African almost-Moderns was incredibly abrupt.[9] Imaginaries and idealisations of Africa in this period are, thus, ideally placed to highlight this important transition in race-thinking. The outcome of the transition was a desperate search for Africans who would affirm the key tenets of White vitality and Western civilisation as understood by the self-proclaimed agents of progress and modernity, namely individualism, state capitalism, Christianity and urbanity. Even though this is a fair description of the majority of African nationalists during this period, the latter's growing popular appeal was constructed to represent a threat to the supremacy of White historical genius in Africa and globally, and thus, as we saw particularly in Chapter 5, had to be resisted. It was only later, once the inter-racial associations had failed in their efforts to bring majority African opinion into their circle, that African nationalists were socialised and incorporated into the logics and codes of White supremacy – or assassinated.

The protagonists of Chapters 4 and 5 were not always necessarily representative of broader and contemporaneous societal attitudes. And David Stirling, the key Capricorn protagonist, for all his liberal pretensions, soon returned to the trenches, this time fighting labour

---

[9] This was, of course, also a move that negatively inverted the position of rural Africans in Western imaginaries of the continent to a position of obstructing, rather than safeguarding White vitality. See Chapter 4 for more on this.

and Black Power resistance in the United Kingdom in the 1970s as part of a secretive right-wing cabal of former military personnel and financiers. Nonetheless, the inter-racial associations and the bleak and anxious liberalism they channelled provided a bridge from the eugenicism of the 1920s to the much more full-throated incorporation of Africa we find in contemporary cultural industries and political and economic debates concerning the continent's rise. For if the inter-racial associations of British Southern Africa were often frustrated in their search for the idealised White norm-affirming African, then in the post-crash conjuncture such examples abounded and have been foregrounded in the various ways in which Africa is consumed by audiences constructed as majoritarian white in Western societies. Africa takes its place in these societies in pre-conceived terms, defined by logics and rationalities that maintain Whiteness as a socially conditioning formula. This is, of course, not to suggest that challenges to this form of conditioning are not to be found; indeed, they proliferate.[10] This is, however, a question of foregrounding, and as we saw(particularly in Chapter 6) artistic, cultural and literary representations of Africa that get most commonly foregrounded in societies constructed as majoritarian white are precisely those that affirm the vitality of Whiteness, that illustrate the manner by which Whiteness is 'catching on' and transcending territorial and even phenotypical boundaries. The specifics and mechanics of this process were laid out in much fuller detail in Chapter 7, where the political and economic commentary on Africa that emerged after the global financial crash of 2007–8, and that catalysed this book project, was deconstructed in such a way as to bring into the foreground the image of the (White) enlightenment liberal subject, phenotypically black, but parading all of the achievements and genius of Whiteness that seem to be in such disrepair in the West. Finally, after a century of searching, phenotypically white elites had found their holy grail; affirmation that the logics and codes of Whiteness could now finally be loosed from their phenotypical racial

---

[10] One example can be found in the lyrics to the track, *Did You See?*' by the black British rapper JHus. Rather than celebrating the responsible Black British subject, the lyrics instead valorise insurgent antisocial behaviour, for instance *'Came looking like a ganga farmer; Your daddy betta hide his daughter'*. The track, at the time of writing, had nearly 30 million views on YouTube, and is available at: www.youtube.com/watch?v=3rk6_Ax0mQo, accessed on 11 July 2017. I am indebted to Emma Dabiri for this insight.

categorisations and fly untethered into a glorious White future where individualism, materialism, rationalised bureaucracy and deregulated entrepreneurialism could all flourish, everywhere.

And yet, what of the vignettes that opened this chapter? What do they tell us about the success of this long search for the ideal White African subject? Each of these vignettes opens up a portal to a different set of subjects, driven by the very modes of incorporation that the phenotypically white elites considered throughout the book had hoped would socialise Africans into Whiteness.

Vignette #1 for instance reveals those same rural Africans who were held to be suspicious of Indians and affectionate towards their white settler masters as being far from that, at least in this instance. The very edifice of white settler and British government power in its settler colonies, to rule indirectly and mark out the rural African as a noble, savage and essentially different form of subject from the white European citizen, was ripped down by this report. This was the supposedly docile rural African occupying an intensely political form of subjectivity – one that entirely contradicted the predictive idealisations of settlers, government officials and humanitarians alike. The alliances and movement that Harry Thuku was at the centre of *was* popular and, in this instance at least, transcended the supposed inter-communal tensions between Indians and Africans in the colony.

Vignette #2 is illustrative of the extremely fragile idealisations deployed by David Stirling in particular, but the inter-racial associations in general, concerning the likelihood of 'partnership' being embraced by Africans still living under minority or external rule. According to Capricorn in particular, Africans would rush into the arms of the inter-racial associations, having become more socially, culturally and politically appropriate (i.e., more White) to the perpetuation of settler political economy across the colonies that the associations operated in. That settler political economy was so important to these associations is precisely because of the abject prospects (such as they were held to be) for political economy and broader social standards in the West. Whereas the nearly-Modern, bureaucratic African was expected to be economically self-interested and embrace partnership through a means of rational, economic calculation and emotional attachment to inter-racialism, the reception given to Stirling in this vignette suggested that the opposite was taking place – a conclusion confirmed by the rapid deterioration of the inter-racial associations over the following years.

The screenshot of Vignette #3 is just one of many everyday examples of how the very processes held by contemporary commentators to herald Africa's 'rise' are simultaneously driving what such commentators would presumably hold to be more nefarious manifestations of neo-liberal capitalist expansion in parts of Africa. That such manifestations, delivered to millions, if not billions, of email inboxes every single day, could be Othered from the narrative of Africa's rise, entirely absent from popular book-length treatises on the state of African societies and political economy, is perhaps indicative of the fragile state of the celebratory tone of such pronouncements and the anxieties that fed them.

Ultimately, a Western gaze so implicated in logics associated with historical phenotypical white supremacy and their universalisation (a set of logics and an impulse that I have called 'Whiteness' in this book) will never be able to produce an imaginary of Africa that is devoid of generalisations and crucial absences. Whether driven by a greater sense of racial supremacy or racial deterioration, the result has been, and will be, the same – the idealisation of particular forms of African subjectivity that can serve to reaffirm a sense of historical White genius. It is, therefore, not so much that Western imaginaries of Africa have to be deracialised, in order to avoid telling what the novelist Chimamanda Ngozi Adichie famously called a 'single story' of the continent,[11] but rather Whiteness itself. Africa, that cognitive space that has been so central to imaginations of Western racial exceptionality and international order, will always be a single story if Whiteness remains a form of implicit social self-categorisation that rests on a sense of linear historical, social and racial homogeneity, a 'geo and body-politics'[12] that assigns historical development to originally European, phenotypically white bodies, even where those bodies become deemed no longer to be the best-placed carriers of White vitality. To repeat, it is Whiteness that most urgently needs to be deracialised, and as such, as much as this book has explored different and evolving imaginaries of Africa, I would like to end it where it began; for Whiteness does indeed need 'to be made strange'.[13]

---

[11] Chimamanda Ngozi Adichie, 'The Danger of a Single Story', *Ted Global*, July 2009, available at: www.ted.com/talks/chimamanda_adichie_the_danger_of_a_single_story, accessed on 13 July 2017.

[12] Mignolo, 'Delinking', p. 453.

[13] Dyer, *White*, p. 10.

References

Archives

Brent Archives

- 1924 British Empire Exhibition
- WHS Wembley History Society Collection

Central Research Library, University of Chicago (CRL)

- MF2811 Eileen Haddon Collection of Southern Rhodesia

Imperial War Museum (IWM)

- Oral History Collection

Institute of Commonwealth Studies, Senate House, University of London

- PP.KE.CAS Capricorn Africa Society

Kenya National Archive (KNA)

- PC/CP.18/3/2 Political and other deportees, 1929–1941
- PC/CP/8/5/2 Kikuyu Central Association Papers 1925–1927
- MSS/123/104 Capricorn Africa
- MSS/129/18 Capricorn Africa

Margaret Herrick Library, Academy of Motion Picture Arts and Sciences

- Core Collection Production Files

The National Archive (TNA)

- CO 533/267 Offices: Foreign, Home, India
- CO 533/262 Colonial Office: Kenya Original Correspondence Despatches
- CO 822/340 Activities of the Capricorn Africa Society in connection with native affairs in East and Central Africa
- CO 967/294 Capricorn Africa Society: future
- DO 35/3603 Formation of the Capricorn Africa Society
- DO 35/6731 "Salisbury Declarations" by Capricorn Africa Society; correspondence with Reverend Michael Scott
- DO 35/4705 Work of Capricorn Africa Society
- DO 35/4706 Work of Capricorn Africa Society
- FCO 141/6441 Kenya: Deportation of Harry Thuku
- FCO 141/6440 Kenya: Harry Thuku, Kikuyu native agitator
- FCO 141/17796 Tanganyika: Capricorn Africa Society, Tanganyika National Society and Tanganyika National Party
- PREM 11/3031 Prime Minister met members of New Kenya Party on 17 and 20 February 1960

Weston Library Commonwealth and African Collections

- MSS.Afr.s.594 C. K. Archer Papers
- MSS.Afr.s.633 Papers of Canon Harry Leakey and Charles Richards
- MSS.Afr.s.746 Michael Blundell Papers
- MSS.Afr.s.1829 J. H. Oldham Papers
- Mss.Brit.Emp.s.22/G135 H. S. L. Polack Papers
- MSS.Brit.Emp.s.390 C. E. V. Buxton Papers
- Mss.Brit.Emp.s.405 Papers of Charles Roden Buxton
- s.22/G135 Anti-Slavery and Aborigines Protection Society Papers

Primary Sources

Adichie, Chimamanda Ngozi. 'The Danger of a Single Story' *Ted Global*, July 2009, available at: www.ted.com/talks/chimamanda_adichie_the_danger_of_a_single_story, accessed on 13 July 2017.

Almond, Gabriel. 'On Revisiting the Civic Culture: A Personal Postscript' in Gabriel A. Almond, and Sidney Verba (eds.), *The Civic Culture Revisited* (London, New Delhi: Sage Publications, 1989), pp. 394–410.

Almond, Gabriel, and Verba, Sidney. *The Civic Culture: Political Attitudes and Democracy in Five Nations* (London, New York, NY: Sage Publications, 1963).

Atta, Sefi. *A Bit of Difference* (Boston, MA: Interlink Books, 2012).

Barnebys UK Press Release. 'Spotlight Is on African Art – Growth Greater than Gold: Barnebys, the World's Largest Art and Auction Search Engine, Notes Tenfold Growth in Value of African Contemporary Art', 21 September 2016.

Bell-Grosvenor, Elsie May. 'Safari through Changing Africa' *National Geographic Magazine*, 104, 1953, pp. 145–198.

Blair, Tony. 'Speech Text: Tony Blair: Making Government Work Will Transform Africa', Speech at Center for Global Development, 17 December 2010, available at: www.cgdev.org/article/speech-text-tony-blair-making-government-work-will-transform-africa, accessed on 3 July 2017.

Blair, Tony. 'A New Approach to a New Africa' Tony Blair Africa Governance Initiative, 19 March 2012, available at: www.africagovernance.org/africa/news-entry/a-new-approach-to-a-new-africa/, accessed on 17 March 2014.

Burke, Jason. 'Has Africa Had Its Fill of Strongmen?' *The Guardian*, 11 December 2016, available at: www.theguardian.com/world/2016/dec/11/africa-strongmen-angola-dos-santos-zimbabwe-mugabe-uganda-sudan, accessed on 20 December 2016.

Carlos, Marjon. 'Inside Nigeria's It-Bag Obsession' *Vogue*, 2 November 2016, available at: www.vogue.com/13498878/nigeria-lagos-fashion-and-design-week-prada-gucci-hermes-chanel-accessories-alara/, accessed on 5 December 2016.

Cell, John W. (ed.). *By Kenya Possessed: The Correspondence of Norman Leys and J.H. Oldham, 1918–1926* (Chicago, IL: University of Chicago Press, 1976).

Child, Ben. 'Matt Damon Apologises for Diversity in Film Gaffe as #Damonsplaining Trends' *The Guardian*, available at: www.theguardian.com/film/2015/sep/17/matt-damon-damonsplaining-apology-diversity-race, accessed on 3 May 2017.

Chown, Daisy M. *Wayfaring in Africa: A Woman's Wanderings from the Cape to Cairo* (London: Heath Cranton Limited, 1927).

Cleland Scott, S. R. 'Travelling through Africa' *The Fortnightly*, 1951.

Cloette, Stuart. *The African Giant: The Story of a Giant* (London: Collins, 1957).

Courlander, Katherine. *I Speak of Africa* (London: Robert Hale Ltd, 1956).

Cox, Daniel, Lienesch, Rachel, and Jones, Robert P. 'Beyond Economics: Fears of Cultural Displacement Pushed the White Working Class to Trump' *Public Religion Research Institute*, 9 May 2017, available at: www.prri.org/research/white-working-class-attitudes-economy-trade-immigration-election-donald-trump/, accessed on 22 August 2017.

Dabiri, Emma. 'Why I'm not an Afropolitan' *Africa is a Country*, 21 January 2014, available at: http://africasacountry.com/2014/01/why-im-not-an-afropolitan/ accessed on 2 December 2016.

Daybreak in Udi, Crown Film Unit Production, in collaboration with SDO ED Chadwick, and Nigerian Government, 1949, Dir. Terry Bishop.

Defries, Amelia. 'Craftsmen of the Empire: A Comparative Study of Decoration and Industrial Arts' *Architectural Review*, June 1924.

Deloitte. 'The Rise and Rise of the African Middle Class' available at: www2 .deloitte.com/content/dam/Deloitte/au/Documents/international-specialist/deloitte-au-aas-rise-african-middle-class-12.pdf, accessed on 15 January 2015.

Dowden, Richard. *Africa: Altered States, Ordinary Miracles* (London: Portobello Books, 2008).

Dowden, Richard. 'What Will Brexit Mean for Africa?' available at: www .royalafricansociety.org/blog/what-will-brexit-mean-africa, 24 June 2016, accessed on 23 August 2017.

Dowden, Richard. 'Britain Must Seize the Chance for More Trade with Africa' *The Times*, 25 January 2017, available at: www.royalafricansociety .org/blog/britain-must-seize-chance-more-trade-africa, accessed on 23 August 2017.

Dronamraju, Krishna R. *If I Am to Be Remembered: The Life and Work of Julian Huxley with selected correspondence* (Singapore, New Jersey, London, Hong Kong: World Scientific Publishing, 1993).

Dudley Stamp, Laurence. *Africa: A Study in Tropical Development* (New York, NY: John Wiley and Sons Inc., 1953).

Dulani, Boniface, Mattes, Robert, and Logan, Carolyn. 'After a Decade of Growth in Africa, Little Change in Poverty at the Grassroots' Afrobarometer, October 2013, available at: www.afrobarometer.org/ files/documents/policy_brief/ab_r5_policybriefno1.pdf, accessed on 1 November 2013.

The Economist Newspaper Limited, 'The Hopeless Continent', London, 13 May 2000.

'Africa Rising', London, 3 December 2011.

'The Hottest Frontier: Strategies for Putting Money to Work in a Fast-Growing Continent', 6 April 2013, available at: www.economist.com/ printedition/2013-04-06, accessed on 30 July 2013.

Elliot, Chris. 'The Readers' Editor on ... Showing That Black Writers Can Write about Far More Than Race', 2 November 2014, available at: www .theguardian.com/commentisfree/2014/nov/02/guardian-readers-editor-black-writers-write-about-anything, accessed on 11 July 2017.

Freedland, Jonathan. 'If Donald Trump Wins, It'll Be a New Age of Darkness' *The Guardian*, 4 November 2016, available at: www.theguardian .com/commentisfree/2016/nov/04/if-donald-trump-wins-new-age-endarkenment, accessed on 23 August 2017.

Freedland, Jonathan. 'The 1930s Were Humanity's Darkest, Bloodiest Hour. Are You Paying Attention?' *The Guardian*, 11 March 2017, available at: www.theguardian.com/society/2017/mar/11/1930s-humanity-darkest-bloodiest-hour-paying-attention-second-world-war,accessed on 23 August 2017.

Friedman, Thomas. 'Where Did "We the People" Go?' *New York Times*, 21 June 2017, available at: www.nytimes.com/2017/06/21/opinion/where-did-we-the-people-go.html, accessed on 23 August 2017.

Flynn, Gerard, and Scutti, Susan. 'Smuggled Bushmeat Is Ebola's Back Door to America', 29 August 2014, available at: www.newsweek.com/2014/08/29/smuggled-bushmeat-ebolas-back-door-america-265668.html, accessed on 5 September 2015.

Goldman Sachs. 'Africa's Turn', Equity Research Fortnightly Thoughts (Goldman Sachs newsletter), Issue 27, 1 March 2012, available at: http://allafrica.com/download/resource/main/main/idatcs/00031978:a2187 04b4806a5136c18f03d75a4529c.pdf, accessed on 15 January 2015.

Gunther, John. *Inside Africa* (London: Hamish Hamilton, 1955).

Hance, William A. 'Economic Change in Africa' *Journal of Geography*, 58, 1959, pp. 180–195.

Harris, John H. *Africa: Slave or Free?* (London: Student Christian Movement, 1919).

Heseltine, Nigel. *Remaking Africa* (London: Museum Press Ltd, 1961).

Hill, Robert A. (ed.). *The Marcus Garvey and Univesal Negro Improvement Association Papers, Volume IX, Africa for the Africans 1921–1922* (Berkeley, CA, Los Angeles, CA, London: University of California Press, 1995).

His Majesty's Government, *Indians in Kenya* (London: His Majesty's Stationary Office, 1923).

Hobson, John A. *Imperialism, A Study* (London: George Allen and Unwin, 1938/1968).

Hollande, Francois. 'Speech by M. François Hollande, President of the Republic, to the National Assembly of Senegal', 12 October 2012, available at: https://uk.ambafrance.org/President-Hollande-s-keynote, accessed on 3 July 2012.

Huxley, Elspeth. *White Man's Country: Lord Delamere and the Making of Kenya* (London: Macmillan and Co, 1935).

Jarvis, W. J. *Planning from a Multi Racial Aspect in Africa* (Salisbury: Government House Publications, 1951).

Jewkes, John. *Ordeal by Planning* (London: MacMillan, 1948).

Johnson, Colonel Jim. 'Obituaries' *The Telegraph*, 13 August 2008, available at: www.telegraph.co.uk/news/obituaries/2553726/Colonel-Jim-Johnson.html, accessed on 19 January 2017.

Johnston, Harry. 'The Africa of the Immediate Future' *Journal of the African Society*, 18:71, 1919, pp. 161–182.

Kimble, George H. T. 'How Free Are the New Countries?' 1963.

Laurence, Jonathan, and Vaïsse, Justin. *Integrating Islam: Political and Religious Challenges in Contemporary France* (Washington, DC: Brookings Institution Press, 2006).

Lewis, William H. *Emerging Africa* (Washington, DC: Public Affairs Press, 1963).

Leys, Norman. *Kenya* (London: Leonard and Virginia Woolf at the Hogarth Press, 1924).

Lievesley, Nat. 'The Future Ageing of the Ethnic Minority Population of England and Wales' *Runnymede Trust*, 2010, available at: www .runnymedetrust.org/uploads/publications/pdfs/TheFutureAgeing OfTheEthnicMinorityPopulation-ForWebJuly2010.pdf, accessed on 1 March 2017.

Lugard, Frederick D. *The Dual Mandate in British Tropical Africa*, Fifth Edition (London: Frank Cass & Co. Ltd, 1965/1922).

MacMillan, William. *Africa Emergent* (Harmondsworth: Pelican Books, 1938/1949).

'African Growing Pains' *African Affairs*, 52:208, 1953, pp. 192–201.

Mahajan, Vijay. *Africa Rising: How 900 Million African Consumers Offer More Than You Think* (New Jersey: Pearson Education, 2009).

Manchester, Julia. 'Bill Kristol: US Reliving Decline and Fall of Rome under Trump' *The Hill*, 2 July 2017, available at: http://thehill.com/blogs/ blog-briefing-room/news/340443-bill-kristol-us-reliving-decline-and-fall-of-rome-under-trump, accessed on 23 August 2017.

Mataen, David. *Africa: The Ultimate Frontier Market* (Peterman: Harriman House, 2012).

Mbeki, Thabo. 'The African Renaissance Statement of Deputy President, Thabo Mbeki, SABC, Gallagher Estate, 13 August 1998', available at: www.dfa.gov.za/docs/speeches/1998/mbek0813.htm, accessed on 1 October 2015.

Mbembe, Achille. 'Afropolitanism' in Njami Simon, and Lucy Durán (eds.), *Africa Remix: Contemporary Art of a Continent*. (Johannesburg: Johannesburg Art Gallery, 2007), pp. 26–30

McGregor Ross, William. *Kenya from Within: A Short Political History* (London: George Allen and Unwin, 1927).

McKinsey & Company. 'The Rise of the African Consumer: A Report from McKinsey's Africa Consumer Insights Center', available at: www.mckinsey.com/~/media/McKinsey%20Offices/South%20Africa/ PDFs/Rise_of_the_African_consumer-McKinsey_Africa_Consumer_ Insights_Center_report.ashx, accessed on 14 January 2015.

Meeker, Oden. *Report on Africa* (London: Chatto and Windus, 1955).

Mockerie, Parmenus Githendu. *An African Speaks for His People* (London: Leonard and Virginia Woolf at the Hogarth Press, 1934).

MoMa, 'King Britt Presents MOONDANCE, A Night in the AfroFuture', 13 April 2014, available at: http://momaps1.org/calendar/view/498/, accessed on 4 February 2016.

Nippert, Matt. 'Revealed: How Peter Thiel Got New Zealand Citizenship' *The New Zealand Herald*, 1 February 2017, available at: www.nzherald .co.nz/business/news/article.cfm?c_id=3&objectid=11790034, accessed on 20 February 2018.

No author. *Can Africa Claim the 21st Century?* (Washington, DC: World Bank, 2000), available at: http://siteresources.worldbank.org/INTAFRICA/Resources/complete.pdf, accessed on 22 August 2017.

No author. 'How Fair Is Britain?' *Equality and Human Rights Commission*, 2010, available at: www.equalityhumanrights.com/en/publication-download/how-fair-britain-report, accessed on 22 August 2017.

No author. 'Africans Still Seething over Sarkozy Speech' *Reuters*, 5 September 2017, available at: http://uk.reuters.com/article/uk-africa-sarkozy-id UKL0513034620070905, accessed on 3 July 2017.

No author. 'Population Structure and Aging' *EuroStat*, available at: http://ec.europa.eu/eurostat/statistics-explained/index.php/Population_structure_and_ageing, accessed on 1 March 2017.

No author. 'The Unofficial English Translation of Sarkozy's Speech' available at: www.africaresource.com/essays-a-reviews/essays-a-discussions/437-the-unofficial-english-translation-of-sarkozys-speech?showall =&limitstart=, accessed on 3 July 2017.

Oldham, Jospeh H. *Christianity and the Race Problem* (New York, NY: George H. Doran Company, 1924)

Oldham, Joseph H. *White and Black in Africa: A Critical Examination of the Rhodes Lectures of General Smuts* (London, New York, NY, Toronto: Longmans, Green and Co, 1930).

Oldham, Joseph. *New Hope in Africa* (London: Longman, 1955).

Oldham, Joseph H., and Gibson, Betty. *The Remaking of Man in Africa* (London: Oxford University Press, 1931).

Oxfam, 'Show Africa's Potential Not Just Its Problems, Says Oxfam', 28 December 2012, available at: www.oxfam.org.uk/media-centre/press-releases/2012/12/show-africas-potential-not-just-its-problems-says-oxfam, accessed on 23 August 2016.

Peel, C. V. A. *Through the Length of Africa: Being an Account of a Journey from Cape Town to Alexandria and Sport in Kenya Colony* (London: Old Royalty Book Publishers, 1927).

Pfeiffer, Alice. 'A Closer Look at South Africa's "Afropolitan" Chic' *Elle*, 1 August 2014, available at: www.elle.com/fashion/news/a25076/a-closer-look-at-south-africas-afropolitan-chic/, accessed on 5 December 2016.

Radelet, Steven. *Emerging Africa: How 17 Countries Are Leading the Way* (Washington, DC: Center for Global Development, 2010).

Ranger, Terence. 'Obituary: Eileen Haddon' *The Guardian*, 22 July 2003, available at: www.theguardian.com/news/2003/jul/22/guardianobituaries .southafrica, accessed on 28 June 2017.

Ranger, Terence. *Writing Revolt: An Engagement with African Nationalism, 1957–1967* (Woodbridge, Suffolk: James Currey, 2013).

Rask Knudsen, Eva, and Rahbek, Ulla (eds.). *In Search of the Afropolitan: Encounters, Conversations and Contemporary Diasporic African Literature* (London, New York, NY: Rowman and Littlefield, 2016).

Robertson, Charles. *The Fastest Billion: The Story behind Africa's Economic Revolution* (London: Renaissance Capital, 2012).

Rostow, Walt W. *The Stages of Economic Growth: A Non-communist Manifesto*, Third Edition (Cambridge: Cambridge University Press, 1990/1953). *Politics and the Stages of Growth* (Cambridge: Cambridge University Press, 1971).

Rotberg, Robert. *Africa Emerges* (Cambridge: Polity Press, 2013).

Rotberg, Robert. Robert 'Will Africa Keep Rising?' 19 September 2016, available at: https://robertrotberg.wordpress.com/2016/09/19/will-africa-keep-rising/, accessed on 23 August 2017.

Salami, Minna. '32 Views on Afropolitanism' *MsAfropolitan*, 7 October 2015, available at: www.msafropolitan.com/2015/10/my-views-on-afropolitanism.html, accessed on 1 December 2016.

Scipio, *Emergent Africa* (London: Chattum and Windus, 1965).

Selasi, Taiye. 'Bye-Bye Babar' *the Lip*, 3 March 2005, available at: http://thelip.robertsharp.co.uk/?p=76, accessed on 11 July 2017.

Selasi, Taiye, and Sy, Stephanie. 'Taiye Selasi Talks to Stephanie Sy' *Al Jazeera*, 19 february 2015, available at: http://america.aljazeera.com/watch/shows/talk-to-al-jazeera/articles/2015/2/19/taiye-selasi-talks-to-stephanie-sy.html, accessed on 11 July 2017.

Severino, Jean-Michel, and Ray, Olivier. *Africa's Moment* (Cambridge: Polity Press, 2011).

Shay, Felix. 'Cairo to Cape Town, Overland: An Adventurous Journey of 135 Days, Made by an American Man and His Wife, through the Length of the African Continent' *National Geographic Magazine*, 47:2, 1925, pp. 123–260.

Shorthouse D.S.O., F.R.G.S., Capt., W. T. *Sport and Adventure in Africa: A Record of Twelve Years of Big Game Hunting, Campaigning and Travel in the Wilds of Tropical Africa* (London: Seeley, Service and Co. Limited, 1923).

Smuts, Jan. *Africa and Some World Problems, Including the Rhodes Memorial Lectures Delivered in Michaelmas Term1929 by General J. C. Smuts* (Oxford: The Clarendon Press, 1929).

Spencer Chapman, F. *Lightest Africa* (London: Chatto & Windus, 1955).

Stoddard, Lothrup. *The Rising Tide of Color against White World Supremacy* (London: Chapman and Hall, 1920).

Reforging America: The Story of Our One Nationhood (New York, NY: Scribners, 1927).

Time Out, 'V&A Friday Late: Afropolitan', Thursday 11 October 2012, available at: www.timeout.com/london/shopping/v-a-friday-late-afropolitan, accessed on 4 February 2016.

Thiel, Peter. 'The Education of a Libertarian', 13 February 2009, available at: www.cato-unbound.org/2009/04/13/peter-thiel/education-libertarian, accessed on 20 February 2018.

Thuku, Harry. *Harry Thuku: An Autobiography* (Nairobi, Lusaka, Dar Es Salaam, Addis Ababa: Oxford University Press, 1970).

Todd, Judith. 'Obituary: Guy Clutton-Brock' *The Independent*, 16 February 1995, available at: www.independent.co.uk/news/people/obituary-guy-clutton-brock-1573319.html, accessed on 28 June 2017.

Tutton, Mark. 'Young, Urban and Culturally Savvy: Meet the Afropolitans' *CNN*, 17 February 2016, available at: http://edition.cnn.com/2012/02/17/world/africa/who-are-afropolitans/index.html, accessed on 5 December 2016.

United Nations. Human Development Report 2014, Sustaining Human Progress: Reducing Vulnerabilities and Building Resilience. Explanatory note on the 2014 Human Development Report composite indices for Mozambique, available at: http://hdr.undp.org/sites/all/themes/hdr_theme/country-notes/MOZ.pdf, accessed on 22 June 2015.

Wa Thiong'O, Ngugi. *A Grain of Wheat* (Edinburgh: Pearson Education International, 1967/2008).

Ward, William. *Emergent Africa* (London: George Allen and Unwin Ltd, 1967).

Waugh, Evelyn. *A Tourist in Africa* (London: Chapman and Hall Ltd, 1960).

Woolf, Leonard, et al. 'Natives in Africa, the Policy of Equal Rights: To the Editor of *The Times*' *The Times*, 12 November 1930.

Wyndham, Hugh. 'The Colour Problem in Africa' *Journal of the British Institute of International Affairs*, 4:4, 1925, pp. 174–190.

Secondary Sources

Achebe, Chinua. *An Image of Africa* (London: Penguin, 1977/2010).

Adeyanju, Charles, T.. *Deadly Fever: Racism, Disease and a Media Panic* (Blackpoint, NS: Fernwood Publishing, 2010).

Ahmed, Sara. 'A Phenomenology of Whiteness' *Feminist Theory*, 8:149, 2007, pp. 149–168.

Ajulu, Rok. 'Thabo Mbeki's African Renaissance in a Globalising World Economy: The Struggle for the Soul of the Continent' *Review of African Political Economy*, 28:87 (2001), pp. 27–42.

Allen, Theodore. *The Invention of the White Race, Vol. 2: The Origin of Racial Oppression in Anglo-America* (London: Verso Books, 1997).

Anderson, Amanda. *Bleak Liberalism* (Chicago, IL: University of Chicago Press, 2016).

Anievas, Alex, Manchanda, Nivi, and Shilliam, Robbie. *Race and Racism in International Relations: Confronting the Global Colour Line* (London: Routledge, 2014).

Archibugi, Daniele. *The Global Commonwealth of Citizens: Toward Cosmopolitan Democracy* (Trenton, NJ: Princeton University Press, 2015).

Ayers, Alison, 'Beyond the Imperial Narrative: African Political Historiography Revisited' in Branwen Gruffydd-Jones (ed.), *Decolonizing International Relations* (Lanham, MD: Rowman and Littlefield, 2006), pp. 155–179.

Bayart, Jean-Francois. *The State in Africa: The Politics of the Belly*, Second Edition (London: Polity Press, 2009).

Belich, James. *Replenishing the Earth: The Settler Revolution and the Rise of the Anglo World, 1783–1939* (Oxford: Oxford University Press, 2009).

Bell, Duncan. 'The Project for a New Anglo Century: Race, Space and Global Order' in Peter Katzenstein (ed.), *Anglo-America and Its Discontents: Civilizational Identities Beyond West and East* (Abingdon: Routledge, 2012).

Berman, Bruce. *Control and Crisis in Colonial Kenya: The Dialectic of Domination* (Rochester, NY: James Currey, 1990).

Berman, Bruce, and Lonsdale, John. *Unhappy Valley: Violence and Ethnicity Book II: Conflict in Kenya and Africa* (Athens, OH: Ohio University Press, 1992).

Beswick, Danielle. 'Managing Dissent in a Post Genocide Environment: The Challenge of Political Space in Rwanda' *Development and Change*, 41:2 (2010), pp. 225–251.

'Genocide and the Politics of Exclusion: The case of the Batwa in Rwanda' *Democratisation*, 18(2): 2010, pp. 490–511.

Bhabha, Homi. *The Location of Culture* (London: Routledge, 1994).

Bhambra, Gurminder K. 'Historical Sociology, Modernity, and Postcolonial Critique' *The American Historical Review*, 116:3, 2011, pp. 653–662.

Bourne, Stephen. *Black in the British Frame: The Black Experience in British Film and Television* (London: Continuum Press, 2001).

Bradford, Phillips Verner. *Ota Benga: The Pygmy in the Zoo* (New York, NY: St Martin's Press, 1992).

Brautingam, Deborah. *The Dragon's Gift: The Real Story of China in Africa* (Oxford: Oxford University Press, 2009).

Brownell, Josiah. 'Out of Time: Global Settlerism, Nostalgia, and the Selling of the Rhodesian Rebellion Overseas' *Journal of Southern African Studies*, 43: 4, pp. 805–824.

Büscher, Bram. 'The Political Economy of Africa's Natural Resources and the "Great Financial Crisis"' *Tijdschrift voor Economische en Sociale Geografie*, 103:2, 2012, pp. 136–149.

Bush, Barbara. *Imperialism Race and Resistance* (Abingdon: Routledge, 1999).

Cannadine, David. *Ornamentalism: How the British Saw Their Empire* (London, New York, NY: Penguin, 2001).

Carmody, Padraig. *The New Scramble for Africa* (Cambridge: Polity Press, 2011).

Centre for the Study of Financial Innovation, 'Microfinance Banana Skins: Facing Reality' (New York, NY: CSFI, 2014).

Chakrabarty, Dipesh. *Provincializing Europe: Postcolonial Thought and Historical Difference* (Princeton, NJ: Princeton University Press, 2000).

Cheeseman, Nic. 'Does the African Middle Class Defend Democracy? Evidence from Kenya' Afrobarometer, Working Paper No. 150, December 2014,

Clements, Keith. *Faith on the Frontier: A life of J. H. Oldham* (Edinburgh: T&T Clark/Geneva: WCC Publications, 1999).

Cobain, Ian. *The History Thieves: Secrets, Lies and the Shaping of a Modern Nation* (London: Portobello Books, 2016).

Cockett, Richard. *Thinking the Unthinkable: Think Tanks and the Economic Counter Revolution, 1931–1983* (London: Harper Collins, 1994).

Comaroff, Jean, and Comaroff, John. 'Introduction' in John Comaroff, and Jean Comaroff (eds.), *Civil Society and the Political Imagination in Africa: Critical Perspectives* (Chicago, IL, London: University of Chicago Press, 1999), pp. 1–44.

Cornelissen, Scarlett, Cheru, Fantu, and Shaw, Timothy. 'Introduction – Africa and International Relations in the Twenty First Century: Still Changing Theory?' in Scarlett Cornelissen, Fantu Cheru, and Timothy Shaw (eds.), *Africa and International relations in the Twenty First Century* (New York, NY: Palgrave MacMillan, 2012), pp. 1–12.

Cox, Michael. 'Is the United States in Decline – Gain?' *International Affairs*, 83:4, 2007, pp. 643–653.

Curtin, Phillip. *The Image of Africa: British Ideas and Action 1780–1850* (Madison, WI: University of Wisconsin Press, 1964).

Derrida, Jacques. *Spectres of Marx* (London: Routledge, 1994).

DiAngelo, Robin. 'White Fragility' *International Journal of Critical Pedagogy*, 3:3, 2011, pp. 54–70.

Du Bois, W. E. B. *The Souls of Black Folk* (New York, NY: New American Library, Inc, 1903).

  Black Reconstruction in America: An Essay toward a History of the Part Which Black Folk Played in the Attempt to Reconstruct Democracy in America, 1860–1880 (San Diego, CA: Harcourt Brace, 1935).

  'The Negro and the Warsaw Ghetto' in Phil Zuckerman (ed.), *The Social Theory of W. E. B. Du Bois* (Thousand Oaks, CA: Pine Forge Press, 2004), pp. 45–47.

Dyer, Richard. *White: Essays on Race and Culture* (London, New York, NY: Routledge, 1997).

Ellis, Stephen. *Season of Rains: Africa in the World* (C Hurst and Co, London, 2012).

Engelbert, Pierre. *Africa: Unity, Sovereignty, and Sorrow* (Boulder, CO: Lynne Reinner, 2009).

Escobar, Arturo. *Encountering Development: The Making and Unmaking of the Third World* (Princeton, NJ: Princeton University Press, 1994).

Fanon, Franz. *Black Skins White Masks* (London: Pluto Press, 1968/ 2008).

Ferguson, James. *Global Shadows: Africa in the Neoliberal World Order* (Durham, NC: Duke University Press, 2006).

Ferguson, Niall. *Colossus: The Rise and Fall of the American Empire* (London: Penguin, 2009).

Frankenberg, Ruth. *White Women, Race Matters: The Social Construction of Whiteness* (Minneapolis: University of Minnesota Press, 1993).

Fukuyama, Francis. *The End of History and the Last Man* (New York, NY: Free Press, 1992).

Furedi, Frank. *The Silent War: Imperialism and the Changing Perception of Race* (New Brunswick, NJ: Rutgers University Press, 1998).

Fusco, Coco. 'Fantasies of Opportunity' *Afterimage Magazine*, December 1988.

Gabay, Clive. *Civil Society and Global Poverty: Hegemony, Inclusivity, Legitimacy* (London: Routledge, 2012).

  'Decolonising Interwar Anti-colonial Solidarities: The Case of Harry Thuku' *Interventions: International Journal of Postcolonial Studies*, 2018, 20:4, pp. 549–566.

Gallagher, Julia. 'Healing the Scar? Idealizing Britain in Africa 1997–2007' *African Affairs*, 108:432, 2009, pp. 435–451.

Gikandi, Simon. 'The Ghost of Matthew Arnold: Englishness and the Politics of Culture' *Nineteenth-Century Contexts*, 29:2–3, 2007, pp. 187–199.

Goldschmidt, Henry, and McAlister, Elizabeth. 'Introduction' in Henry Goldschmidt, and Elizabeth McAlister (eds.), *Race, Nation, and Religion in the Americas* (New York, NY: Oxford University Press, 2004), pp. 12–13.

Griffin, Penny. 'The World Bank, HIV/AIDS and Sex in Sub-Saharan Africa: A Gendered Analysis of Neoliberal Governance' *Globalizations*, 8(2), 2011, pp. 229–248.

Grovogui, Siba. 'Regimes of Sovereignty: Rethinking International Morality and the African Condition,' *The European Journal of International Relations*, 8:3, 2002, pp. 315–338.

Gruffydd Jones, Branwen. ' Race in the Ontology of International Order' *Political Studies*, 56(4), 2008, pp. 907–927.

Gupta, Partha Sarathi. *Imperialism and the British Labour Movement, 1914–1964* (New York, NY: Holmes & Meier Publishers, 1975).

Hall, Stuart. *The Whites of their Eyes: Racist Ideologies and the Media* (New York, NY: Lawrence and Wishart, 1981).

'The West and the Rest: Discourses and Power' in Stuart Hall, David Held, Don Hubert, and Kenneth Thompson (eds.), *Modernity: An Introduction to Modern Societies* (Cambridge, MA: Blackwell, 1996), pp. 275–331.

Hammond, Dorothy, and Jablow, Alta. *The Myth of Africa* (New York, NY: The Library of Social Science, 1977).

Harman, Sophie, and Brown, William (eds.). *African Agency in International Politics* (Abingdon: Routledge, 2013).

'In from the Margins? The Changing Place of Africa in International Relations' *International Affairs*, 89:1, 2013, pp. 69–87.

Harrison, Graham. *The World Bank and Africa: The Construction of Governance States* (Abingdon: Routledge, 2004).

The African Presence: Representation of Africa in the Construction of Britishness (Manchester: Manchester University Press, 2013).

Harvey, David. 'Globalization and the "Spatial Fix"' *geographische revue*, 2, 2001, pp. 23–30.

Heartfield, James. *The Aborigines' Protection Society: Humanitarian Imperialism in Australia, New Zealand, Fiji, Canada, South Africa, and the Congo, 1837–1909* (London: Hurst Publishers, 2011).

Hegel, Georg. *The Philosophy of History* (New York, NY: Dover Publications, 1837/1956).

Held, David. *Cosmopolitanism: Ideals and Realities* (Cambridge: Polity Press, 2010).

Henderson, Errol. 'Hidden in Plain Sight: Racism in International Relations Theory' in Robbie Shilliam, Alex Anievas, and Nivi Manchanda (eds.), *Race and Racism in International Relations* (Abingdon: Routledge, 2014), pp. 19–43.

Hobson, John H. The Eurocentric Conception of World Politics: Western International Theory 1760–2010 (Cambridge: Cambridge University Press, 2012).

Hobson, John H. 'Re-embedding the Global Colour Line within post-1945 International Theory' in Alexander Anievas, Nivi Manchanda, and Robbie Shilliam (eds.), *Race and Racism in International Relations* (Abingdon: Routledge, 2014), pp. 81–97.

Hochschild, Adam. *King Leopold's Ghost* (New York, NY: Mariner Books, 1998).

Hughes, Richard. *Capricorn: David Stirling's Second Africa Campaign* (Milton Keynes: Radcliffe Press, 2003).

Huntington, Samuel. *The Clash of Civilizations and the Remaking of World Order* (New York, NY: Simon & Schuster, 1996).

Ignatiev, Noel. *How the Irish Became White* (London, New York, NY: Routledge, 1995/2009).

Ikenberry, John. 'Is American Multilateralism in Decline?' *Perspectives on Politics*, 1:3, 2003, pp. 533–549.

Isin, Engin F. and Ruppert, Evelyn S. *Being Digital Citizens* (London: Rowman & Littlefield International, 2015).

Jackson, Robert. *Quasi-States: Sovereignty, International Relations and the Third World* (Cambridge: Cambridge University Press, 1991).

Jeater, Diana. *Law, Language and Science: The Invention of the 'Native Mind' in Southern Rhodesia, 1890–1930* (Portsmouth, NH: Heinemann, 2007).

Jutersonke, Oliver, and Kartas, Moncef. 'The State as Urban Myth: Governance without Government in the Global South' in Robert Schuett, and Peter M. R. Stirk (eds.), *The Concept of the State in International Relations: Philosophy, Sovereignty, Cosmopolitanism* (Edinburgh: Edinburgh University Press, 2015) pp. 108–135.

Kagan, Robert. 'Not Fade Away: The Myth of American Decline' *The New Republic*, 11 January 2012, available at: https://newrepublic.com/article/99521/america-world-power-declinism, accessed on 21 August 2017.

Kaplan, Robert. 'The Coming Anarchy: How Scarcity, Crime, Over-population, Tribalism, and Disease are Rapidly Destroying the Social Fabric of our Planet' *The Atlantic*, 1994, available at: www.theatlantic .com/magazine/archive/1994/02/the-coming-anarchy/304670/ accessed on 3 July 2017.

Kennedy, Dane. 'Introduction: Reinterpreting Exploration' in D. Kennedy (ed.), *Reinterpreting Exploration: The West in the World* (Oxford: Oxford University Press, 2014).

Kenny, Michael G. 'Racial Science in Social Context: John R. Baker on Eugenics, Race, and the Public Role of the Scientist' *Isis: A Journal of the History of Science Society* 95: 3, 2004, pp. 394–419.

Kiely, Ray. 'Development and Modernisation' in J. Scott ed. *Key Sociological Concepts* (Abingdon: Routledge, 2006) pp. 107–110.

Kirby, Jack Temple. *Darkness and the Dawning: Race and Reform in the Progressive South* (Philadelphia, PA: Lippincott, 1972).

Krishna, Sankaran. *Globalization and Postcolonialism: Hegemony and Resistance in the Twenty-First Century* (Boulder, CO: Rowman and Littlefield, 2008).

Kupchan, Charles. *No One's World: The West, the Rising Rest, and the Coming Global Turn* (Oxford: Oxford University Press, 2012).

Lake, Marilyn, and Reynolds, Henry. *Drawing the Global Colour Line* (Cambridge: Cambridge University Press, 2008).

Larner Wendy, and Walters, William. 'The Political Rationality of "New Regionalism": Toward a Genealogy of the Region' *Theory and Society*, 31, 2002, pp. 391–432.

Lester, Alan. *Imperial Networks: Creating Identities in Nineteenth-Century South Africa and Britain* (Abingdon: Routledge, 2001).

Little, Jo. *Against Meritocracy: Culture, Power and Myths of Mobility* (Abingdon, New York, NY, Routledge: 2017).

Lowry, Donal. 'Ulster Resistance and Loyalist Rebellion in the Empire' in K. Jeffrey (ed.), *'An Irish Empire'? Aspects of Ireland and the British Empire* (Manchester: Manchester University Press, 1996), pp. 191–216.

Ndjio, Basile. 'Overcoming Socio-Economic Marginalisation: Young West African Hustlers and the Reinvention of Global Capitalism' in Ebenezer Obadare, and Wendy Willems (eds.), *Civic Agency in Africa: Arts of Resistance in the 21st Century* (Suffolk: James Currey, 2014), pp. 85–104.

No author. 'After the "Rising" – now Reform and Realism' *Africa Confidential*, 57:2, 2016, available at: www.africa-confidential.com/article/id/11448/After_the_'rising'_%E2%80%93_now_reform_and_realism accessed on 28 January 2016.

Maclean, Nancy. *Democracy in Chains: The Deep History of the Radical Right's Stealth Plan for America* (New York, NY: Viking Press Inc, 2017).

Mamdani, Mahmood. *Citizen and Subject: Contemporary Africa and the Legacy of Late Colonialism* (Princeton, NJ: Princeton University Press, 1996).

When Victims Become Killers: Colonialism, Nativism, and the Genocide in Rwanda (Princeton, NJ: Princeton University Press, 2002).

Martin, Guy. *African Political Thought* (London, New York, NY: Palgrave MacMillan, 2012).

Maxon, Robert. *Struggle for Kenya: The Loss and Reassertion of Imperial Initiative, 1912–1923* (London and Toronto: Associated University Presses, 1993).

Mayer, Jane. *Dark Money: The Hidden History of the Billionaires behind the Rise of the Radical Right* (New York, NY: DoubleDay, 2016).

Curtis, Adam. (Dir) The Mayfair Set, British Broadcasting Corporation (1999), available at: www.youtube.com/watch?v=234H8X1-JiA, accessed on 23 May 2016.

Mazrui, Ali Al'Amin. 'The Re-invention of Africa: Edward Said, V. Y. Mudimbe and Beyond' *Research in African Literatures*, 36:3, 2005, pp. 68–82.

Mbembe, Achille. 'Nicolas Sarkozy's Africa' Africultures, 2007, Available from www.africultures.com/php/index.php?nav=paper&no=6816, accessed on 20 September 2015.

McCracken, John. *A History of Malawi, 1859–1959* (Suffolk: James Currey, 2012).

McIntosh, Peggy. 'White Privilege and Male Privilege: A personal account of coming to see correspondences through work in Women's Studies' Wellesley: Center for Research on Women, 1988, Working paper 189.

Mies, Maria. 'Colonization and Housewifization,' in Rosemary Hennessey, and Chris Ingraham (eds.), *Materialist Feminism: A Reader in Class, Difference, and Women's Lives.* (Abingdon: Routledge, 1997) pp. 175–185.

Mignolo, Walter. 'Delinking' *Cultural Studies*, 21:2, 2007, pp. 449–514.
   The Darker Side of Western Modernity: Global Futures, Decolonial Options (Durham, NC: Duke University Press, 2011).

Mignolo, Walter, and Vasquez, Rolando. 'Decolonial AestheSis: ColonialWounds/Decolonial Healings' Social Text, 2013, available at: http://socialtextjournal.org/periscope_article/decolonial-aesthesis-colonial-woundsdecolonial-healings, accessed on 14 May 2015.

Mills, Charles. *The Racial Contract* (Ithaca, NY: Cornell University Press, 1997).

Mkandawire, Thandika. 'Rethinking Pan-Africanism, Nationalism and the New Regionalism' in Sam Moyo, and Paris Yeros (eds.) *Reclaiming the Nation: The Return of the National Question in Africa, Asia and Latin America* (Chicago, IL: University of Chicago Press, 2011), pp. 31–54.

Molz, Jennie Germann. '"Watch us Wander': Mobile Surveillance and the Surveillance of Mobility" *Environment and Planning A*, 38, 2006, pp. 377–393.

Morrison, Toni. *Playing in the Dark: Whiteness and the Literary Imagination* (Cambridge, MA: Harvard University Press, 1992).

Mouffe, Chantal. *On the Political* (London, Routledge, 2005).

Mudimbe, Valentin Yves. *The Idea of Africa* (Bloomington, IN: Indiana University Press, 1994).

Murray-Brown, Jeremy. *Kenyatta* (London, George Allen and Unwin: 1972).

Nederveen Pieterse, Jan. *White on Black: Images of Africa and Blacks in Western Popular Culture* (New Haven, CT: Yale University Press, 1992).

Padmore, George. '"Left" Imperialism and the Negro Toilers' *Labour Monthly*, 14 (5), 1932, available at: www.marxists.org/archive/padmore/1932/left-imp.htm, accessed on 9 August 2018.

Pasha, Mustapha Kamal. 'The "Bandung impulse" and international relations'in Sanjay Seth (ed.), *Postcolonial Theory and International Relations: A Critical Introduction* (Abingdon: Routledge, 2013), pp. 144–166.

'Religion and the Fabrication of Race' *Millennium: Journal of International Studies*, 2017, Vol. 45(3) pp. 312–334.

Power, Joey. *Political Culture and Nationalism in Malawi: Building Kwacha* (Rochester, NY: University of Rochester Press, 2010).

Price, Richard. *Making Empire: Colonial Encounters and the Creation of Imperial Rule in Nineteenth-Century Africa* (Cambridge: Cambridge University Press, 2008).

Prior, Christopher. *Exporting Empire: Africa, Colonial Officials and the Construction of the Imperial State c.1900–39* (Manchester: Manchester University Press, 2013).

Read, Jason. 'A Genealogy of Homo-Economicus: Neoliberalism and the Production of Subjectivity' in Sam Binkley, and Jorge Capetillo (eds.), *A Foucault for the 21st Century: Governmentality, Biopolitics and Discipline in the New Millennium* (Cambridge: Cambridge Scholars Publishing, 2010), pp. 2–15.

Reid, Richard. *Warfare in African History* (Cambridge: Cambridge University Press, 2012).

Rich, Paul B. *White Power and the Liberal Conscience: Racial Segregation and South African Liberalism, 1921–60* (Manchester: Manchester University Press, 1984).

Richey, Lisa Ann, and Ponte, Stefano. 'Brand Aid and the International Political Economy and Sociology of North-South Relations' *International Political Sociology*, 7:1, 2013, pp. 92–93.

Roberts, Andrew. 'The Imperial Mind' in Roberts, Andrew (ed.), *The Colonial Moment in Africa: Essays on the Movement of Minds and*

Materials, 1900–1940 (Cambridge: Cambridge University Press, 1986), pp. 24–76.

Robinson, Keith. *The Dilemmas of Trusteeship: Aspects of British Colonial Policy between the Wars* (London: Oxford University Press, 1965).

Roediger, David. *The Wages of Whiteness: Race and the Making of the American Working Class* (London: Verso, 1992/2007).

Working toward Whiteness: How America's Immigrants Became White: The Strange Journey from Ellis Island to the Suburbs (New York, NY: Basic Books, 2006).

Roitman, Janet. 'New Sovereigns? Regulatory Authority in the Chad Basin' in T. Callaghy, R. Kassimir, and R. Latham (eds.), *Intervention and Transnationalism in Africa: Global-Local Networks of Power* (Cambridge: Cambridge University Press, 2001), pp. 240–263.

'A Successful Life in the Illegal Realm: Smugglers and Road Bandits in the Chad Basin' in Peter Geschiere, Birgit Meyer, and Peter Pels (eds.), *Readings on Modernity in Africa* (Bloomington, IN: Indiana University Press, 2008), pp. 214–220.

Rosberg, Carl G., and Nottingham, John. *The Myth of Mau Mau: Nationalism in Kenya* (New York, NY, Washington, DC: Frederick A. Praeger, 1966).

Rosenblum, April. 'The Past didn't Go Anywhere: Making Resistance to Antisemitism Part of all of our Movements', 2007, available at: www .buildingequality.us/prejudice/antisemitism/rosenblum/the-past.pdf, accessed on 11 January 2018.

Ross, Alistair. 'The Capricorn Africa Society and European Reactions to African Nationalism in Tanganyika, 1949–60' *African Affairs*, 76:305, 1977, pp. 519–535.

Sabaratnam, Meera. 'Avatars of Eurocentrism in the Critique of the Liberal Peace', *Security Dialogue*, 44:3, 2013, pp. 259–278.

Said, Edward. *Orientalism* (London: Vintage Books, 1978).

San Juan Jr, Epifanio. 'Postcolonialism and the Problematic of Uneven Development,' in Crystal Bartolovich, and Neil Lazarus (eds.), *Marxism, Modernity, and Postcolonial Studies* (Cambridge: Cambridge University Press, 2002), pp. 221–240.

Shadle, Brett. *The Souls of White Folk: White Settlers in Kenya, 1900s–1920s* (Manchester: Manchester University Press, 2015).

Shilliam, Robbie (ed.). *International Relations and Non-Western Thought: Imperialism, Colonialism and Investigations of Global Modernity* (London: Routledge, 2010).

'Intervention and Colonial-Modernity: Decolonising the Italy/Ethiopia Conflict Through Psalms 68:31' *Review of International Studies* 39:5, 2013, pp. 1131–1147.

The Black Pacific: Anti-Colonial Struggles and Oceanic Connections (London: Bloomsbury Academic, 2015).

Shutt, Allison K. *Manners Make a Nation: Racial Etiquette in Southern Rhodesia, 1910–1963* (Rochester, NY: University of Rochester Press, 2016).

Sklair, Leslie. *The Transnational Capitalist Class* (Oxford: Wiley-Blackwell, 2001).

Slabodsky, Santiago. *Decolonial Judaism: Triumphal Failures of Barbaric Thinking* (New York, NY: Palgrave MacMillan, 2014)

Snead, James. *White Screens/Black Images: Hollywood from the Dark Side*, Colin MacCabe, and Cornell West (eds.) (Abingdon, New York, NY: Routledge: 1994/2016).

Somerville, Keith. 'Africa Emerges, but from What into What?', available at: http://africanarguments.org/2013/09/04/africa-emerges-but-from-what-and-into-what-a-triumph-of-hope-over-experience-in-robert-rotbergs-new-assessment-of-contemporary-africa-by-keith-somerville/, accessed on 18 November 2014.

Sontag, Susan. *AIDS and Its Metaphors* (New York, NY: Farrar, Straus, Giroux, 1999).

Spengler, Oswald. *The Decline of the West* (Oxford: Oxford University Press, 1918/1991).

Staniland, Martin. *American Intellectuals and African Nationalists, 1955–1970* (New Haven, CT, and London: Yale University Press, 1991).

Stephen, Daniel Mark. '"The White Man's Grave": British West Africa and the British Empire Exhibition of 1924–1925' *Journal of British Studies*, 48:1, 2009, pp. 102–128.

The Empire of Progress: West Africans, Indians and Britons at the British Empire Exhibition, 1924–25 (London, New York, NY: Palgrave MacMillan, 2013).

Stocking, George W. *Race, Culture, and Evolution* (Chicago, IL: Chicago University Press, 1982).

Stoler, Ann L. *Along the Archival Grain: Epistemic Anxieties and Colonial Common Sense* (Princeton, NJ: Princeton University Press, 2010).

Taiwo, Olufemi. *Africa Must be Modern: A Manifesto* (Bloomington, IN: Indiana University Press, 2014).

Taylor, Ian. *Africa Rising? BRICS – Diversifying Dependency* (Oxford: James Currey, 2014).

Tignor, Richard L. *Colonial Transformation of Kenya: The Kamba, Kikuyu and Maasai from 1900–1939* (Princeton, NJ: Princeton University Press, 1976).

Tilly, Helen. *Africa as a Living Laboratory: Empire, Development, and the Problem of Scientific Knowledge* (Chicago, IL: University of Chicago Press, 2011).

Todorov, Tzvetan. *The Conquest of America: The Question of the Other* (New York, NY: Harper and Row, 1984).

Vale, Peter. 'The Movement, Modernity and New International Relations Writing in South Africa' *International Affairs*, 78:3, July 2002, pp. 585–593.

Vansina, Jan. *Being Colonized: The Kuba Experience in Rural Congo, 1880–1960* (Madison, WI: The University of Wisconsin Press, 2010).

Vigne, Randolph. *Liberals against Apartheid: A History of the Liberal Party of South Africa, 1953–1968* (Basingstoke: MacMillan Press Ltd, 1997).

Vitalis, Robert. 'The Graceful and Generous Liberal Gesture: Making Racism Invisible in American International Relations' *Millennium – Journal of International Studies*, 29:2, 2000, pp. 331–356.

    White World Order, Black Power Politics: The Birth of American International Relations (Ithaca, NY: Cornell University Press, 2015).

West, Michael O. *The Rise of an African Middle Class: Colonial Zimbabwe, 1898–1965* (Bloomington, IN, and Indianapolis, IN: Indiana University Press, 2002).

Williams, David. 'Constructing the Economic Space: International Organisations and the Making of Homo Oeconomicus' *Millennium - Journal of International Studies*, 28(1) 1999, pp. 79–99.

Williams, David, and Young, Tom. 'Civil Society and the Liberal Project in Ghana and Sierra Leone' *Journal of Intervention and Statebuilding*, 6:1, 2012, pp. 57–72.

Wolton, Suke. *Lord Hailey, the Colonial Office and Politics of Race and Empire in the Second World War* (London: Palgrave, 2000).

Woodham, Jonathan. 'Images of Africa and Design at the British Empire Exhibitions between the Wars' *Journal of Design History*, 2:1, 1989, pp. 15–33.

Younge, Gary. 'Being a Black Man in White America: A Burden even Obama Couldn't Escape' available at: www.theguardian.com/us-news/2017/jan/17/obama-legacy-black-masculinity-white-america accessed on 26th January 2017.

Index

For EU product safety concerns, contact us at Calle de José Abascal, 56–1°, 28003 Madrid, Spain or eugpsr@cambridge.org.